The BEATLES
an oral history

The BEATLES
an oral history

David Pritchard and Alan Lysaght

HYPERION

New York

First published in Canada by Stoddart Publishing Co. Limited, Toronto, Ontario

Library of Congress Cataloging-in-Publication Data
The Beatles : an oral history / [compiled by]
David Pritchard and Alan Lysaght.
        p.   cm.
        Includes index.
        ISBN 0-7868-6436-2
    1. Beatles—Interviews.   I. Pritchard, David.
        II. Lysaght, Alan.
    ML421.B4B413   1998
    782.42166'092'2—dc21
        [B]   98-19090
            CIP
            MN

First U.S. Edition
1 3 5 7 9 10 8 6 4 2

Contents

Acknowledgments   *vii*

Introduction   *ix*

Cast of Characters   *xi*

List of Illustrations   *xvii*

Chapter One
Rockin' the Casbah   *1*

Chapter Two
Growing Up on the Reeperbahn   *33*

Chapter Three
To the Toppermost of the Poppermost   *57*

Chapter Four
Mathew Street to Manchester Square   *79*

Chapter Five
Thank Your Lucky Stars   *111*

Chapter Six
What Will You Do When the Bubble Bursts?   *143*

Chapter Seven
Eight Arms to Hold You   *185*

Chapter Eight
Pop Art, *Pepper,* and Post-Touring   *215*

Chapter Nine
Revolution, Evolution, and Apple Corps   *249*

Chapter Ten
And in the End   *297*

Index   *321*

Acknowledgments

This book, and the radio program on which it is based, could not have been done without the generous contributions of time from each and every one of the interviewees included. Without exception we were treated warmly by each person.

For their help in shaping the content of both the radio show and this book, we must acknowledge the kind assistance of the following: Shirley Burns, Michael Carroll, Chris Charlesworth, CHUM-FM, Davida Clarke, Dr. Sara Cohen, Andrew Croft, Chris Edwards and family, Gary Ferrier, Richard Foreman, J. P. Finnigan, Vera and Archie Hudson, Liz and Jim Hughes, Bongo Kolycius, Brad LeMay, Jim and Ethel Levins, Mary Frances Lysaght, Magnos Brasserie, Paul McGrath, Alan Michaels, Peter Miniaci, Lynn Nicolai, Pomegranates Restaurant, Libby Pritchard, Randy Richardson, Dimo Safari, Neil Sargent, Karen Schaus, Gary Slaight, Victor Spinetti, Ron Stermac, Rogan Taylor, and Ritchie Yorke.

We would also like to acknowledge the profound debt we owe to our friend and colleague Doug Thompson, who has been unfailingly generous in sharing his own huge archive of material.

DAVID PRITCHARD
ALAN LYSAGHT

Introduction

Writing this book seemed a natural next step for us after collecting hundreds of wonderful stories over the years from the men and women who knew The Beatles, and from The Beatles themselves. My co-author, David Pritchard, started collecting Beatle material on family trips from Canada to his native England in 1963. He saved articles and papers throughout the 1960s while at art college and then as a top-rated radio DJ. I was a music fan from an early age and became hooked on the group after first hearing "She Loves You" in September 1963. Fascinated as much by The Beatles' sociological impact as by their musical evolution, I started to collect stories and anecdotes during my days as a university student.

When David and I met in the late 1970s, we agreed to pool our resources and collaborate on what we hoped would be the most complete and accurate Beatles radio documentary ever done. Noting the many inaccuracies that had been perpetuated through the years, we began the first of many trips to England to track down anybody who had ever worked with The Beatles or had been their friend. We wanted to get their stories on tape. This personal approach resulted in the debunking of several myths and the clarification of stories that had been misconstrued over the years. Through these interviews we captured the human side of the story. We learned of John Lennon's excitement as he held, and smelled, the first acetate copies of "Love Me Do." We heard about The Beatles jumping around their Parisian hotel room after being informed that they had finally reached "number one" in the United States, land of their musical heroes. We felt the fatigue that ended their touring career.

Years of research and preparation were virtually complete in December 1980 when John Lennon was killed. Out of respect, the finished 24-hour radio documentary, called *The Beatles: The Days in*

Their Life, was not released for six months. It was eventually heard in more than 30 countries.

This effort turned out to be just the beginning. While researching programs on other artists, we kept meeting people who had worked with The Beatles, all of whom had great stories. We ended up with a treasure trove of material, much of which had never been heard before. As only a fraction of that material could be used in the radio documentary, we have now put together this book, allowing us to tell the whole story for the first time.

We are deeply grateful to the many people who have contributed their stories to our radio documentary, and now, this book. They have allowed us to tell one of the most fascinating stories of our time, and to shed some light on the environment that produced the unparalleled phenomenon of The Beatles.

ALAN LYSAGHT
TORONTO, CANADA

Cast of Characters

Keith Altham: British rock music publicist and writer

Don Arden: Promoter, agent, and one of the owners of the Star-Club in Hamburg, Germany

Jane Asher: Girlfriend of Paul McCartney

Peter Asher: Brother of Jane Asher and, with Gordon Waller, part of British duo, Peter and Gordon

Julia Baird: John Lennon's half sister; author of *John Lennon, My Brother*

Tony Barrow: Public relations manager for The Beatles

Sid Bernstein: New York music promoter who booked The Beatles' first American concert performances

Mona Best: Mother of Pete Best and owner of Liverpool's Casbah Club

Pete Best: Mona Best's son and onetime Beatle drummer

Peter Blake: British artist; designer of *Sgt. Pepper's Lonely Hearts Club Band* album cover

Bob Bonis: American tour manager

Ken Brown: Musician and friend of George Harrison who performed with The Quarry Men

Peter Brown: Apple Corps executive

John Burgess: British record producer

Tommy Charles: Right-wing American radio announcer who initiated controversy during the "Bigger Than Christ" affair

Alan Civil: Classical French horn player

Dick Clark: Television host of popular U.S. music show

Maureen Cleave: British newspaper writer

Phil Collins: British drummer, composer, and vocalist

Les Condon: British jazz trumpet player

Spencer Davis: British vocalist and guitarist with the Spencer Davis Group

Dave Dexter: Capitol Records A&R man in the 1960s

Alan Durband: Teacher at the Liverpool Institute

Peter Eckhorn: Manager of the Top Ten Club in Hamburg

Geoff Emerick: Recording engineer at Abbey Road Studios

Brian Epstein: Manager of The Beatles

Clive Epstein: Brother of Brian Epstein

Horst Fascher: Former Hamburg boxer, bouncer, and nightclub manager

Len Garry: School friend of John Lennon and member of The Quarry Men

Billy Graham: American evangelist

Jim Gretty: Salesman and guitar teacher at Hessey's Music Store in Liverpool

Tom Halley: Animator on the movie *Yellow Submarine*

Peter Halling: Classical cello performer

George Harrison: Liverpool Institute student and musician

Louise Harrison: George Harrison's sister

Bill Harry: Liverpool Art College student and editor and founder of *Mersey Beat,* a Liverpool music paper

Ronnie Hawkins: Rock-and-roll performer

Dezo Hoffman: Beatle photographer

Mary Hopkin: Apple-signed singer

Liz Hughes: Regular patron of the Cavern Club

Dick James: British music publisher

Stephen James: Son of Dick James

Glyn Johns: Engineer/producer of The Beatles, The Rolling Stones, and The Who

Peter Jones: British writer for *Beatles Book Monthly*

Murray Kaufman (Murray the K): New York radio disc jockey

Freda Kelly: British Beatles Fan Club president

Astrid Kirchherr: Hamburg art student, photographer, and fiancée of Stuart Sutcliffe

Billy J. Kramer: Liverpool-born performer

Sam Leach: Liverpool music promoter

Donovan Leitch: Scottish rock vocalist

Cynthia Lennon: Art student and John Lennon's first wife

John Lennon: Art student, performer, and musician

Julian Lennon: Son of John Lennon and his first wife, Cynthia

Sean Lennon: Son of John Lennon and Yoko Ono

Richard Lester: American film director; directed *A Hard Day's Night* and *Help!*

Little Richard: American rock-and-roll performer

Maharishi Mahesh Yogi: Indian guru

George Martin: The Beatles' record producer

David Mason: Classical horn player

Michael McCartney: Art student and Paul McCartney's brother

Paul McCartney: Liverpool Institute student, musician, and performer

Bill Medley: Vocalist with the American "white soul" group, The Righteous Brothers.

Jay Nelson: Rock and Roll Hall of Fame disc jockey

Norman Newell: British record producer

Philip Norman: London *Times* journalist; author of *Shout! The True Story of The Beatles*

Sean O'Mahony: Publisher of *Beatles Book Monthly*

Yoko Ono: Conceptual artist and performer; John Lennon's second wife

Roy Orbison: American musician and performer

David Ormsby-Gore: British ambassador to the United States in 1964

Alan Parsons: British rock musician and performer

Harold Pendleton: Owner of London's Marquee Club

Carl Perkins: American rockabilly performer

André Perry: Montreal recording engineer on "Give Peace a Chance"

Gene Pitney: American rock-and-roll performer

William Popjoy: Headmaster of Quarry Bank Grammar School

Cliff Richard: British rock-and-roll performer

Keith Richards: Rolling Stones guitarist

Red Robinson: Rock and Roll Hall of Fame disc jockey

Dick Rowe: A&R manager for Decca Records

John Rowlands: Photographer

Del Shannon: American rock-and-roll performer

Walter Shenson: American film producer of *A Hard Day's Night* and *Help!*

Tony Sheridan: British musician and Hamburg friend of The Beatles

Pete Shotton: Teenage friend of John Lennon

Mimi Smith: One of John Lennon's aunts who became his guardian

Norman Smith: Recording engineer at Abbey Road Studios

Ronnie Spector: Recording artist

Victor Spinetti: British actor; starred in *A Hard Day's Night, Help!,* and *Magical Mystery Tour*

Ringo Starr: Liverpool drummer and performer

Ed Sullivan: Television host of popular U.S. variety show

Millie Sutcliffe: Mother of Stuart Sutcliffe

Alistair Taylor: Brian Epstein's personal assistant

Derek Taylor: Journalist, personal assistant to Brian Epstein, and Apple Corps press officer

Iain Taylor: Liverpool historian and Liverpool Institute student

James Taylor: American rock performer and early Apple Records artist

Chris Thomas: British producer during *White Album* sessions

Ken Townshend: EMI employee at Abbey Road Studios

Klaus Voorman: German artist and musician

Paul White: A&R director for Capitol Records, Canada

Bob Whitaker: British photographer

Allan Williams: Liverpool club owner and promoter

Lord Woodbine: West Indian friend and business associate of promoter Allan Williams

Beryl Wooler: Assistant to Brian Epstein and wife of Bob Wooler

Bob Wooler: The Cavern Club's disc jockey and friend of The Beatles

Bill Wyman: The Rolling Stones' bassist

List of Illustrations

Chapter One: The Quarry Men in performance at St. Peter's Church Fête, Woolton, Liverpool, July 6, 1957: Eric Griffiths, left (guitar), Colin Hanton (drums), Rod Davis (banjo), John Lennon (guitar, vocals), Pete Shotton (washboard), Len Garry (tea chest bass). It was after this performance that Paul McCartney met John. Geoff Rhind. Ponopresse/L.F.I.

Chapter Two: Rare shot of The Beatles performing in Hamburg: George Harrison, left, John Lennon, Paul McCartney, Pete Best. As Paul is playing bass, this must be from the group's second German residency. Archive Photos

Chapter Three: The Beatles playing The Cavern Club in 1961: George Harrison, left, Paul McCartney, Pete Best, John Lennon. Archive Photos

Chapter Four: Performing for a BBC radio broadcast in London, 1963: George Harrison, left, Paul McCartney, John Lennon, Ringo Starr. Ponopresse/L.F.I.

Chapter Five: A police cadet protects his ears from the screams of surrounding female fans at a Beatles performance in Manchester, November 20, 1963. Canapress Photo Service

Chapter Six: Manager Brian Epstein, left, and three of The Beatles watch as Ed Sullivan gets a lesson in playing bass guitar before The Beatles' historic appearance on Sullivan's national television show, February 9, 1964. It is estimated that 60% of all television viewers in the U.S., or 73,000,000 people, were watching. George Harrison, recovering from the flu, missed this audition. Archive Photos

Chapter Seven: The Beatles display their medals after being awarded membership in the Order of the British Empire by Queen Elizabeth at Buckingham Palace, October 26, 1965. Canapress Photo Service

Chapter Eight: Celebrating the launch of *Sgt. Pepper's Lonely Hearts Club Band* at Brian Epstein's London residence, May 1967. Ponopresse/L.F.I.

Chapter Nine: Business pressures begin to take their toll. Ponopresse/L.F.I.

Chapter Ten: Outtake from The Beatles' last photo session, taken at John's house, Tittenhurst Park, August 22, 1969. © Ethan A. Russell

Chapter One

Rockin' the Casbah

Crossing the Mersey River today is quite different from those noisy days in the mid-1950s. Back then Liverpool was an industrial seaport where ships from around the world made regular visits. The city was dull, damp, and dirty. It was working-class, but in the 1950s it raised a generation of young people not content to finish their education merely to take over traditional jobs. They wanted their freedom and independence, which was revealed in the way they acted and in the way they dressed. They wore the British tough-boy clothes of the day known as the Teddy Boy look: crepe-sole or winkle-picker shoes, drainpipe pants, long, draped jackets, and "slim-jim" ties. Their hair was long and greased back in the Elvis/Little Richard style, and they were drawn to the aggressiveness of rock and roll, a lot of which was brought into Liverpool by the ships from America. One of those disaffected teenagers growing up in Liverpool was John Winston Lennon.

Mimi Smith: I loved John [Lennon] from the first moment I saw him in the hospital. Of course, George [my husband] and I never had any children, so when my sister, Julia, had John, I was thrilled. I remember running quickly home from the maternity hospital the night he was born to beat the start of the nightly German bombing raids. I was out of breath and excitedly told everyone, "He's the most beautiful baby in the hospital." My father said, "Well now, Mimi, all women say that about their babies." So I said, "No, no, he's not like the others. They're all red and wrinkly and he's smooth and beautiful."

Julia was a wonderful girl, all full of fun and life, and though she loved John dearly, it was clear after Freddy [Julia's husband] left on the ships that it was really better that he stay with George and me. Of course, things couldn't have worked out better if we'd planned it, because George and I loved him madly, and every day Julia would come over and play with him, so he really had two mothers in a way.

Julia Baird: Mimi is the eldest of five girls and apparently decided right from the start never to have children. When she got married, there was this understanding that there would be no children.

John was brought up by his [and my] mother, Julia, although Mimi did the "bread and butter" of the daily upbringing. My mother had all the fun with him, I think. She taught him all the musical stuff. Mimi was a bookworm, an absolute reader. My mother read a lot, too, but also played lots of instruments and sang. She played the piano, the accordion, the harmonica, and the banjo. She was a lot of fun. She played with us a lot, which I thought was normal for a parent to do, but I don't think it actually is. She gave us a lot of her time. A lot of time in the park, a lot of time just walking, a lot of time going on the river boats. And it gives us so much more to remember her by.

Aunt Mimi has been maligned by journalists and authors over the years, and it just isn't fair. Mimi is a great lady. There isn't anyone in the family who hasn't fallen on her for support whenever they needed to. She's as strong as a rock. Now you can't expect someone as strong as that not to have her own very firm ideas about how things should be done. My sisters have lived with her. My cousins have lived with her. She's great, absolutely great. She is a very strong disciplinarian, but it fits in with enough love. We all used her when we were growing up to bounce ideas off. She's a great listener. If you've got problems, she sits and she listens. She's also a very witty, highly intelligent woman. She can cut with her words.

I think the whole family has got a sense of humor, but then, if you live in Liverpool, everybody has it. If you get on a bus to go into town, the bus conductor will say, "Who let you out looking like that!" This is just part of the life in Liverpool. It really is!

Paul McCartney: They used to call Liverpool the capital of Ireland, so you were always around a lot of music. In some ways it was a very musical city. Glasgow is just like it, with lots of musical history combined with all the old music hall stuff, which my dad played in a band at one time. Before that he worked on a spotlight in the music halls. His background certainly influenced me. He worked on the limelights when it was actually a piece of lime that they burned. He was the guy who trimmed the pieces of lime after they were finished. He would bring home used programs after the first shows, tidy them up, then take them back and sell them again for the second show.

From childhood John had to be the leader, whether in a gang or in his first musical groups.

Mimi Smith: He [John] loved to draw and paint as a child, and he was always reading. He would be content for hours at a time drawing in his room above the porch. We put an extension speaker from the hi-fi in the lounge in his bedroom so he could listen to some of his favorite shows. He loved *The Dick Barton Show,* which was that very popular thriller series, and he was crazy for *The Goon Show.* He loved to imitate the accents and replay all the skits for me. I think this is where he really developed his love of words and those horrible plays on words.

Julia Baird: Where did John get his musical talents? Oh, from my mother definitely. Some people, like my cousin, Leila, said that my mother had far more talent than John ever had because he only inherited a slight spot of it. The whole family is biased toward my mother, of course, beautifully so. But she did really have enormous talent. She was a very creative person. She did paintings on the wall, directly on the wall. We grew up with all that around the kitchen chimney. And she would always play. If she was reading us something like "The Teddy Bear's Picnic" [a children's story], we'd get the *da, da, da, da* and the mouth organ and stuff like that. We got it all. Everything was well decorated.

Of course, John was six and a half years older than me, so she was beginning to teach him. She'd been taught the banjo by her grandfather. She'd inherited this beautiful mother-of-pearl, four-string banjo, a very big one. She used to play "That'll Be the Day" by Buddy Holly, one of the ones John sang later. I remember us standing over him, making him play it again and saying, "Yes, it will hurt. Press harder. Press harder. Yes, it hurts. Get the tone clear." When I was talking to Paul [McCartney] recently, I asked, "Do you remember the banjo?" He said, "Oh, yeah, of course I remember it." Later, in the studios, when they'd actually started recording, sometimes they had to cut, cut, cut, cut because John was back on banjo chords. My mother must have taught him well.

John was always practicing, and Mimi banished him and his friends out to the porch. I can't blame her. Only two could get into the porch, so if they wanted more than two, they would come to my mother's house and she would let them into the bathroom. Well, only four could get in there at a squash, but they used to play the guitars, the harmonica, a washboard, and cymbals. Skiffle was very big at the time. They used to play there a lot. They would bang around in the kitchen because they could use different utensils. Then they would go up to the bathroom, which was a good echo chamber. The walls were all tiled and the bath was enamel and very small. It was very noisy. We lived in a corner house with a big garden. But we used to hear, from outside, the thumping of it. Never meant any music to us. It was just a noise, a real noise. You'd never expect a big group to come out of it.

John was playing instruments for as long as I can remember. In the end he was in groups — so-called groups in those days. Everyone who had a brother, and there were lots of big families, had someone in a group. I mean, we were three. There were families of five, seven, eight, nine. It was nothing. Liverpool is a very Catholic city. That's the Irish influence for you. And huge families. I mean, it wasn't odd to have a brother nearly seven years older than you at all. And sisters and brothers younger and more on the way. They all played something. The guitar, the piano or the "gob iron," which was the harmonica. Everybody played it. Children would get little mouth organs in Christmas socks, and by the time they were nine, they were little Larry Adlers going around. I mean, they all knew how to play. It was just a lovely instrument because you could stuff it into your pocket, couldn't you? You had your own music entertainment wherever you went. And then there was a bus driver who gave John a really good harmonica.

So, as I say, getting back to brothers. It wasn't unusual to have one playing things and getting together with other people to play. Just wasn't unusual at all. John was going to art school and stuff like that. Mimi was desperately worried all the time that he wasn't doing enough drawing, enough painting, enough, you know, work. He was going to be a commercial artist. I always thought that meant that he would stand up on the big billboards and actually paint the adverts on. That's what I wanted it to be. But he was going to be a commercial artist.

Mimi Smith: He used to drive me mad with his guitar playing, and I'll always remember telling him, "The guitar's all right for a hobby, John, but it won't earn you any money."

Harold Pendleton: I can tell you exactly how skiffle started. It was with the Chris Barber Jazz Band. Sometimes they would just be fooling around, playing "rent party" music or "whisk broom" music or whatever. They didn't know what to call it until somebody said it was sort of like a skiffle music, which was one of the various names, and it caught. Decca Records decided to produce an LP of Barber's band. On that LP was a song called "Jingle Rock Island Line" by one of the members, Lonnie Donegan. The reason that it was recorded in the first place was only because they didn't have enough tunes, so they did this song simply to fill up the record. Two years later somebody discovered it and issued it as a single, "Rock Island Line." Bingo, it became a big hit, and Lonnie Donegan became a star. It was, simply, because they hadn't enough material to complete an LP, so they did a couple of skiffle numbers to fill the hole.

Sam Leach: I started promoting in 1957, and skiffle was what caused me to get into it. Skiffle was the beginning of the whole Liverpool scene in the end, because once the bands realized that they could form a group cheaply, just washboards and tea chests, it was next to nothing and you could have a band. So, from the 600 or 700 skiffle groups came the nucleus of about 300 rock-and-roll bands two or three years later. And that's sort of how it evolved!

John Lennon: It was just before the time rock and roll started getting big in Britain. I think I was around 15, so it would be 1955. Everyone was crazy about skiffle, which was a kind of American folk music, and it sort of went like *ging ging-e-ging, ging ging-a-ging,* using washboards. And all the kids who were 15 and 16 used to have these groups, and so I formed one at school.

William Popjoy: I became headmaster at Quarry Bank during John Lennon's last year. My first year was his last year — by coincidence, I might say. I knew John very well indeed because he and his friend, Pete Shotton, were notorious long before I came to the school. They had set out to make as much a nuisance of themselves as possible, and they were the two boys I was principally warned about before I arrived. And they did get up to a number of tricks, but John was a boy of great talent, as others of his friends were. The interesting thing was that skiffle was not his main interest at the time. It was a strong interest, but I asked him to write out for me what were his principle interests in order and he began with salmon fishing. Now sometimes people think it's a joke, but no, his aunt enabled him to go up to Scotland and fish for salmon and he liked that very much. Then he was keen on poster designing. He was very keen on painting, he was keen on writing poetry, and then in the middle of the second line came skiffle.

Yoko Ono: He used to tell me about his salmon fishing. One of his aunties lived in Scotland and married a Scottish man, so whenever John visited them, he went salmon fishing. Not often. I think that this man really liked salmon fishing and he did that by himself usually, but sometimes John was allowed to join him. And salmon was a big thing. John used to say, "Oh, salmon . . . Scottish salmon. There's nothing like it." And when I visited this auntie with him, I did get to eat the salmon, and it was very fresh. We used to get smoked salmon to eat here in New York, but most of them were so salty we didn't like it. The ones that we got in Scotland were really good. I don't know why they don't export them. Salmon was one of the things that we really enjoyed eating.

John and friend Pete Shotton formed their first group, The Quarry Men, in early 1956, named after their school, Quarry Bank Grammar School.

William Popjoy: Several of John's friends were interested in skiffle and also wrote lyrics and played the guitar, as he did. In those days he hadn't thought of making money out of it. For example, he came to me and asked for permission to play with The Quarry Men, his skiffle group, in the interval of the sixth-form dance. I said that I'd think about it and then perhaps reluctantly I'd agree. Then John and his friends would play during the dance, but it would never occur to him to ask for money. When The Beatles and other groups became popular, there was a craze for forming groups. Boys would come along and ask for money, which they wouldn't get. John in those days certainly wasn't mercenary and he didn't have his eye on making money.

He was loyal and very generous to his friends at school. I do know that. Interestingly, I ran into his aunt once while visiting a sick friend, and she told me that John slept with a picture of the school over his bed, which rather impressed me. And he used to send messages through old friends. He would say — even after I'd been here for more than 20 years — "Oh, do look in and see how that new fellow Popjoy is getting on." I remember that he wrote a letter to one of my students who had written a fan letter to him saying, "Remember me to anyone who is still there, even to Popjoy. After all, it was he who got me into art school so I could fail there, too, and I can never thank him enough," which I thought was very witty.

Julia Baird: John was a rebel. I'm not denying that. He was a pack leader. We were very, quite strictly, brought up, yes. And when you're kept too tight, you spring an awful long way when you go. We all went back, of course, because you do, don't you? Oh, he did. There was always that restraint there. When you think of his talent and the pressures he was under from the media, he always conducted himself very well. He kept his cool in interviews. It wasn't John who lost his cool ever. He would be snarky sometimes and talk his way through it because we can all talk our way out of anything, but he would never, he never, lost his rag in an interview, did he? Even when he was being pushed to the ultimate. He might give a quip. He had that common decency of restraint. The social graces were laid down well enough. He never did the Keith Moon thing, for example, or anything like that. He never bashed up hotel rooms or left them with a wreck and then just sent a check the next day, which was commonplace with lesser groups at that time. That was because he'd been brought up with that sort of standard.

We've all sprung out and now we're all coiling back again. In fact, you're looking for the center again as you get older and you get your own children. Now there was John with Sean. He started looking for a family [again]. He always said that he would never bring his own children up as strictly as we were brought up, including himself. He said that's not for children. You don't treat them like that, you know. And then when he had Julian, he actually sent Julian down to Mimi and asked, "Mimi, will you do something with him?" It didn't take John long to realize what children do need — firm guidelines and all the rest of it. And he was always strict with him. Julian was eating boiled eggs at mahogany tables when he was 18 months old, feeding himself. Because John knew it was the right thing for him to be doing.

Len Garry: We got on because of our sense of humor and also because of music. We'd laze about on the bank of the river every day in the summer. That was our meeting place. The gang consisted of Lennon, [Pete] Shotton, Ivy [Ivan Vaughn], myself, Nigel Whalley, and a guy called Billy Turner. The music we were listening to was Guy Mitchell, and Bill Haley was coming in. In fact, all the music from the United States was coming in at the time. I'd take off Johnny Ray and Lennon would take off Elvis and somebody would take off someone else, but it was only Lennon and me who actually could sing, to be honest with you. We used to take off and laze about on the bank on a summer afternoon. Just absolute wasters, we were.

John was doing cartoons then at the age of 14, you see. We had a book called the "Daily Howl," where he'd do cartoon characters of his teachers at Quarry Bank and that sort of thing. So the outlet for his talent was even coming in those days. One was in the music and the other was in the arts, which in the cartoons was his humor coming through. Very quick with the one-liners. I mean, I was quite quick with the one-liners, too. I still am but I've mellowed over the years because I don't like hurting people, but in those days we didn't care who we hurt, if you know what I mean. As to why people were drawn to Lennon, it's an undefinable gift. Some people really have that certain charisma or magnetism and people are drawn to it. And there's not that many on the planet, to be honest with you, like that. But he was one of them. It's inexplicable.

Ivan [Vaughn] was a zany character with a great sense of humor. When we were on the stage, I linked with Ivan. We were in form 3A in the Liverpool Institute and we studied Latin. Ivan was very bright. I think his mother was widowed and she had a daughter called Bernice, who Lennon was always "taking the piss" out of. She was a lovely girl, however. Ivan was very studious, very good on the languages side, and went on to higher forms. I dropped down because of The Quarry Men and Lennon. I'll blame it all on Lennon. Blame everything on Lennon. No, but seriously, I went lower and he went higher, though we were still friends. That's how Ivan linked up with Paul [McCartney] because Paul went higher on the languages side, you see. That's where the link, the friendship, came with Ivan and Paul.

But Ivan was a character. Ivan used to stand in on the teacher's space when he didn't feel like turning up. He'd get up and do a couple of stints now and again. Oh, yeah, he fitted in the gang because it was the humor that linked us all together initially. That's what it was. Anything for a laugh. Do anything, you know. Liven the place up. Go to a cinema and let's liven it up. Lennon would be rolling on the floor and be kicking the hell out of him, you know, begging him to stop. Everywhere was a laugh. We just took everything so flippantly really.

Iain Taylor: Ivan was a tall, good-looking guy with dark hair. I remember him in our last years at school when we would go down to the Central Reference Library and he would always park himself next to these circular stairs where the cute young librarians would walk up the stairs and he could get a better view of them. He was always able to get dates and he was certainly a very witty guy. He was funny and he had a certain way with the one-liners that Paul and John developed, as well.

Paul McCartney: Ivan was a great guy. He was the leader of "the gang," if you will, and all the lads followed him around because he was just a lot of fun to be with, you know, always making crazy jokes. He was really hilarious, yet he was never mean to anyone, and so he had a lot of friends. The other thing was that he knew a lot about music, you know, skiffle and rock and roll.

My dad was a pretty musical guy, and one day he bought me a trumpet. I started playing around and eventually learned "When the Saints Come Marching In" and a couple of other standards. But I couldn't make my lip do quite what it was supposed to, and I realized that I wouldn't be able to sing if I was playing the trumpet, and I liked singing. So I decided to try the guitar, but it was a right-handed one because they hardly ever made left-handed guitars then. I couldn't figure out how to play it correctly. Eventually I turned the strings around and finally it felt good and I could play.

I remember watching telly one day and on comes the movie *Blackboard Jungle,* which is where Bill Haley performs the song "Rock Around the Clock." And I remember it very clearly because it was the first piece of music that ever sent a tingle up my spine.

Len Garry: Well, you see, Paul was quite artistic. And academically Paul was very, very bright. He was good on languages. He was good on art. He was good on English. Good at maths. I mean, academically he could have gone to university, which is what his dad would have liked. My memories of Jim [Paul McCartney's father] were him sitting there doing his crossword puzzles in the chair. Always doing the crossword was Jim. Of course, Jim had, I think, a link with the bands in the 1930s.

On July 6, 1957, Paul went with Ivan Vaughn to see The Quarry Men perform at an outdoor party at the Woolton Parish Church.

Pete Shotton: His name was Paul McCartney. We spent 20 minutes talking to him, and at first it was very reserved because John was a bit careful about meeting new people. He liked to suss them out first. He never liked to make the first move. People always had to come to him. Eventually Paul came to him by getting out his guitar and playing, I think, "Twenty Flight Rock" by Eddie Cochran, and it was *good!* So, as I say, we chatted for about 20 minutes and then we split up and John and I walked home together. While we were walking, John asked me, "What do you think of him then?" And I said, "I think he's okay. I like him." And John said, "Well, should we ask him to join the band then?" And I said, "Yeah, it's okay by me if it's okay by you." So that was that.

Len Garry: Yeah, I knew Paul would come that day from Ivy Vaughn. Because Paul used to, prior to coming to meet us, bring his guitar in at Christmas time. There was a guy called Ian James who Paul was friendly with. Now Ian James was a better guitarist than Paul. I think Ian helped Paul on his guitar a great deal because you always learn from one another. He was quite instrumental. No one's mentioned him, but Ian James was a good guitarist. Anyway, at Christmas time, and the end of term, I remember Paul bringing his guitar in. This is before he joined The Quarry Men. Ivan had seen this and said, "You've got to come around and see this other guy." Ivy was the one who spotted Paul's interest and talent. Of course, there were loads of bands starting up at the time. There must have been about 300 or 400 bands within the Liverpool area. There were loads and loads of them. Some of them far better than us instrumentally, you know. Let's face it. We were pretty basic. And with the joining of Paul it was just what was needed, wasn't it? Sparked us off and here we are.

John Lennon: Paul met me the first day I did Gene Vincent's "Be Bop a Lula" live onstage. Ivan Vaughn, a mutual friend of both of us, brought him to see my group, The Quarry Men. We met and we talked after the show. He was playing guitar backstage and doing "Twenty Flight Rock" by Eddie Cochran, and I saw he had talent. After talking about all the music and artists we liked, I turned round, and right there at this first meeting I asked, "Do you want to join our group?" And he looked down at his feet for a minute or so and said, "Um, um, ah, yeah!"

Paul McCartney: John was onstage with The Quarry Men singing "Come little darlin', come and go with me," but he didn't know the proper words, so he just started making them up, like "Down, down, down, down to the penitentiary." I remember I was impressed, and I thought, They're good. That's a great band. I met them in the church hall later and I sang a few songs to them, and John was impressed because he didn't know that many. He played some songs to me and we had some fun, but the other thing I remember is that he smelled a bit drunk.

Julia Baird: Yes, we all went — Nanny, everybody but Mimi. She didn't go, and I don't know why. She was probably disgusted with them playing in public or something like that. But we all went. My mother, my dog, and everybody. That was the day that John and Paul met. And that was when Paul said that he was thoroughly impressed by John totally improvising all the words because he could never remember them. He was improvising like crazy and lots of *whoa, whoa, whoas*. Well, he just couldn't remember the words. And Paul impressed them all thoroughly by knowing all the words to everything. Well, he was a musician, Paul. I'd say if you ever were going to split them up — this is my own viewpoint — John was the lyricist and Paul was the musician.

Len Garry: As I say, there was a fear that he [McCartney] could oust Lennon. I mean, that was the fear to start with. Of course, it didn't work out like that. They gelled, didn't they?

Paul McCartney: We used to sag off school together and go back to my house because there was nobody home in the afternoons. We'd sit around smoking and talking and then we'd play a bit on my dad's piano and our guitars. We would try different songs that either of us knew, and John would teach me the ones he knew and I would show him the ones I knew. But, actually, we ended up playing a lot of Buddy Holly's stuff, mostly because he had the least number of chords and we could get through them. We wrote a lot of songs then like "Love Me Do" and "Too Much About Sorrows." There was a lot from then, about 100 that we've never recorded. We would have friends who were getting blues records from family members. Remember, Liverpool was a seaport, and a lot of imports like blues records, country-and-western and rock-and-roll records, would come into Liverpool through the ships. Records by Hank Snow, Hank Williams, Chuck Berry, Ray Charles, Little Richard and, of course, Elvis Presley. He was my boy, as we used to say. The main man, the lad, and I also loved Little Richard, too. I never thought that this music was rebellious. My dad would tell me he didn't like much of it, but then his dad did the same to him. He would call the music that Dad liked tin-can music, because mainly he was a brass-band musician. You know, the McCartney family tree has a line of music in it that goes back quite a way. My grandfather used to play an E-flat bass in a brass band, and as I said, he didn't like the music my dad did, so my dad became a lot more tolerant with my musical tastes and likes. I've always loved bass, and I remember my dad making me listen, or making me aware, of the bass coming through on the radio, and saying to me, "Hear that? It's the bass part." And then he would show me how the bass is used in a band.

Early in 1958, when George Harrison was only 15, he was asked to join The Quarry Men by Paul McCartney. At first John was opposed until George flawlessly played Bill Justis's "Raunchy."

George Harrison: When I was a kid growing up, the guitar was the main thing that saved me from boredom. It was the only job I could think of that I really wanted to do — playing guitar and getting in a rock band. Then, through the Beatle years, it was the way I made my living. The guitar has always been important to me. I think 1956 was when I first got a guitar. That was around the same time I met Paul McCartney in school. He used to live near me and we used to take the same bus ride home. After we started hanging around together, I found out that his father used to have a little band. So there was a bit of music in his family. He had a trumpet, so we used to hang out and try and play things like "When the Saints Go Marching In."

Paul McCartney: I mean, everything just sort of happened in The Beatles. We didn't really ever plan anything. John had a group before The Beatles and, through a friend of mine, I happened to meet him. I knew George at school, and I happened to introduce him. It all just fell in.

Louise Harrison: I don't think of ourselves as being any kind of a class. I mean, we were just us. My father drove a bus and Mom looked after us at home. Occasionally she would take a job at about Christmas time, you know, to get a bit of extra money for Christmas. But we never ever thought of ourselves as poor or anything. Afterward you read these stories about The Beatles growing up in the slums and all this kind of stuff. I think the way our parents treated us, and the way they handled themselves, was that they had great self-esteem, and we grew up with great self-confidence and self-esteem. You don't think about whether you're deprived or underprivileged. We were just a normal family. We had a good, warm, friendly family life.

Dad would save up his overtime money and his winnings from snooker tournaments. He was a very, very good snooker player, and he would get into the tournaments with the men at his job, the other bus drivers, and he would invariably win because he was such a good player. So he would save the money from that, along with some extra overtime money, and then every year he would take us over to north Wales, or somewhere like that, and rent a little cottage for a couple of weeks and have a vacation. And, you know, a lot of kids in the same income bracket as ours probably didn't see as much of the world as we did, but Mom and Dad were very much into taking us for days out, taking us to different parts of the country. Anywhere that was within a day's outing on a bus or a train or whatever. So although we didn't have a great deal of money, we didn't realize that we didn't.

We did see a lot of what was going on around us. Mom and Dad were both very intelligent people, although neither one of them had the opportunity to be educated to the point that they could have been. When I came along, one of the major goals in their lives was to make sure I was able to get a good education, and as luck would have it, I won a scholarship.

And we always had a gramophone, as it was called back then. Dad had brought a nice rosewood one back from the States when he was away at sea, when I was a little baby. And so we always had loads and loads of records, you know, those little 78s, when I was growing up. Of course, you used to have to wind the gramophone up to play it. We also used to sing a lot. Mom and Dad would sing around the house. We had a radio, as well, which was always going. And Mom, when she was pregnant with George, used to have a program on from Radio India on a Sunday morning. I often think now, you know, that he [George] heard the sitar music, that Indian music, from before he was born.

Members of The Quarry Men were constantly changing. Many couldn't take John's attitude. Eventually it was just George, Paul, and John. One of the first big engagements of this new combination was on August 29, 1959, at the basement Casbah Club in Liverpool.

Mona Best: At that time Pete and [his brother] Roy had their own friends, and they all came and went through the house like it was a railway station. I wanted a little bit of privacy for myself because we had just moved in. The boys eventually said, "Why can't we have the cellar to make into a den?" I said it was a very good idea. So they set up a den down there, and instead of using the house like Victoria Station or Liverpool Central, they'd all troop down to the cellar and natter-tatter downstairs. Then they said, "We've got so many friends, and they bring their friends, so why don't we open a little club?" And I said, "Well, I don't know whether it would pay. Is it big enough?" And they said, "Only a small place, just for our friends, you know, just a place where we can collect. We have no other place where we can congregate." So I said okay, and then everybody said they'd help, and away we went.

We started brushing out and cleaning and designing the club. We had coffee and prepacked sweets and sandwiches, Coca-Cola and juices. And on hot days when the take wasn't very good, the boys would stoke up the fire and everyone would say, "God, it's hot. Coke, please." It was all done in good fun, and we all used to laugh about it. In the midst of us starting off and trying to get the club organized, word got out. It was like a Russian whisper. You know, you say something, then someone else passes it on and they'll add to it. Well, I had a friend staying with me named Ruth. She was a young girl, and she mentioned to some friends that we were opening a club and eventually someone said, "Well, you have to have a group." We said, "Who can we get?" And Ruth said, "I know a boy named Ken Brown, and he's a marvelous guitarist. We'll get him down." I said, "Fair enough," and Ken came down. We had a natter, and I asked, "Do you think you could possibly get a group going by opening night?" He said, "Oh, I'm sure I can if you give me a few days." Well, the next night he came back and said he had a group prepared to play. Now this group consisted of George Harrison, John Lennon, Paul McCartney, and Ken Brown, and that's how it started.

One by one, George, then John, then Paul came over to see me, and they said, "Can we help get the club ready?" I said, "If you want, because there's a lot to do to complete everything for opening night." In fact, we weren't entirely finished when we opened. We all tucked into it, and George, Paul, and John all came over to help. John was the funniest of the lot because, you know, his eyes were terrible. We told him to paint something this color, and needless to say, when he finished it, he'd done it all in a different color. Also, he wasn't too careful when he painted. There were places where we told him not to paint somewhere because the girls would lean against it and get paint on their clothes. And sure enough, John got paint on those places and the girls got splatters of paint on their lovely dresses. But it was all taken in good fun. The club had a fantastic atmosphere. I've not been to a club anywhere in Liverpool or, for that matter, have never heard of any other club that had the same atmosphere as this club.

Pete Best: We were about 15, 16, 17, that age group. Virile young teenagers, so to speak. We were music-mad, and we used to come home and put the record player on or whatever was there to crank up. [He hums.] So Mo [my mother], in her wisdom, turned around and said, "Look, you know we've got a cellar downstairs. Why don't you go down and kick it around? You know, take the stuff down and blow the roof off the cellar, and we did. And then all of a sudden we had people knocking on the door and turning around and saying, "What's going on? We're hearing sounds." And in those days, and I'm talking around '58, '59, coffee bars were very much in.

I don't know whether America knows what coffee bars are. They're slightly different from what we would address as coffee bars. But it was an "in" scene in London. It was coming into Liverpool, and Mo turned around and had an idea. We'd already started. We'd been throwing paint on the wall and doing our little things to make it into our den, so to speak. And Mo took it into another dimension. She started to do it up. She put timber cladding on the wall, turned little units into a bar, and all of a sudden we had a membership of over 1,500, 2,000 people knocking on the door. So we had this little club, but we needed a name. Because of the Eastern influences, with it [the coffee bar] being born out in India, we wanted something to reflect that. There was that famous phrase that Charles Boyer was supposed to have said — "Come to the Casbah." That was how the Casbah Club got its name.

Now we needed a band. There was one that used to play in a little club down the road. They were called the Les Stewart Quartet, and we booked them to open the club. A couple of days before the Casbah was due to open, Ken Brown and George Harrison, who were two members of the band, came round and told Mo, "We've got bad news. The group has broken up, so we're unable to open the club." But George turned round and said that he might be able to save the situation. He happened to know two guys, who turned out to be Paul McCartney and John Lennon, and he said, "I'll talk to them and see if they're interested." So he got in touch with them, and the following day they came down.

Mo talked with them and said that she needed a band to open in about two weeks' time. They said, "Yeah, we'd love to do it!" She said, "Okay, what's going to be the name of the band?" And they said, "The Quarry Men." The lineup was Ken Brown, with

George Harrison, Paul McCartney, and John Lennon. That was the first time that I got to know them, and I eventually became friends with them. They also helped in decorating the club. John did some painting on the ceiling. He painted gloss where it should have been matte and vice versa. And then the fateful night came. The Quarry Men played and the place was crowded. They started off as more or less the resident band, if I could put it that way, and they stayed there for about 12 months.

Ken Brown: At that time George Harrison and I were playing with the Les Stewart Quartet. The most we ever got was two pounds for playing at a wedding reception. Working-men's clubs never paid us more than 10 bob. It was George's girlfriend, Ruth Morrison, who told us that Mrs. Best was opening this coffee bar. I went round to see Mrs. Best, and we helped her get the coffee bar ready, installing lighting, covering the walls with hardboard to prevent condensation, painting the place orange and black. In return Mrs. Best promised that we could play in the Casbah when it finally opened. On the Saturday it opened I went round to see Les Stewart. George was there, too, practicing his guitar. Les and I got into an argument, and Les said he wouldn't appear at the club. So George and I walked out, and I asked him if he knew anyone who could help us out. He said he had two mates and went off on a bus to fetch them. He came back in a couple of hours with his friends, John Lennon and Paul McCartney.

Paul was still at school, with a schoolboyish haircut, and seemed rather neat. But even then John was a bit of a beatnik, wearing his hair very long over his collar and an old pair of jeans. Among the songs we performed on the opening night of the Casbah Club were "Long Tall Sally," which is one of Paul's favorite pieces, and "Three Cool Cats," which John sang, rolling his eyes. This made one chap start to laugh, and John just stopped playing and said, "Belt oop, lad!" John never took any nonsense from anyone even in those days. He was a lonely youngster who didn't talk much about his family. He seemed in need of affection and dependent on Cynthia, who was his steady girlfriend even when I was with them. She used to come along to the Casbah in the evening and sit by the stage. Paul didn't bother about girls at all in those days.

Cynthia Lennon: The chemistry was very strange because my upbringing was a very basic and a very secure and happy family in a semi-detached house on the Wirral, which is across the water from Liverpool. John was also brought up in a semidetached house by his auntie. It was sort of a middle-class upbringing. I dressed middle-class, but John didn't. He dressed like a Teddy Boy, but underneath that exterior, that rough and aggressive exterior, was a middle-class John Lennon. Because I had such a secure upbringing, I think it was the attraction of opposites. I mean, I had to find out what this person was all about, and I think he felt from me the same way. Of course, the glasses were the catalyst, or whatever it is, that brought us together. His rough exterior was for self-defense, and it also had a lot to do with not wearing glasses because he couldn't see. He felt he was being preyed upon the whole time by someone who was going to punch him in the nose because he didn't wear his glasses. If he had worn his glasses, he would have been able to see that nobody would have been there to do it. He wanted to stand out. He needed an audience, and he always got an audience because he shocked. John didn't let anyone off lightly. He was on many levels. John's attitude was to fight insecurities, hence the aggression that came out in different ways. He would never allow people to see his insecurities. John had a lot more tragedies in his life than most. I think the fact is that he didn't want people to see his weaknesses. He was always battling against that. He never stopped all his life, right up to the end.

Mona Best: The boys used to play every Saturday and Sunday, and we had a membership of over 2,000 people in our little club. Luckily they all didn't come at once! But every weekend we'd be packing in about 300, 400 people. Sweat would be pouring off them. We had a little dance area, and they'd all be shoulder to shoulder, but they loved it. One night Ken Brown was sick with flu, so I thought I'd keep his pay and give it to him later. I said, "I'll pay Ken when he's better." And they [the rest of the group] said, "No, you won't. He wasn't here. We'll take his share." They didn't have much money in those days, so they'd fight over a halfpenny. And I said, "That's a bit mean, isn't it? He's ill and can't play and you begrudge him his pay?" They said, "No!" So I said, "I'll give the money to Ken and you sort it out among you." The next week I gave Ken the money, and there was a real showdown. Ken said, "If that's your attitude, then I don't want to play with you." As soon as he left, and word got out that he'd left because they begrudged him the money when he was sick, their appeal was gone. No one seemed to care about them. So they decided that it was time to move on, and we were without a group.

Ken Brown: Mona Best came up to us to pay me the 15 shillings for the night I was sick. The other three looked round and said nothing. Then Paul shouted, "Right, that's it then!" And all three of them stormed off.

The Quarry Men started to play different venues, sometimes changing their name.

George Harrison: We did this one talent show thing where we were called Johnny and the Moondogs, which was really just John standing at the front with no guitar and singing. Paul and I played guitars at the back doing, "Ba ba ba."

Bill Harry: At the Liverpool Art College I heard of this "brilliant" new student who everyone was talking about because they thought his art was unique. He was young and quite introverted. That was Stuart Sutcliffe. I used to go round to his place and talk. After we became friends, we were appointed to the Art College Students' Union Committee, and he wanted to make a friend of another new student, John Lennon. Well, at first I thought John was a bit different from everybody else. When I first saw him, he was quite an imposing figure in Teddy Boy jacket and sideburns. He looked like a right Teddy Boy, because everyone else [at the art college] at the time wore duffel coats and very arty-type things with dark, long, droopy sweaters and tight trousers. Very artsy-craftsy. Of course, the influence at the time was the Beat Generation of America — [Jack] Kerouac, [Allen] Ginsberg, and all the rest. After getting to know John, I began to like him very much. There was this sort of creative side about him. I think John was a bit shy at the time, because even though he came on like a rocker, I'd been told, probably by Stuart, that he wrote poems.

Across from the art college in Rice Street there was a pub called Ye Cracke, which we often used to go to. I'd sit there with John and we'd have half bitters and things. One time I said, "Look, I've heard that you write poetry. Can I see some of it?" I eventually talked him into showing me some of it and I thought the humor was very strange and different. What impressed me about it was that it wasn't derivative of the Beat Generation, the West Coast type thing that was going down in California, which a lot of the people in Britain were doing at the time.

Millie Sutcliffe: Poor Stuart. In my stupidity I sent him to learn the piano when he was only nine. It was only later that I realized how stupid it was because a boy feels rather "soft" learning the piano. His father was a wonderful pianist, a classical musician, though not commercial or anything like that. He played just for his own pleasure, which is a Scottish thing. In the Scottish middle-class families, if you didn't have a piano, you weren't middle-class, you see. There was always a member of the family who played the piano or the violin or the cello or something. Banjos and things like that, they never came into our life at all!

John Lennon was teaching himself the guitar. He was such a wonderful personality — oozing with it! And such a contrast to Stuart. John did all the things that Stuart would have loved to have done if he had the courage. John was a real extrovert and a natural wit. It was true that they were great friends, but in a nice way. Some people would like to put an evil construction on it, a homosexual slant, which was very far from the truth. Not true at all! John nearly killed somebody one time when it was hinted. Besides, there were too many lovely girls.

They admired each other's talent. John admired Stuart's ability, his intelligence, his honesty, and his refined manner. He was very gentlemanly indeed! Stuart, likewise, admired John's "Don't give a damn about it, why should I do this just because that's what everybody else does" attitude. He refused to be conventional, to conform.

Len Garry: I was at the [Liverpool] Institute. John had started at the art college, which is right next door to the institute. At lunchtime Paul and I would just whip in and see John. We met this guy called Stuart, who was a very morose, quiet sort of character. Very much an introvert, I would say. I never really got to know him all that well because he was heavily into his art.

Alan Durband: Paul was always liked by the other lads. He was friendly and well behaved but, at the same time, he was always very private. He was very funny at times and could make his mates at school collapse with laughter. He had what people often refer to as a "Liverpool wit," yet he was also rather withdrawn. He had a lot of natural charm, which endeared him to his teachers. In fact, he was consistently voted the "head boy" of his class, which meant he was responsible for organizing the class.

I was sad to hear of his mother's death because I know, as it would be for any other youngster, it was very tough on him. I know it shattered him, though. As far as his behavior in class, he remained pleasant and charming. The other thing was that I think it [Paul's mother's death] was probably the reason he turned to playing the guitar. Although I could hardly believe that he would one day become a rock-and-roll performer.

Iain Taylor: There were some teachers who were extremely good. "Dusty" Durband, who taught Paul McCartney and myself for two years, was great. He taught us geography and English. There were also some terribly boring ones, and there were some who should have been put out to pasture years before. But I think the mix was of high scholarship and riot. It was almost like the 18th century sometimes. Kids put silver paper into the light sockets and fused every electrical outlet in the school. They put flower or soot into the organ, and when it was played, it dropped soot or whatever all over us. You looked forward to something happening and you usually weren't disappointed. Baz, our headmaster, was hated. Everyone said that Baz stood for bastard. He was greatly disliked. On George Harrison's *Dark Horse* album cover there's a section taken out of our school magazine, and it's possible to identify a lot of our teachers at the institute. George's picture from the magazine has been sectioned out and put into the middle of this collection of teachers. Baz has a bull's-eye and George has his finger up because he didn't enjoy the school. It wasn't very good to him.

I got to know Paul McCartney in my last two years at the Liverpool Institute. I had seen him around, but I didn't know him very well. Someone dug me in the ribs and said, "We're in for a couple of good years here," because Paul already had a reputation for being a guy who could create quite a bit of mayhem. Butter wouldn't melt in his mouth. He was able to turn it on and off. He could look as sweet as an angel just after he'd done the most incredibly disruptive things, and usually the blame went to someone else. Paul loved watching performances. He and I were in *Saint Joan,* the George Bernard Shaw play, which was put on by the school. Paul would endlessly change his makeup from night to night. Since we were playing [different] jurors, he was able to do this. He would come up with a new look every night.

I knew George very well. I went to Dovedale Primary School with him. He was a quieter, more taciturn kind of guy, but he was pretty tough, as well. And for a lot of those kids like George, getting a guitar and the skiffle boom was a way of directing their energies and their creativity. So if they hated the boring school stuff we were being fed, then there was an outlet in the literally scores of groups that formed at that time in the institute.

In January 1960, Stuart Sutcliffe sold a painting for 65 pounds sterling at an art exhibition. John Lennon convinced him to use the money to buy a bass guitar.

Millie Sutcliffe: Well, I didn't know what had gone on with the guitar or anything else. What Stuart did was his own business, because he was too sensible and responsible to be stupid. He'd gotten to know John, and John had been running around with McCartney and Harrison. They were at the college [Liverpool Institute], a school that was joined to the art college. George Harrison had left, but McCartney had gone on, thinking he'd do English or something. I think that George Harrison's father played banjo and McCartney's father played in a band. So they were both in that sort of atmosphere or level or whatever you'd like to call it. On the other hand, Stuart was from a very Victorian background with a schoolteacher mother and a civil servant father, who was now in the merchant navy. I had to keep very strict, tight reins on my three children who, very fortunately for me, were excellent and cooperated with me in every way. They never put a foot wrong.

Bill Harry: Well, with Stuart, his art was his passion. When I used to visit with him at his flat in Percy Street, watching him paint, I could never understand why he got involved with The Quarry Men. He wanted to be involved. But, in fact, that only happened after he managed to get one of his paintings sold at the John Moores Exhibition and got the money for the guitar. To me it was very strange. He fell in love with The Quarry Men. He was enraptured by them and wanted to become a member. Yet I knew it was doomed to fail from the start, because he was such a great artist. His mind was constantly ticking over about paintings and art all the time.

Jim Gretty: When the rock-and-roll craze started after skiffle, all the kids wanted to learn how to play guitar. I used to teach every Monday night in a little shop just along the road in Whitechapel between six and half past seven. When you bought a guitar at Hessey's, you got free lessons, and I was the teacher. [There were] 50, 60, 70 people in one night, learning the basic chords of the guitar. I used to have a big blackboard with six lines that were the strings and big dots, and I'd say, "That's the key of so-and-so and that's the key of so-and-so." I would sing a song, and we had a right good time. We had all sorts of kids in for lessons. We had Gerry Marsden of Gerry and the Pacemakers. We had people from The Fourmost — kids from all kinds of groups and bands. Everybody in the Liverpool groups who made the top came for lessons. It got very, very popular.

Allan Williams: Way back in 1959 I had a coffee bar club in downtown Liverpool and I called it the Jacaranda. There was a reason why we had a coffee bar club. It was like the 2-Is Coffee Bar in London. It was a way round the law so that you could open a club as long as you didn't sell alcohol. You just registered it as a club. We had no fire exit. We had nothing, except sweat from the ceilings and the walls. Those days were known as "rock and dole." Fortunately for me, the Jacaranda was about three minutes away from the local unemployment exchange. So all the groups used to collect dole money and then they would come to my coffee bar. I used to let them play for free in the basement. But about five minutes away was the art college and the Liverpool Institute.

Stuart Sutcliffe and John Lennon were from the art college, and from the institute there was George Harrison and Paul McCartney. Anyway, Sutcliffe was John Lennon's best friend. Stu had just won an award for an exhibition of his art. He got paid some money, like 65 pounds, and John persuaded him to buy a guitar — a bass guitar. Now Stu was never really a Beatle. When he played, he was so embarrassed he used to turn his back to the audience because he really couldn't play. But he was John Lennon's mate, and it was John's group, not Paul's.

I was a promoter in the 1960s, and I'd just put a big promotion in Liverpool with Gene Vincent and Eddie Cochran. Well, those who know the history of rock and roll will probably remember that Eddie Cochran was tragically killed in a car accident in England. And so I had the problem of how to promote this show without Cochran. So I phoned up Larry Parnes, who I'd booked the show from — he was the big impresario of the 1960s — and I said, "Look, what's happening?" He said, "You can have your money back or Gene Vincent will do it on his own." I thought, Wow, wouldn't it be great for the first half of the show to showcase all our Liverpool groups? And I put on groups like Gerry and the Pacemakers and Rory Storm and the Hurricanes.

The Beatles had always liked the name of Buddy Holly's band, The Crickets, especially John Lennon. Stuart Sutcliffe loved the name of The Beetles, which he thought was the rival gang in Marlon Brando's movie, *The Wild One*. Much later they realized that "The Beetles" actually referred to the girlfriends of the bike gang. Stuart came up with the name Beetals. Then John changed it to "Beatles." When Allan Williams objected, it became The Silver Beatles.

John Lennon: I was looking for a name like Crickets that meant two things. Then from Crickets I eventually got to Beetles. I changed the *bee* part of the word because it didn't mean two things on its own. So I changed the *e* to an *a* and then it meant two things. It contained *beat*, which is what we were — a beat group. When you said it, people thought of crawly things. And when you read it, it said beat music.

Millie Sutcliffe: At this time, before they went to Germany, Paul McCartney sang most of the numbers and he sometimes played bass, but when Stuart was brought in by John, Stuart was to be the bass player. Paul couldn't play Stuart's bass because he was left-handed. Stuart's father and I always listened to the bass in an orchestra. The bass fascinated us. So we were very pleased when

Stuart decided he'd play the bass guitar. When he asked John to teach him to play the bass, John replied, "It takes all my time to teach myself. I hardly know two chords. I'm only guessing as I go!" So Stuart always played with his back to the audience, when there was an audience. As one writer very aptly put [it], "So the experts wouldn't see how badly he played" — as if there would be any "experts" in those audiences. I thought that was priceless! Stuart was also very shy. He really didn't like the whole performance thing. He didn't like it at all, but he needed the money, even though it was only five shillings they were getting at the time. But when they played at Pete Best's mother's club, she gave them a really good meal, which was nice because they were always hungry.

Pete Best: Yeah, I mean there were influences. The American influences were there. They were attainable. All the Liverpool seamen would come back from America and say, "Hey, listen to this one." So we started to hear sounds long before the rest of Europe and London got to hear them. And people copied it. It was prevalent even going back to the early 1950s stuff and bebop and all those types of music. Then, in the mid-1950s and 1960s, everybody got into Little Richard, Fats Domino, Duane Eddy, and all those different sounds popping over from across the Atlantic. You could say that, right from an early age, the musicians were influenced by American artists.

Lord Woodbine: Allan Williams and I used to run some clubs together, and The Beatles used to play in one of the clubs. There were actually two clubs. In the first one they used to play at dinner time [noon] until 3:00 p.m. The second one was a striptease club in a basement. [It was] called the Cabaret Artists' Social Club [and was] in Liverpool's Chinatown district. Their job was to play music for the strippers. The strippers used to get them to play very slow numbers, which The Beatles really didn't like. There was only one [stripper] who wanted an uptempo song. She used to use a hula hoop in her act. The Beatles weren't interested in the strippers or the music. They just did it for the money.

Paul McCartney: We all had to wear pink shiny suits and had to play weird music. And it was really funny, actually, because every time Janice [a stripper] finished her act, she'd turn right around, stark naked, and look us straight in the eye. We were still only lads back then and had no idea what to do with ourselves. She gave us music sheets, but none of us could read it, so we just made do with things we knew from memory such as "The Harry Lime Theme." She also gave us some classical music, and one of the pieces she wanted us to play was *The Spanish Fire Dance.*

George Harrison: During this period, we never really had a drummer. They would constantly come and go, so Paul decided to play the drums for certain jobs that we would get.

The Silver Beatles played off and on until Larry Parnes, a big British promoter, came to Liverpool to audition bands to back Billy Fury, a very popular star of the day who was also from Liverpool. Billy and Larry Parnes were impressed with The Silver Beatles but would give them the job of backing Billy only if they dropped their bass player, Stuart Sutcliffe. John, Paul, George, and Stuart were very loyal to one another, and so they turned down the offer. Parnes did, however, give them a job backing a lesser known act, Johnny Gentle, for a week in Scotland.

Millie Sutcliffe: Stuart brought home a sketch he'd done of Larry Parnes. I remember it well. He was quite upset, really heartbroken, and he said, "Mother, I think I've let the boys down." Billy Fury was looking for a band, and after the audition, Larry Parnes had said that the bass guitar and percussion were weak, but that could be sorted out. He could get somebody else, as long as he got John, Paul, and George. So John Lennon said, "No go. No Stuart. No go!" Stuart said, "I'm sorry about this," to John. And John said, "Forget it, Stu." That was John's attitude and, time has proved, they didn't need Larry Parnes. I suppose, later on, he was to become the sorriest man in the world for turning down The Beatles.

Chapter Two

Growing Up on the Reeperbahn

Allan Williams: The scene in Liverpool was swinging, and there were about 300 groups playing in church halls, town halls, and clubs. I had a steel band working in the basement, a calypso band, rather, and they went over to Hamburg. Apparently, with Liverpool being a seaport, some German seamen came and told the band that they would get plenty of work in Hamburg. So off they went. By the way, they didn't even tell me. I just went down there one night and there was no steel band. They wrote to me about a month later because they knew that I was promoting, as well, and they said, "Why don't you come over here and look at the scene? It's exploding. There's plenty of work for your bands." So off I went to Hamburg with a character called Lord Woodbine, who was also in a steel band. Apparently, if you're in a calypso band, you have the title of being the lord. Lord Woodbine and I went to Hamburg, and we found this club called the Kaiserkeller. The next thing I knew, I was exporting all the Liverpool groups over there. I told them that the groups were the best in England and that they were very famous. In those days The Beatles worked for five and 10 bob a night [pocket change]. I said, "It will cost you 100 pounds a week, plus my commission of 10 pounds!"

Millie Sutcliffe: Stuart and John got together with Allan Williams and said, "We hear you're taking groups to Hamburg. What about us?" Allan said, "What about you?" Stuart and John said, "Well, why can't we go?" Allan said, "You haven't got a drummer. You can't go professional until you have a drummer." Well, they couldn't afford a drummer, but Pete Best was around at that particular moment and he had the whole drum kit, the lot. Pete was definitely willing to go with them. So that's how they came to get Pete.

Mona Best: After The Quarry Men left us, we needed to find another group for our club. Luckily for us, Ken Brown stepped in and said, "Don't worry. We'll get Peter [Best] and a couple of his friends and we'll put another group together. We'll call them The Blackjacks. We'll play next week and teach Pete the beats. That's how Pete started with The Blackjacks. From that moment on The Blackjacks pulled in bigger crowds than we'd ever had. Unfortunately it was only a temporary group. First, one of the boys announced he was going on a course in London, and another was going back to university, then Ken's parents moved to London and took him with them. That left only Peter.

Paul McCartney had called up just prior to this and said they needed a drummer desperately. George's brother, Peter Harrison, had spoken highly of The Blackjacks. George had seen them and couldn't believe what a good group they were, so they asked Pete if he would like to join them. Pete said, "Okay." That's how he joined The Beatles and how they all went off to Germany.

I wasn't pleased at Peter leaving home at that time because I didn't know what he was stepping into, but he said, "I do want to go into show business, and this will give me a little bit of experience as to what it's all about." So off they went, and Pete had to work very, very hard with the other boys. Germany played a big part in their lives. I think it was the combination of the long hours of playing and the really hard life they had there that made them so good as musicians.

Pete Best: By this time they [The Beatles] had auditioned for Larry Parnes. Stu had joined the band and they were The Silver Beatles. They had been to Scotland to back Johnny Gentle and had come back. Tommy Moore was then playing drums for them but turned around one day and said, "I've had enough." It wasn't quite the Beatle phenomenon yet. The boys had been back down to the club [the Casbah] in their spare time. They saw me playing drums and I got a phone call from Paul. He said, "Pete, we've got the offer to go to Germany. Would you be interested in going?" So I said, "Yeah, sounds good." He said, "Check it over with your family." I had a word with Mo [my mother] and she said, "My boy, if that's what you want to do, do it." So Paul said, "Okay, come down and audition." We went off to a little club, which was later to become the Blue Angel, and we blasted off about six numbers. All standard stuff, cover versions, 12-bar blues, and all of that. Six numbers afterward, the consensus opinion was "You're in, Pete." A week or so after that we were on our way to Hamburg.

The funny thing I meant to mention was that by this time the Casbah was starting to become a showcase for all the bands in Liverpool. Ninety-nine percent of the bands in Liverpool went through and played the Casbah. Mo would give them the chance. They were all starting off. She would say, "Okay, come down and play. We'll give you a break. In the view of the bands it became quite a venue to actually play. And you had Gerry and the Pacemakers, Derry and the Seniors, Rory Storm and the Hurricanes and, of course, The Beatles.

Michael McCartney: On top of the 86 bus coming home to Forthlin Road was when Paul mentioned to me about the Hamburg trip. He was very clever in getting his own way. He just said, "Hey, we're going to Hamburg." I said, "Fantastic. That's amazing. Are you sure?" He said, "Yeah, we're booked. Allan Williams has got this thing over in Hamburg and we're sort of going over there." I said, "Beautiful." Then he inferred, "If I went to Hamburg, I could buy you that blue plastic mac and leather trousers and a camera and things like that. That's what I could buy if I went." I said, "Of course, yes, you could, great!" He said, "There's only one thing, though." I said, "What's that?" [Paul said], "Dad will never go for it." Then there's me going, "Oh, yeah, sure. That's right. That's true." Then Paul said, "Well, maybe if you and me went in together." And I said, "Oh, yeah, okay." And that's how *we* went in and convinced Dad that it would be the greatest thing since sliced bread if his son went to Hamburg and starved for a couple of months, which he did.

I remember when Paul came home from Hamburg. He sat down and made the mistake of putting his leg up on the table. You could see how thin his leg was sticking out between the trouser and the boot, betraying his story or image of how well they did there. You know, "Really doing well. Got all these things

— a new guitar, new this and new that and the other." But this little pipe-thin, pipe-cleaner leg appeared and betrayed him.

My dad's catch phrase was always "Get a job first . . . a serious job. All this poncing round with a guitar and pop singers. . . . Get a job first." Actually my mother was the one that would have been most instrumental in my and my brother's lives. If she had lived, she would have wanted both of us sons to be in the professions, like a doctor, a vicar, or a priest. I often imagine how it would have ended up: "Dr. McCartney?" "Yes, Nurse?" Or "Father McCartney?" "Yes, my son?"

Even though my father was very musical and appreciated our love of performing, it didn't matter. Dad loved his piano and his cornet. He used to play a cornet when he couldn't put a piano on his back and take it round the dances. It didn't matter how much he loved music and parties, though. Me mom would have stopped Paul's career in The Beatles. So there would have been no Beatles and no career [for me] in The Scaffold, the comedy group I was part of. There would have been neither of those entities because we would have been "The Professions."

The Silver Beatles, now renamed The Beatles, left for Hamburg on August 16, 1960.

Lord Woodbine: The five boys, Allan, his wife, Beryl, myself, and Allan's brother-in-law, all piled into this little van for the trip. Allan and I shared the driving, so we had the good seats. I don't know how comfortable it was for the ones in the back seat. [He laughs.] I was fine while I was driving and the time went by quickly. When I wasn't driving, I was resting. Then we had the boat trip and we stopped at a number of places like Arnhem [in Holland]. None of us had ever been out of the country before, so everything was all new. Just outside of Arnhem we stopped for a break, and John was by himself in a store. We were all looking for fruit and vegetables and stuff, but John found a mouth organ and stole it. Allan got really upset, because if we'd gotten caught we would have been deported immediately. Once we got to Hamburg we were tired and just wanted to get our accommodations together. They turned out to be just a couple of rooms in an attic. Nothing in them but a couple of beds. It was really poor, but at the same time it was fun because we didn't know what to expect and it was exciting.

Julia Baird: They went to Germany for the first time, and this was big stuff. John had dropped out of art college to go, and there were riots at home, I can tell you. It wasn't an easy thing for him to do. This is where John the rebel came in. "But I want to, Mimi," he said. "I want to go." She didn't want him to, but he went to Germany, anyway. That's where George [Harrison] says they did all the groundwork for the group. I suppose it's like a manager of a shop where he goes in and spends months learning each department. By the time he gets to the top, he knows the ins and outs of the job. Well, they were doing that bit. Because they'd had a smaller repertoire in Liverpool. They certainly didn't have the huge repertoire that they had to get together when they went to Hamburg.

The first Hamburg club The Beatles played was the Indra. At first they got a cool reception, but gradually their show improved. Their audience went from a group of five to the point where they were packing them in. The first contract had them playing seven nights a week, performing a minimum of four-and-a-half-hour sessions, which was quite a change from the one-hour sets back in Liverpool.

Horst Fascher: Many people called me a bouncer, and I was a bouncer at some of the clubs, but I was also a manager and a friend of the bands. When the [British] groups came to Hamburg, I tried to learn English because I loved the music they were playing. As a result, I became good friends with The Beatles. I was a "Hamburger," like we say, and they were Liverpudlians, so I took care of them. I knew what was going on, especially in the St. Pauli area with all the prostitution and pimps, all the sailors and foreigners. I told them what was dangerous and how to take care of themselves. I said, "If you get into trouble, let me know and I'll try to solve it for you."

When The Beatles first arrived, we were downstairs at the Kaiserkeller, and all of a sudden a rumor got around that a new group was here. We were all nosy and went upstairs to see what this new group looked like. They were playing further down [the street] at the Indra. Tony Sheridan was playing at the Kaiserkeller, so we went downstairs again. When Tony was finished that night, we met The Beatles at Harold's, which was a club where we could eat good chicken soup. We went there and met The Beatles and that was when I found out who was who. Later I found out that the other musicians had told The Beatles, "It's good to stay with Horst. He's a good friend. He takes care of the musicians here!" And that's why we first became friends. I never thought in the first place that they would get so big. If I'd known, then I would have collected more things that they threw away, like drumsticks and guitar strings.

Paul McCartney: Hamburg was our real introduction to the world of show business. People would appear at the door of the club, and our job was to convince them to come in and see us so that they would buy beer from the guy who was paying us. So this is obviously very important when it comes to show business. You're basically there as a means to sell beer. So we'd see someone at the door and we'd really turn it on. One of us would say quietly, "Hey, guys, this is it." And we'd launch into one of our big numbers like "Twenty Flight Rock," or one of our other big numbers. We would make like we hadn't seen them, and we would be just rocking! And you'd see them walk in. Eventually we would fill the club up, and when that started to happen regularly, I would say then we started to know that we were going to make it.

Pete Best: When we first went out there, we were 17 and 18 and we'd never been away from England. We didn't expect anything at all, and we didn't know what Hamburg was like. Of course, when we got there and found out it was a sin city, we were just blown away. We were actually playing in the St. Pauli area, which was the entertainment area for that part of Hamburg, and the Reeperbahn. Gangsters, booze, drugs, prostitution, everything evolved out of there. It was all around and, of course, we were young kids or young men. The booze flowed thick and fast, simply because of the fact that the more we played onstage, and the more the German audiences liked us, they would show their appreciation by sending drinks up to us.

Not surprisingly, during those sets there was often complete mayhem. We used to do crazy things because we were identified as "The *Verrueckt* Beatles," which was "The Crazy Beatles." That was our nickname. We had to perform wild antics onstage. We used to jump off the stage, and John would split his jeans and there would be mock fights onstage. We'd jump off the stage and dance with the audience and run around and stamp our feet. It really became a release valve for us. The faster the music, the faster the German crowd went wild, and Horst Fascher was pleased. So we would do crazy, off-the-wall stuff, like rolling in the streets, getting up to crazy antics onstage, dressing up in funny things, doing things that were totally "crazy" because that's what they wanted to see. That was what we were getting paid for. It became second nature for us and, in a way, because of the state we were in, and the long hours we were playing, it became our release from some of the frustrations we had. Basically we were doing it because it gave us a lot of laughs. It just went on from that really.

Horst Fascher: When The Beatles first came to Hamburg, they behaved quite politely. But when they got used to Hamburg, found out what they could do, and how safe their asses were, then they got a little more fresh. Later on they did many funny things and did much crazier things than in the early days.

George Harrison: In Hamburg we got very good as a band because we had to play eight hours a night and we started building a big repertoire of some of our own songs, but mainly we did all the old rock songs. In fact, we did everything. We used to play "Moon Glow" and lots of other old songs, whatever we could come up with in order to try not to repeat too many. Of course, we had our favorites, which we'd play a couple of times in the night in the main sets when most of the crowd were there. But we got very tight as a band. And it was the period in England when it was all "matching ties and handkerchiefs" and doing [really safe] routines like The Shadows, and we weren't there for that. So we just kept playing the rock-and-roll things and the stuff from records we used to get from Brian Epstein's shop before we met him.

Allan Williams: I think it's recognized now that without Hamburg we'd never have had The Beatles. Hamburg was the training ground for the band. When I sent them over, I already had a group working there, and I informed them that I was sending The Beatles. Back came a nasty letter saying, "You've got something really good going here, Allan. Why are you going to spoil it by sending over that bum group The Beatles?" This was because they were sort of a crappy group. The big names in Liverpool were Rory Storm and the Hurricanes with Ringo [Starr] as their drummer, Gerry and the Pacemakers, The Big Three. The Beatles only played at the art college every Saturday until I became their manager and started getting them work. When the job came up in Hamburg, I thought they were ready to go. And history has proven me right.

It was really . . . well, it wasn't a Sunday school, believe me. Hamburg was *the* place. It was a 24-hour scene, nonstop, and it kicked off at something like 8:00 in the morning and carried on till 8:00 the next morning. It was dark everywhere, and you had no idea what time it was. You just went from one club to another. This is where The Beatles got into amphetamines. Remember that the group was working seven and eight hours a night. They'd finish at 2:00 or 3:00 in the morning and then they'd go to a club where all the other rock-and-roll stars congregated afterward. Then they'd move to another club. I actually tried it one night and did the 24 hours. It was incredible. I'd start on Saturday, and because all the clubs were pitch-black, you couldn't tell whether it was night or day. You'd come out into brilliant sunshine and find that it'd be 11:00 in the morning. The next thing you know, you're going home while people are going to church. Can I tell you the story about John urinating on the nuns as they were going to church? No, I won't tell that story.

It was really wild. Apparently when the Berlin Wall went up, all the gangsters from East Germany moved into the West and into the Hamburg scene. So it was a big gangster town and, of course, they ran all the clubs. There was also a lot of gun running going through Hamburg. The Algerian war was going on, so there was a big gun-running scene. Then along come these little innocent Liverpool lads . . . but we soon learned.

Philip Norman: Hamburg lends itself to the feeling of being able to do anything you want to do. You never have to go to bed. There's a standard of living and a standard of liberality that is quite different from that in England. There seems to be two ways of looking at the world. There are those countries, like England, France, and Russia, that say no on principle, and those, like America, Holland, and Germany, that say yes on principle. You just feel that whatever you ask, people will be nice and try to help. Combined with the raunchy, sexy atmosphere of Hamburg, it must have been wonderful for The Beatles. All of the so-called "wildness" comes down to a lot of alcohol and sex. In England at the time there was not a lot of sex going on. It would have mostly been restricted to heavy petting and so on. There was no birth control, and everyone was terrified of getting girls pregnant. So, to arrive in a place where the girls were very good-looking and forthright with very little hypocrisy, must have been tremendous for them.

Pete Best: The first trip to Hamburg, we were playing six and seven hours a night, six nights a week. That's an hour on, 15 minutes off. The thing was that we were young, we were hungry, and it was our first time out in Hamburg. We'd say, "How many hours are we playing?" They'd say, "You're on all night." We'd say, "Oh, Jesus, what do you mean we're on all night?" It was, however, because of those long, grueling hours, because of the tedium, that we developed the sound that later captured the world. All of a sudden the leather jackets were there and the polo neck shirts, because you could buy them in the shops. We all wore jeans, because any stage suits would fall apart from the sweat. Hamburg was the foundation. It made everything tight. Hamburg helped create an image. I often sit back and say, "If we'd never gone to Hamburg, would it have all transpired?"

On the first trip we were very much a cover band with some differences. We weren't a Cliff Richard-type of band with a soft-shoe-shuffle type of sound. We were into the American stars — Carl Perkins, Little Richard, and Fats Domino. It was the meaty stuff that you could get going with. But we were always looking for something different. We were listening to any records we could find, trying to be a little different. We'd meet people like Tony Sheridan and listen to his repertoire and then our repertoire began to grow. It was only when we went back to Liverpool that we realized how different we'd become.

Most of the bands in Liverpool were called middle-of-the-road, you know, very clean-cut. Suddenly they all turned around and said, "My God, who the hell are these guys?" All of a sudden stage suits went out the window. Everyone was walking around in jeans or motorcycle jackets, whatever the case might be, and it was then that people started really going through the new releases, looking for what was different — the blues and jazz type of thing. Everyone was trying to get different material, to be different from everyone else. Consequently we, in our wisdom, turned around and said, "Let's be a little different. We've written some material. It'd be nice to go back up onstage and say, 'Here's a number that we've written.'" We started doing that. It was nice, and it gave us a good feeling to do some of John and Paul's material. Of course, when we started doing that, lo and behold, everyone else started to follow suit. But we were the first. We were the flagship. As a result, we started to introduce more and more original material into the act.

Cynthia Lennon: Hamburg was decadent. It was sleazy. It was disgusting and it was wonderful at the same time. I was an art student and Dot [Dorothy Rohne], Paul's girlfriend, was working in a chemist's shop at the time. She took time off and I had my holidays, and we went to visit the boys. Now Liverpool was quite decadent, but no comparison to Hamburg. It was a real eye-opener and, of course, when you're young, you have no fear. None of us had any fear at all. I mean, going back now, you watch your back and you're very careful about what's going on. It's just as dangerous now as it was then, but I think it was the experience of a lifetime. I loved it.

After about two months, the Indra was closed because of complaints from neighbors about the noise, and The Beatles moved to another club called the Kaiserkeller. It was a larger place, but had the same tough crowd as the Indra. In this new venue they had to do alternate hours with Rory Storm and the Hurricanes, whose drummer was none other than Richard Starkey, better known as Ringo Starr. The Beatles didn't have much time to socialize during these Hamburg visits, but one day a few German arts students began visiting the Kaiserkeller and they soon became friends. Klaus Voorman was the first to see them and then he took along his girlfriend, Astrid Kirchherr, and Jurgen Volmer. They were immediately attracted to The Beatles and could see something special in their show. Astrid was an excellent photographer. She and Jurgen were the first people to take professional pictures of the band.

Klaus Voorman: I often went for walks in that area [St. Pauli] because I lived pretty close and I had a small apartment there. I walked there because I liked going to the harbor. It wasn't the normal area for art students like me to hang out. As I walked along, I heard this rock music. All the rest of the places were mostly strip clubs and such. I heard this band playing and thought it sounded great. I was scared to go into the place. I sometimes went into jazz clubs, but I never went into rock clubs because I never knew what to expect. I wasn't used to them.

So I went in and sat down at a table. I was scared stiff and ordered a beer. Rory Storm and the Hurricanes were playing, with Ringo Starr on drums. I didn't know he was called Ringo. I just saw this band with this weird-looking singer and thought it was fantastic. And when they were finished, the next band immediately came on. Sometimes a jukebox played between acts, but this time the next band came on. Stuart Sutcliffe came out first and looked really stunning. I thought he was the bandleader because he looked it. He was the most interesting. Then, one after the other, the rest of the band came out. They picked up their instruments, plugged in, and started playing. It sounded amazing, fantastic. I loved it from the first moment. I don't know how long I stayed, but when I went home I said, "You all have to come!" I lived upstairs in a little attic at Astrid's home, so I first took her. She didn't want to go. I really had to convince her, because people were really scared to go there. It was just not the place to go. It was like Soho in London. It wasn't the area you normally went to.

They were a tight little band playing pieces I knew, like Chuck Berry and Little Richard. I thought, Wow, it's so simple. Remember, they rehearsed a hell of a lot and they were quite young. Young kids, really. George was only 17. It was exciting for them. They were having fun. They were giving a lot of enjoyment to the audience, which was a hard thing to do. They just wanted to give pleasure, and that's what they did.

It took more time before we actually met them. We sat there and sat there. We didn't talk with them because we were scared. It was alien and strange for us. Don't forget, we were Germans and they were English. The most outgoing was Paul, like he always was. They didn't strike up a conversation. They were talking about us and seeing us sitting there and saying, "Oh, look at him. He's here again." Then, maybe after six or seven times in the club, the first person I talked to was John. I don't know why. John immediately said I should go and talk with Stuart because he was the arty one in the band. Eventually we somehow became friends, and when they had time to leave their little rooms, which wasn't often, we asked them to come for dinner, go out for a walk, go to the harbor, or drive to the Baltic Sea. We became good friends and saw them a lot.

They definitely wanted to become famous. They had the urge and I think they had the will. You could see that. The other bands that played in the clubs were good, but none were as good as them. Even if they hadn't become a huge success, I would still say they were the best band that played around there at that time.

Astrid Kirchherr: Hamburg has got an area called the Reeperbahn, and it's just nightclubs. In the early 1960s there were strip clubs, prostitutes, and the whole bit. So if you were born in Hamburg as I was, and lived there all your life, it wasn't a place to go for a young girl. I think I'd been to the Reeperbahn once before I went with Klaus. I was pretty frightened when he asked me to go. It took me a couple of days to really make up my mind and agree to go there. We both weren't very comfortable the first couple of times. My English was very poor, just school English. I had little experience talking to English people. I was very shy, as well, and frightened of making mistakes.

Klaus first introduced me to Stuart. He knew Stuart by then because he had been to the club three or four times before he took me. I didn't converse with The Beatles the first time, but I immediately thought how wonderful they were and how much I would like to really get to know them. For me, seeing them was like a dream come true. I was always longing to take pictures of boys who looked like them, but I had never met any before. I was very nervous and excited, and very young and innocent, but my whole life changed in a couple of minutes. All I wanted was to be with them and to know them.

I had never seen performers like them before. I was into jazz and classical music and, of course, a bit of Nat King Cole and The Platters. Don't forget, in the late 1950s and the beginning of the 1960s, anything that came from the States or from England was so far away. The only thing we could get hold of was music from France, like *chansons,* and a lot of French movies. I'd heard rock and roll before because I'd been to England once and had loved it. I really, really loved it, but I'd never seen it performed onstage. It was like a merry-go-round in my head — seeing The Beatles perform and liking them as people. They looked absolutely astonishing.

Pete Best: Stu was a great "little" guy. I call him little, simply because of the fact that he was the smallest in stature in the band. But I refer to him with a great deal of affection. When I first got to know him, he was playing bass in the band, and he realized that his musical talents weren't up to the same level as the others. But he was a brilliant artist, and that became apparent when I used to watch him in Germany. In between the sets in the clubs — I mean, we were playing long hours, six to seven nights a week, six, seven, and eight hours a night — he'd take out a piece of chalk, a drawing pencil, or something like that and a sketch pad. He'd see a face in the crowd and sketch it. It was just incredible to watch him work. Then, of course, he met and fell in love with a very beautiful German girl called Astrid Kirchherr. I'm certain the world knows about her photography with The Beatles. So Stu fell madly in love with her, and it was great to watch because it was like one of those fairy stories — a love-at-first-sight type of thing.

Astrid Kirchherr: Well, one day I asked Stuart if they would like to be photographed by me. I was so frightened they would say no, but they were excited about it. So we made a meeting point. They had to work very late, up to four o'clock in the morning, and I only used daylight film, so we had to meet at twelve o'clock in the day. They were there right on the spot, all nicely combed in their little suits and polished shoes, and acted from the first minute like professionals. I was really the first professional photographer who took pictures of them. Nobody told me to. I wanted to do it. They didn't pay me to do it, nor did any magazine pay me. It was just for my own pleasure.

They were attracted to my looks because I looked weird then or different. I used to wear black only and had very short hair. I wore these collarless jackets and leather suits, big velvet capes, boots, and things like that, but I was so attracted to the way they looked with their tight jeans and leather jackets. It was a sort of give-and-take, from me to them and back. We influenced one another.

Peter Eckhorn: The Beatles were working at the Kaiserkeller, but they didn't like it. So they came to see me and asked if there was any work to be had at the Top Ten Club. To show what they could do, they played a couple of numbers for me. I liked them and said, "Okay, I'll give you a job." But before I could hire them, the owners of the Kaiserkeller, principally Bruno Koschmeider, made a complaint about them to the police, saying they had tried to burn down his theater. It wasn't true, of course, but the complaint had the desired effect. The Beatles were deported to England. It was more than seven months before I was able to have them at the Top Ten.

George Harrison: We got ourselves together enough for a manager of another nightclub called the Top Ten. He wanted us to work there, which was the reason we were deported in the first place. We tried to leave at the end of our engagement at the Kaiserkeller and go and work for this other club for more money. The manager of the original club got a bit uptight and had us all deported.

Pete Best: The Kaiserkeller and the Top Ten were the two main clubs in Hamburg, and there was a lot of competition between them. The Top Ten was around the corner from the Kaiserkeller, where we were playing. We had an offer from Peter Eckhorn to play at the Top Ten with Tony Sheridan. He offered us more money, and that was a fair deal in itself. So we went in to see Bruno Koschmeider, who was the manager of the Kaiserkeller, and said, "Look, we've asked you to decorate things and you haven't done it. Our living conditions are horrible. We've asked you to fix the stage for us and you just said, 'Booooop! On your bikes!' Well, we're finishing up and then we're going to play at the Top Ten Club." Bruno told us, "If you play at the Top Ten, you'll never play in Germany again!" So we said, "Boooooo to you, Bruno Koschmeider," and off we went.

About the same time George was deported to Liverpool after it was discovered he was underage. So the rest of us started playing at the Top Ten. Because of the way we just basically up and left, Paul and I still had all our clothes in what we called "the Black Holes of Calcutta." These were the two dungeons at the back of the Bambi Kino where we stayed. It meant we had to go back. The Bambi Kino was a movie theater, and we lived right at the back. There was a corridor that ran from the back of the urinal, just off the fire exit, and there were two rooms there that Paul and I had. One was the "palatial suite," as we used to call it, which was the one that had the electric lightbulb in it.

When we got back, we needed a bit a of light so we could see to get our stuff together. Paul had some condoms on him, so he stuck them on the wall and tied them together with a little bit of tapestry. Then he lit them so they would split away, as condoms on fire do. This gave us enough light to actually throw things together. The condoms must have scorched the wall slightly, and the following morning we were picked up at the Top Ten by the German police and taken to the Hamburg Police Station. After being grilled for two or three hours, we were told that Bruno Koschmeider had charged us with trying to burn down the Bambi Kino, then we were thrown in jail. Paul and I were terrified because we thought, God Almighty! What the hell's happening? We've been thrown in jail and no one knows where the hell we are. We're probably going to spend the rest of our lives in the Hamburg jail. But what happened was that we spent about two to three hours there and then we were deported.

We contested it when we got back home, and it was resolved in a couple of weeks. We wrote to the German embassy and police and eventually cleared it up. All the charges were dropped. But as Paul and I have always said, "How the hell can you burn down a stone cinema with a couple of condoms? It just doesn't make sense."

George Harrison: In my opinion our peak for playing live was in Hamburg because at that time we weren't famous. So the people who came to see us were drawn in by the music or by whatever atmosphere we created. Also, at that time, with us being from Liverpool, it was a big scene because people would always say, "You've got to be from London to make it." They always thought we were hick or something. But when we played in Hamburg, they kept wanting us back because we would pull in lots of people.

We first went to a place called the Indra, which was shut down. Then we went to the Kaiserkeller, and then the Top Ten, which was probably the best club on the Reeperbahn. At that time it was really fantastic. There was echo on the microphones and it was really a gas. So we'd go in there and spend afternoons rooting through all those old songs like, you know, "Money," and all the sort of tunes that weren't popular particularly but were quite heavy. We'd do all those ones by Chuck Berry and Little Richard, all the rock-and-roll things. We just kept doing that, even though that sort of period had died out.

The Hamburg days, in retrospect, were probably the most important times of our lives because it was what you could call our apprenticeship. We worked very hard and we worked long hours. We played for eight hours a night, seven days a week for over four and a half months on our first go-round there. We really got a lot of material down, a lot of material we would never have learned if we hadn't gone there. It was one great rehearsal and it really got the group going. Yes, those days were very important to The Beatles.

Pete Best: Allan Williams was our first manager, and he took us out to Germany in August 1960. When we got back to Liverpool from Hamburg, we should have played at his club. Unfortunately, before we got home, the club burned down. We went to Allan and said, "Okay, we're back. Start finding us work." But nothing happened, so we split from him.

My mother threw us the lifeline. She let us play at the Casbah Club and billed us as "the fabulous Beatles direct from Hamburg." It was quite funny, actually, because when we went in, the kids were already there. The place was packed to capacity, and they looked at me and said, "Hang on a minute. That's Pete from The Blackjacks." Then they saw John, George, and Paul and said, "That's The Quarry Men. Who are these Beatles 'direct from Hamburg'?" And Mo said, "Wait till you hear them! Just wait till you hear them." Basically that was it. After the first number, the kids went wild. They forgot where we came from and who we were. We were The Beatles. That's all that mattered, and it went on from there.

Since Allan Williams didn't come up with any new bookings, I took it over. Promoters started to get in touch with me, saying, "We want to book The Beatles." So until Brian [Epstein] took over, I took on that particular slant of it.

It's funny. At that time there wasn't a particular person who was the driving force. When I joined them, Stu Sutcliffe was also in the band. He was the bass player. Ken Brown had disappeared from the scene, and when I joined them, everyone basically pitched in. There wasn't one person who made the decisions or anything like that. It was a case of "Okay, what are we gonna do? How are we gonna do it?" It was a consensus of opinion among the boys in the band, and that's how we operated. It was funny. We had this motto. It was a thing we used to do onstage in Hamburg and also in Liverpool. John used to shout it out. He'd yell, "Where are we going, guys?" And we'd stand up and yell, "To the toppermost of the poppermost, Johnny."

Allan Williams: I'd like to be known as the first manager of The Beatles. I saw something in them in those days that nobody else did, and I was part of their formative years, part of the creation of The Beatles. The fact that I say I gave them away isn't really true. I just simply had a row with John Lennon, which wasn't very difficult in those days. I'd opened a club that was swinging in Liverpool — the Blue Angel — and I just decided that I didn't need this hassle from the group. And so, exit. You know, I actually wrote to them and said, "I'll fix it so that you'll never, ever work again."

Bob Wooler: There have been a number of watershed dates in the history of The Beatles. One that figured prominently in my life with The Beatles was undoubtedly Tuesday, December 27, 1960. They'd just come back from Hamburg and had hardly any work. Mona Best had fixed them up with one or two bookings. Allan Williams was supposed to line up jobs for them, but his club had been reduced to ashes. I'd just gotten these one-nighters with Brian Kelly, who operated dance halls around the north end of Liverpool, including Litherland Town Hall. That was the venue in which I was to become aware of Beatlemania. I'd never seen anything like it, and I'd worked with most of the groups around Merseyside for a number of years. And while they were all damn good, The Beatles were a different ball game. They were sensational. They staggered back from Hamburg, but they had learned so much from pounding those Kaiserkeller boards onstage and at the Indra.

They only did a short spot because The Del Renas, The Deltones, and The Searchers were already booked. I prevailed upon Brian Kelly to put them on as an extra. We fought over the fee. I suggested eight pounds. He had a slight attack of heart failure at the prospect of laying out so much money, because in those days the groups were paid a pound a man. Well, there were five Beatles then, and we fought and fought and he only wanted to pay four. I said they've got a driver, which makes six, so we settled for six. I gave them the best spot in the lineup. Now you've got to appreciate that they were an unknown fact to me, but I had heard these reports from Hamburg that they were a powerhouse, and they lived up to it.

Bill Harry: Before Brian Epstein got involved with The Beatles there was a guy called Brian Kelly. He was a very astute promoter at the time, one of the best ones, actually, because most of the promoters were con men who didn't pay the bands their money. There used to be a lot of fights. Promoters used to get bouncers to actually beat up the groups when they asked for their money, but Brian Kelly was straight. He didn't pay very much. Nobody paid much. But he paid a decent whack, and he always gave them cash. He didn't give them any hassles. Brian booked The Beatles a lot. He did all the bookings for the Aintree Institute and Litherland Town Hall, so when they came back from Germany, he put posters all over town screaming, "The Beatles, live from Hamburg." A lot of the kids thought they were a German group and went along thinking that this was a fantastic German group in black leather. The rest of it you know.

Pete Best: It was exciting coming back to Liverpool after virtually being unknown when we went away. Within 48 hours we were performing at the Casbah Club first, then Litherland Town Hall! It was total excitement! We were seeing reactions from the fans in Liverpool that, well, I mean, you'd only see when Bill Haley and His Comets were around. We'd seen some of the films and heard about it, read about it, but we were actually there, seeing the kids going wild in front of us, which gave us great kicks.

Bob Wooler: We had curtains at Litherland, and I said to The Beatles, "As soon as I announce you, go straight into the first number," because that was the "impact" we wanted to have. Paul opened the show with "Long Tall Sally," the Little Richard "stormer." I said, "Direct from Hamburg," which they were, and the song exploded. The crowd was as stunned as I. Now I got quite worried, because when people in these dance halls in those days stopped dancing, it was either to cause a fight or witness one. The policy was that we were to keep them dancing, keep them happy, so they wouldn't get into any "lumber," you know, any fights. But they were transfixed, and they were drawn, as if by a magnet, toward the stage. The stage at Litherland is quite high, so they were all looking up and I was looking down at the sea of bewildered faces. They hadn't seen or heard anything like it. Yet they were familiar with the songs because The Beatles were doing songs by Little Richard, Chuck Berry, and Carl Perkins. They were all familiar with those [songs], but it was that extra something The Beatles always gave to their performances and songs. And that was the beginning of Beatlemania.

Chapter Three

To the Toppermost of the Poppermost

Bill Harry: It was a real buzz. It was real excitement. When I went to The Beatles' gig at Litherland Town Hall after they came back from Germany, I thought, This is tremendous. This is pure excitement. It was like being in heaven. It was on another plane. It was mind-blowing! The kids felt that, as well. But it was growing, and it had been growing in Liverpool for years. It was like an underground movement. The kids had something that belonged to them, and The Beatles were gradually emerging as the big group coming out of the little cesspools like the Casbah Club and the Jacaranda Club into the bigger halls. The kids of Liverpool felt that this belonged to them. This was theirs! Like the philosopher Abraham Maslow once said in the 1950s, "People have peak experiences." When we lived and breathed in the Merseybeat scene, when we went to these gigs and all the kids were there, and the groups were playing onstage, it was explosive! And it happened not only with The Beatles, but with The Flamingos and all the other groups, as well.

I remember being at those gigs at the Aintree Institute and Litherland Town Hall, and Bob Wooler was doing the compering. I remember Cynthia [Lennon] had to sit in the balcony to be out the way. She was told, "Don't go near them 'cause the other girls will kill you." And she had to keep a very low profile because The Beatles were starting to happen very big locally. Of course, Pete Best was a major figure in this because somehow the girls seemed to really go for Pete. Bob Wooler called him "mean, moody, and magnificent." He looked like [actor] Jeff Chandler. He was very handsome [with his] dark hair. [He was] probably the most handsome of The Beatles at the time, and girls used to sleep in his garden at night. They used to go berserk over him.

At one of The Beatles' performances in early 1961, Stuart Sutcliffe was attacked and beaten.

Millie Sutcliffe: When Stuart came back to Liverpool, something terrible happened in January 1961. Stuart always gave Pete his guitar when they were finished playing because Pete had a van for his drum kit and he took their guitars. He looked after them and transported everything for the boys. So Stuart handed his guitar to Pete and went out alone from the bright lights into the pitch-dark. He was hit on the back of the head, knocked out, kicked, and beaten . . . brutally beaten up in the dark. Some young girl who was coming out saw it, came back in, and called out, "Stuart's been murdered!" You know, she thought he was dead! So the boys ran out. John got the thug and broke his own wrist beating him up! And it's so funny, because when I was speaking to Auntie Mimi sometime later, she said, "So that's where he got the broken wrist. I said to him, 'What have you been up to?' And John said, 'Oh, I fell on it.'"

Pete Best: We'd finished playing onstage. We'd been warned before and we had played there before. It was a rough place to play, but we weren't too worried about it because we could handle ourselves. But this particular night, as Stu was coming through the stage door, a gang of Teddy Boys grabbed and pushed him back through the door and started beating him up. Now John and I saw what was going on and we jumped in and sorted the problem out by returning the punishment and throwing them out. But Stu had taken quite a beating. He had taken a few blows around the head, and we had to make sure he made it out in one piece. We had our van driver, Frank, who was a bouncer in those days, take him home. We made sure he got home as fast as he could. Now a lot of people have said that it was that particular fight that may have led to Stuart's brain hemorrhage, from which he died in Germany later. No one can say for sure, but it may have started something. Who knows?

Millie Sutcliffe: So, anyway, it was about four in the morning when this happened. I always stayed up for Stuart coming home, with the light on. Once Stuart was home I knew I could lock the door. The first thing he would shout was "It's me, Mum," and then put on the kettle and make a cup of tea. Then he'd come up and tell me what happened. But this particular night he looked like death. "Mother," he said, "you've got good reason to wait up tonight. We were attacked." He didn't say, "I was beaten up." He said, "We were attacked!" Then he said, "John broke his wrist when he got the thug who hit me on the back of the head. I was unconscious for a few minutes. Jim Gretty, who was promoting, or looking after things, said he'll replace the glasses. So don't worry, Mother. You don't have to buy new glasses." His skull was fractured that night, and that's what killed Stuart. I shall say that to my dying day.

He wouldn't go to the hospital. During that night, I don't know what possessed me to go into Stuart's room, but the blood — it was everywhere! He said, "Mother, I nearly died. I don't know where that blood came from — my mouth or my nose — but I nearly died." He looked dead, so I turned around and said, "I'm phoning for the doctor, sweet." He said, "If you go to the doctor, Mother, then I shall be gone before he gets here, because I've got too much to do. I can't afford to be ill." So he lived for 10 months with that fractured skull pressing on his brain. The agony must have been indescribable. You see, I was ill all those 10 months, as well. I felt the same pain.

On February 21, 1961, The Beatles made their debut at 10 Mathew Street, the Cavern Club.

Bob Wooler: The Cavern opened in January 1957 as a jazz cellar. It was a disused basement in Mathew Street, one of many in that quarter, because that was the original fruit district of Liverpool. There were lots of these cellars that you could rent for 10 bob a week. Alan Sytner, who opened the Cavern, got the idea from visiting Paris. There was this cellar scene there where jazz artists would perform. There was a place he liked called La Cave, so you can see where the name "Cavern" came from. It opened in a blaze of glory, and it was a big success story. But events overtook Alan Sytner and he bowed out. So Ray McFall took over and, though the jazz scene was healthy, gradually the rock scene, which was developing, started taking over. When I first started working there in January 1961 as the lunch DJ, I only worked with rock groups. I got Ray to book more and more. We had to book them for the lunchtime sessions because the jazz bands simply weren't available at that time of day. And so it became more rock-oriented.

Sam Leach: The Cavern in those days wasn't into rock and roll. Rory Storm, a friend of mine, got fined a pound sterling for playing a Jerry Lee Lewis rock-and-roll number, "Whole Lot of Shakin' Going On." The reason the Cavern became full-time rock and roll was through me, basically. You see, I booked the Casanova Club every Saturday and I had the Iron Door, as well, which wasn't far from the Cavern. I used to have 2,000 people in the Iron Door every Saturday, queuing up at one in the morning like a cinema. The Cavern had about 50 people on a Saturday night. So eventually the Cavern had to turn to rock and roll.

Pete Best: We first started playing the Cavern at lunchtime sessions, and again, my mother, Mo, was very influential in getting the first session down there. She got in touch with Ray McFall. She heard that he was running lunchtime sessions, and the Cavern, which was in the city center, gave people a break. They could come in and listen to a rock-and-roll band and get a bite to eat or a drink of Coke. So we got a booking in there and it was absolutely amazing, because when word got out that The Beatles were going to play the lunchtime show, it went from being a normal session of about 200 people to where the place was heaving with fans. Ray McFall, being a good businessman, started to book The Beatles regularly, and the following grew.

Liz Hughes: Mathew Street back then was a very dark, dingy little road with seven-story warehouses all the way down on either side. Very little light, natural light, got through. It was always sort of dark and dreary-looking. The Cavern door was literally a hole in the wall. It had an arched doorway, painted at the top in red, white, and blue, with "The Cavern" scrawled up on one side. It was originally done by the doorman, Paddy Delaney, who worked there. They couldn't afford a nameplate.

It was number 8 to number 10 Mathew Street. It had a very narrow winding stone staircase going down. It gave about enough room for one person to get down, but you couldn't pass anyone on the stairs. It was that narrow! The stairs went to nothing at one side, so you went down sideways, like a crab, with your feet on these stone steps. You got to the bottom and you were in a basement, a cellar — stone walls, no decor to speak of at all, a very smelly, dingy little place that was always very damp. If you touched the walls, your hands came away wet, because with all the bodies down there the walls used to sweat and the water would run off them.

The stage was built into an arch. The groups playing on the stage didn't have a terrific amount of head room. You usually notice on old Cavern photographs that the two fellows standing nearest the wall would always have their heads bent over because the arch was literally touching the tops of their heads. They probably had six feet of playing space and about 14 square feet of stage to play on. And the kids used to go there for the lunchtime sessions. They used to sit along the front of the stage, and as soon as the group would come on, Bob Wooler would come along and say, "Everyone shift off the stage." There was a row of chairs, but mostly it was standing room only. You had to get in really early to get a chair to sit on. Most times you stood in the arches or you stood around the wall.

But trying to tell you about the atmosphere is impossible. Can't do that! It was absolutely unbelievable! I mean, you went down these steps and you just never noticed that the place smelt, that it wasn't particularly clean, that it was dingy. You didn't notice anything like that because there was this electric atmosphere of all these kids. It was the start, if you like, of hysteria — the first time it had ever been known in Britain, anyway. A sort of rock hysteria. And this rock-and-roll music used to literally blast your eardrums to death! It was so loud. You had about four amps onstage and two spotlights. But the atmosphere was absolutely fantastic, you know. If you could create that again, you really would do some good. You know, for the fans who were too young, or who weren't born at the time, to give them that sense of excitement. It was really unbelievable.

Julia Baird: It was a dark, dingy hole. It was a warehouse that wasn't used as a warehouse anymore because it was too damp. Can you imagine? Nowadays you wouldn't be allowed to hold anything there. There was no fire escape and [it was] totally unsafe. You would go down these steps, really narrow steps, turn the corner, and you were in it. There was the stage and a sort of counter at the back. There was a bar at the back where Cilla Black used to serve the Coca-Cola and sing at odd times. Of course, she made it as a singer, too. I didn't actually go that often because we lived outside of Liverpool. So we had to get the bus into town. The last bus used to leave at ridiculously early times. As I said, it was small and the stage took up a lot of space, but you got a clique of people going there all the time, as you would with any club.

On their days off The Beatles would go into Hessey's Music Store and visit Jim Gretty.

Jim Gretty: You know, they used to come in for a visit, just everyday chaps. They'd just go, "Aye, give me a hello, Jim." They'd sit and we'd have a chat and I'd ask, "Do you want anything?" They'd say, "No, we'll just have a look around, Jim." Then they'd pick a guitar up and away they'd go, you know, just having fun. George Harrison used to come in often, as did John Lennon. The Cavern Club was just two minutes away from the shop, so on the way to play the Cavern, they could drop in and have a little go at the guitars. We never used to chase them out, because we knew that they were good customers. They used to watch my fingers as I played. But, by Joe, I could watch their fingers now!

Across the street from Hessey's was North End Music Stores (NEMS), the department store and record shop owned by Brian Epstein's family.

Alistair Taylor: I vaguely remember the boys coming in. I mean, NEMS, after all, was the busiest record shop in northern England. We didn't stock every record, but our pride and joy, and Brian [Epstein's] boast, was that if a record was made anywhere in the world, and was still available, we'd get it. We had the finest collection of jazz, and I'm willing to bet we had everything that was remotely commercial or big in America. I'll guarantee it was there. We had a vast stock of records.

Paul McCartney: One day my dad had enough and insisted I go out and get a job. So I went down to the Labour Exchange, and they immediately sent me to a firm called Massey and Coggins. They were a firm of electrical engineers. I told the foreman I needed a job and that I didn't care what job I had to do. I'd even sweep the yard if that's what he wanted done. I guess he liked me 'cause, in the end, they gave me a job. I had to wind coils for them, which paid about seven pounds a week, which was big money back then. It was really funny, because I remember they used to call me Mantovani because of my hair, which was long by their standards. When you see pictures of us from the early days of the Cavern, you can see that it really wasn't long at all! Anyway, I wasn't very good as a coiler. Everybody else used to wind 14 coils in an average day while I'd only get through a couple, if I was lucky. The other problem was that it seems most of the ones I did didn't work. It was right about this time that we started getting gigs at the Cavern during the lunch breaks. I had to jump over the back wall at lunchtime to play the gig. The next day I'd have to come in and say that the reason I wasn't around the previous afternoon was that I'd been ill. Well, they didn't believe that one for long. The next job was almost as bad. I worked for a lorry driver for a while. The problem there was that when we played at nights I wouldn't get home till late and the job started at 6:30 in the morning. So that didn't last too long, either.

On March 26, 1961, The Beatles returned to Hamburg.

Peter Eckhorn: When they did return to Hamburg to play the Top Ten Club, they were very good and were very popular with our patrons. The interesting thing about The Beatles was that people liked them more for their engaging personalities, their onstage antics, and smart remarks than for their music. Their music sounded very much like all the other English groups, but as performers they were unique.

Klaus Voorman: I didn't really play guitar until I met The Beatles. I was just messing around at home. I was doing commercial art, but at home I had a little guitar, which somebody gave me as a present. I had records and a record player, so I started playing the guitar and messing around with different speeds and echoes and whatnot. One day Paul said, "Hey, Klaus, come on and play the bass. Stuart wants to sit down." So he gave me the bass and said, "Come up onstage." I said, "No, I can't do that. I'm not going onstage." This was at the Top Ten Club. So I took a chair and sat on the dance floor and the band was playing onstage. I think they played a Fats Domino number. It went okay because playing the bass guitar wasn't difficult for me. I played classical piano when I was young, so it wasn't new to me to play anything. All this technical or musical knowledge was no problem for me. I don't know why, but from the word go I had the sort of feel you need to be a bass player. It's funny, because when Stuart wanted to leave in the days at the Top Ten Club, I went up to John and said, "Look, how about me playing bass in your band?" You mustn't forget. It was just a normal band. It wasn't a famous group or anything then. And John said, "Oh, Paul's already bought his bass guitar." Maybe I should have pressed a little more by saying, "Fuck it! Sell it again." I don't know. He might have said, "Oh, fuck off, we don't want you, anyway!" I'm always a bit shy, and I would never have said, "Oh, listen, can't we try it?" I did play bass on many Beatle solo projects.

Astrid Kirchherr: All these stories of how I invented this [Beatle] hair-style is just a lot of rubbish, because in my art school where Jurgen [Volmer] was, as well, all the boys used to have this haircut. I liked it longer, and because Klaus [Voorman] was my boyfriend, I said, "I want your hair to be longer, not that short." So Klaus had it extremely long. First, Stuart wanted to have the same haircut that Klaus and Jurgen had, so I cut Stuart's hair that way. Then George came along and asked me to cut his hair that way. But Paul and John couldn't decide whether to have the different haircut. It took them quite a long time. I think at least six months or more. They went to Paris to visit Jurgen, who was working there, and they asked him if he would cut their hair for them like his. So I only cut Stuart's and George's hair.

George Harrison: We have always liked our hair long. Even in school our headmaster used to talk to us about having our hair long. We had it back when we first went to Germany and then down and all sorts of ways. Paul and John went to Paris for a holiday and tried to get the French cut, but it didn't work out. Our friends in Germany wore their hair forward, and most art school kids grew their hair long throughout Europe. So it was getting fashionable there in the early 1960s.

Paul McCartney: John and I hitchhiked to Paris once to see our old Hamburg friend, Jurgen Volmer, and we finally decided to change our hairstyle to his. We all did it except for Pete, who preferred his own look. We didn't start the fashion, but I guess we sort of popu-larized it.

Julia Baird: Liverpool had become a hotbed for these [rock-and-roll] groups. They were coming out of the woodwork, and when club owners wanted groups for Germany, they came to Liverpool to look for them. The second time The Beatles were there [in Germany], there was a fellow called Tony Sheridan who was making a revamped version of "My Bonnie Lies over the Ocean." And, of course, that was the record. Somebody told me they made something earlier. I don't know what that was, but as far as I know, that was the first record they made — a backup record.

Bill Harry: At the beginning of the 1960s Bert Kaempfert, the well-known performer and bandleader, was actively looking for artists for Polydor Records. He had a number of big international hit records. One of them was "Wonderland by Night." When The Beatles started to appear in Hamburg, Bert heard a buzz about a group appearing at the Top Ten Club. So he went to the club and listened. In fact, they were backing Tony Sheridan at the time. There were five members. Tony was doing the lead vocals. Bert was very impressed because it was completely different than what was happening in Germany at the time. German bands weren't doing these things. So he thought this was different enough for him to sign up. He knew there was something in this, but he only thought of the German market. He didn't think of the world market. He just thought they were different for Germany.

The way he went about signing them is interesting. He had a word with them and asked if they could come around and meet him at his house. Bert was a little late, so when The Beatles arrived, his housekeeper met them. When Bert got there, she said, "These strange people have come knocking and said they've come to meet you, but I don't like the look of them. I wouldn't let them into the living room. I've stood them on the patio and given them some drinks." That afternoon, however, Bert signed The Beatles to a short contract and arranged for the first recording session. He arranged to meet them one morning, and when he arrived, there was no sign of them. He waited about half an hour and, since he knew their address, he went there. It was a grotty little hole, an attic. So he got to this very small room, with two bunk beds, and they were fast asleep. The only other furniture was a chair with a pile of clothes on it. So he woke them up, got them together, and did the recordings with them.

Tony Sheridan: We all lived in an attic — bare boards, freezing drafts, the lot. Bit like Oliver Twist. There were bunk beds, and I remember John used to have the top bunk. He'd crash around when he got up because he could never see a thing without his glasses. Once he started banging around, we all had to get up. John was a wild character in those days. The others were a little quieter, but there wasn't much in it. They were all ravers. Our day began at about two in the afternoon when we would swagger down to the Seamen's Mission for a meal. I don't know why, but we always used to have the same meal all the time, everywhere — tea and cornflakes.

Pete Best: Just before we actually recorded for Polydor we had this dilemma. We wanted Paul to play bass on the session because we felt it would sound a lot better. He was a more talented bass player than Stu. We were trying, in our minds, to come up with a way to explain this situation to Stu. But he saved us the inconvenience, because a couple of days before we had to actually do that session, he came up and said, "I'm leaving the band. I'm going to stay in Hamburg because I have an offer to go back to school to study under a famous professor at the Hamburg Art College."

Astrid Kirchherr: The band played at the Top Ten, and a lot of art students used to come around and Stuart got friendly with them. One day they said, "Well, Stuart, we're going to bring along Mr. [Eduardo] Paolozzi [the Scottish-born pop art sculptor]. He's our tutor, our teacher." Now Stuart and John knew who Paolozzi was and, of course, they were excited because he was a very famous artist. So the next night Mr. Paolozzi came along. Stuart had a talk with him and told him what he was going to do and that he would love to go to art school again. Mr. Paolozzi had an amazing influence at Hamburg's art college, and he must have seen something in Stuart's work because it was pretty unusual at the time for an English student to get a scholarship in Hamburg. Mr. Paolozzi insisted that Stuart get a scholarship because otherwise he couldn't afford to go there. He was so kind to Stuart and obviously saw a great talent. Later I read interviews that Mr. Paolozzi gave to the press in which he said he saw the enormous quality of Stuart's work and his gift. He said he liked Stuart so much as a person and that he did everything to help him. Stuart was so excited and John was, too! Excited that he got this amazing chance. Mr. Paolozzi being his teacher and getting this scholarship would have been impossible in England.

Millie Sutcliffe: At that time Stuart was still playing all night with The Beatles in the clubs and going to the [Hamburg] Art College in the day, and it really was becoming way, way too much for him. Finally he decided to leave all the performing.

Pete Best: Stu stayed in Hamburg with Astrid Kirchherr. So that solved our problem, and it suited Stu. Even after he left the band, he came over to Liverpool with Astrid, still watching our career. He got a lot of kicks out of finding out what we were up to and actually coming over and watching the performances.

Paul McCartney: Stuart decided to leave the band, and there was this sort of ceremonial handover of the bass to me. But he was only lending it to me, so he didn't want me to change the strings around. Of course, he was right-handed and I'm left, so I had to learn how to play upside down, if you will. Eventually I got my own bass and it was set for a left-hander. Then it felt a lot more natural. But I was a guitar player before that and I kind of inherited the bass position. I was always a kind of frustrated guitarist who played bass.

Pete Best: The Polydor recording session was weird, to be quite honest. You have to imagine that we hadn't recorded before, and when Bert Kaempfert signed us up to back Tony Sheridan — and also to record in our own right — we were expecting to go into a recording studio. You know, this was Bert Kaempfert — "Wonderland by Night" and "That Happy Feeling" — the big

A&R manager in Germany. We actually ended up in a school hall in Hamburg. This absolutely amazed us. It wasn't even a proper studio. So we set up on the stage in the school hall. All the sound equipment was backstage and we took sound levels, then Kaempfert came along and did the sound checks. He turned around and said, "Okay, play the number through." So we ran through "My Bonnie," the levels were taken, and we played another piece through. Basically it was like two or three takes, and *booomp*, it was in the can.

We were excited. Don't get me wrong. Some people said, "Here you are, the lads from Liverpool, recording with Polydor Records. You've made it!" We had gotten a contract and all the rest of it, but it was a case of the surroundings being different from what we had anticipated. It worked out great, though. The sound was good, even on those early recordings. There were two sessions that actually took place. One was in the school hall. Then we went back later and did one in the studio — "Sweet Georgia Brown" — with Tony. Most of the material that was done on those sessions has come out on Polydor and all the American affiliates. And, of course, we don't get any of the royalties. All we did was sign a contract and got sessionman fees, which were about 200 marks in those days. That was it! Royalties might have gone to Tony, but not to us.

Tony Sheridan: The lineup on these sessions recorded at the school was Paul on bass, George and John on guitars, Pete Best on drums, and myself on guitar and vocals. Stuart Sutcliffe had already left, but he was present as a friend. The most famous result of the session was, I suppose, "My Bonnie."

In July 1961 The Beatles returned to Liverpool.

Paul McCartney: Let me tell you the main problem in the old days. When we'd come back from somewhere like Hamburg, we'd have about a month off. We wouldn't play for a bit and then we'd do our first gigs in England, which inevitably would be somewhere like Coventry or Leicester 'cause that's the kind of place that would hire us. It would be a ballroom in Leicester, say, and we'd come on and do the worst show we'd ever done 'cause we'd forgotten how to turn the amps up. You get out of the swing of it, so you forget where your levels are and you forget exactly how near the mike it is you've gotta sing. You're just not together. So we'd always have to do a week of that, those little ballrooms, before we could actually get on to do any good shows. And then we were back in it and we could just go on forever until we took another month's break. Then we would completely forget about it again.

Liz Hughes: The times I saw The Beatles play at the Cavern were very, very exciting. They were raw. Nobody had manipulated them or fashioned them in any way. It was completely raw and it was all their own — this one-two-three-four rock-and-roll beat. They were always in their leather jackets, jeans, Cuban heels, and their hair everywhere. It was so different from the run-of-the-mill groups at the time with their suede-collared jackets and matching colors, all blues and yellows. These four lads just came on in anything. Whatever they happened to get up in that morning, they played in that day. And I think the kids just took to them because they were working-class . . . like them. They were just four boys from the street, around the corner, local lads who got up onstage and did what they wanted to do. I think it meant more to the fans knowing that they could go home and do the same thing maybe. People would shout, "Play this or play that!" They'd answer back, "Ah, shut up!" Or they'd say, "Okay, in a minute." They were always very free with the people and fans who were there. There was a give and take. The other groups would play rehearsed sessions. Then they would say, "Thank you," and leave. Not The Beatles. With them it was a lot different because they didn't have a set routine. They just played because they enjoyed playing.

Bob Wooler: "My Bonnie" came into my possession because I happened to get on the same bus one Saturday night as George Harrison.

He said, "Look at this. I've just received it today." Stuart Sutcliffe, who had stayed behind in Hamburg the second time around, had sent him a copy of the record they had recorded for Bert Kaempfert in the spring of 1961. I grabbed it and said I was working the Aintree Institute that night. They weren't playing on that bill. They were playing the lower ballroom in New Brighton, and I said, "Let me play it tonight because you're playing the Aintree next weekend and this will be great promotion." George wanted to hang on to it because the others hadn't seen it, let alone heard it. But I said, "Look, we'll all be meeting up tomorrow night at Hambleton Hall, so I'll bring it there and play it. Then you can have it back and loan it to me again for the Cavern lunchtime sessions," which I was hosting. So he let me have it, and the first play of the record, outside George's record player, was at the Aintree Institute.

We all wanted it to be a hit, so I used to encourage people to go and order it, even though it wasn't released in England. I said, "Go to your favorite shop and ask them for it, and if they don't have it, have them order it and make sure they get it." There was only one record store that took any interest in it and that was Brian Epstein's [NEMS] shop in Whitechapel. When these fans started to ask him about this group, he became interested in them. He assumed because the record was German that it was a German band. He ordered some copies, and the fans put him straight and said, "No, they're from Liverpool and they play just up the road on Mathew Street at the Cavern lunchtime sessions."

Bill Harry: I got the idea to start *Mersey Beat* in 1960 [the magazine's first issue was dated July 6, 1961]. I had started collecting information about Liverpool groups and the Liverpool music scene in notebooks. There were so many venues and so many groups that I got together with Bob Wooler and we made a list of all the groups we knew. I eventually published it in *Mersey Beat* and found that there were over 350 groups we knew of in Liverpool. We thought,

There couldn't be as many groups as this, even in London. The scene was definitely unique. The Beatles hadn't emerged yet at this time, and so the top groups were people like Cass and the Cassanovas, King Size Taylor and the Dominoes, Howie Casey and the Seniors who, in fact, were the first Liverpool group ever to make a record. And so it evolved. It was only later [in 1961] that groups started to appear at the Cavern when Ray McFall took it over.

I encouraged John to write, and he had his own column called "Beatcomber," with all his . . . what we called "wacky writings," which everyone seemed to fall in love with. We had so many letters about it and then the kids started to write that way! The personalities of all The Beatles sort of developed in *Mersey Beat* week by week. They were the main group I used to feature, though I covered the whole scene. I had such a personal involvement with them and a closeness to them that it virtually was The Beatles all the time. I remember Bob Wooler came to me very irate one day and said, "Bill, these other groups are complaining about *Mersey Beat* because you do so much about The Beatles. You should call it *The Mersey Beatle.*" I thought, That's a good idea! So the next issue I introduced a page called "The Mersey-Beatle," which I ran every single issue.

At about three o'clock in the afternoon on October 28, 1961, legend has it that an 18-year-old boy named Raymond Jones, wearing jeans and a leather jacket, walked into the record store at Whitechapel, Liverpool, and asked for the single "My Bonnie."

Brian Epstein: It was our policy in this division to follow up on any requests from our customers, and when I was asked one day by a young man for a record by The Beatles, I promised to look into it. I didn't know anything about the record at that point and I assumed they were from Germany. It was only a few weeks later that I was told they were, in fact, from Liverpool and frequently played in a club right around the corner from my office.

Alistair Taylor: Raymond Jones came into the NEMS shop and said he was looking for a record by The Beatles. Well, as you know, it wasn't actually by The Beatles. It was by Tony Sheridan. They weren't even called The Beatles on the record. They were called the Beat Brothers. We prided ourselves on the fact that we could find any record that was requested, but it took me quite a long time and a lot of research to find this one. We found it in Germany and we had to import a box of 25, which sold out in about half an hour. Normally, on an average record for the two shops, we would order two to four copies, but Brian had this incredible ability to know how many copies he could sell. And he would say, "Right, let's order 250," which was phenomenal. EMI and Decca got to the point where they waited to see how many records Brian ordered. They would say, "Great, get the presses rolling. Brian Epstein has ordered 250. It's going to be a hit." He was very rarely wrong. We contacted Polydor in London and said, "Look, we've got something happening here in Liverpool. This group is selling large quantities and we are fed up paying through the nose to get these things from your company in Germany." They didn't want to know. They said, "Forget it! We're not interested in pressing them here in England." It took an awfully long time and an awful lot of records before they finally said, "Yeah, all right, let's take a look at it." They started pressing it in England. I don't remember the time span, but it was a long time.

Brian Epstein: It was my grandfather who started the NEMS stores. It was principally a furniture store, and the base was gradually widened to accommodate more general furnishings. We were a middle-class Liverpool family. Perhaps you could say we were slightly better off than middle-class, though not upper-class, by any means.

When I was 16, I left school. At the time the only ambition I had was to be an actor. As a second choice, I would have enjoyed being a dress designer. My family, of course, had different ideas for me and pushed me to join the family business. Although I wasn't very keen on that, I was so anxious to leave school that I let them talk me into it. They initially got me a job as a furniture shop apprentice with another company to prepare me for running our business. After about six months, I had learned everything I was going to from them and I was set up back at NEMS. It was interesting for a while, but eventually I got bored and started to think again about acting.

I met an actor one day who I quite admired, and I remember telling him that I had very much wanted to become an actor, and that I regretted not having done so while I was younger. I remember he looked at me rather incredulously and said, "Why, you can't be any older than your early twenties. There's still plenty of time for you to take lessons and get on the stage." Well, I decided there on the spot that I would take the audition test for RADA [Royal Academy of Dramatic Arts], which I did. And although I passed the test and joined RADA, I'm afraid that after having been away from the strict discipline of schools for such a long time that I found it difficult to adjust to that life again and I left. My family had also offered me the opportunity of rejoining the business in the records division, which greatly appealed to me.

Bill Harry: When I started *Mersey Beat,* I came out with the first issue and took lots of copies round to stores by hand. The main distributors put them in the general news agents shops, but I used to deliver copies to local record shops, clubs, "jive hives," and music stores. I went into NEMS in Liverpool and asked to see the manager, who happened to be Brian Epstein. He knew nothing about the scene at the time. I had a meeting with him, showed him the copies of *Mersey Beat,* and he agreed to take a dozen. The next day he phoned me up. He'd sold out within an hour of taking them. He ordered 12 dozen, sold them out within a day, and then started asking me to have chats with him two or three times a week about this burgeoning scene in Liverpool. He was very interested in it. In fact, in issue one of *Mersey Beat* we had the story of the origin of The Beatles, which John [Lennon] had written for me. In issue number two we devoted the whole front cover to The Beatles, and all about the record they had made with Bert Kaempfert in Germany. It's interesting to note that, according to Brian's book, *A Cellarful of Noise,* it was six months later when this young chap entered his store and asked for a record by The Beatles. That, he said, was when he wondered who they were, found out they were from Liverpool, and decided to find out more about them. Well, of course he'd known about them six months before. He used to discuss the paper with me. In fact, he requested, and I let him have, his own record review column in every issue of the paper!

Bob Wooler: Bill Harry likes to make the point that Brian would have known about The Beatles from reading *Mersey Beat.* I don't think that just because Brian did some plugging for his NEMS record store in his columns, talking about the songs in the Top Ten, that he read the paper from cover to cover and absorbed all those weird group names. It just wasn't his scene at all. He didn't move and groove around the dance halls. Sibelius was more his scene. So I think Bill has put two and two together and not come up with the right answer.

Jim Gretty: Brian Epstein came to me once, since his store was in Whitechapel a few doors away, and said, "Jim, I'd like to get hold of a couple of groups because I think I'd like to manage a couple. You know them all. What's your favorite?" I said, "There's Gerry Marsden, The Fourmost, The Beatles, and Rory Storm. They're the best so far." Brian then asked me where he could see The Beatles and I said, "I tell you what, Brian. I've got a show in a theater called the Albany Cinema at Maghull in a couple of weeks' time [on October 15, 1961]. If you want, I'll get you a couple of tickets." He came to the show and sat in the audience, next to our Member of Parliament, Bessie Braddock, and all those invited guests. The Beatles were supporting Ken Dodd and some others, and it was a proper show act like the Palladium shows. It was really a tip-top lineup. Brian came back to me on Monday morning and said, "Jim, I like those Beatles. I'd like to manage them."

Chapter Four

Mathew Street
to
Manchester Square

Although Jim Gretty, Bill Harry, and others have said that Brian Epstein had already heard of or seen The Beatles, Epstein insisted he saw them first at a lunchtime session at the Cavern Club on November 9, 1961.

Brian Epstein: I went to see them at the Cavern, which was just around the corner from my office. It was very interesting indeed to see all of these teenagers spending their lunch hours in rapt attention to these rather scruffy lads onstage. They put all of their attention into the music, not their appearances, but I liked the way they sounded very much. The first thing that struck me, really, was that they had a very honest and unrehearsed sound. I thought that if I liked it, and all these teenagers liked it, then there was something worth exploring.

Bob Wooler: I had a little back room, a DJ room, where I played the records. At the Cavern the stage was very small. I only had one turntable in those days, no headphones for cueing in, and no flashing lights. I shared that room with the bands playing onstage. The Beatles were onstage [one day] when I was in this back room, and I heard a rattle at the door. Paddy Delaney, who was the chief bouncer of the Cavern, ushered in Brian Epstein. I had seen him on my visits to the NEMS record store, but I didn't know who he was. He said he "was there because I've ordered copies of 'My Bonnie,' which people keep asking for. They tell me you play the record here at the Cavern." I said, "Yeah, that's right and that's good you've got copies because people are always pestering me about where they can get the record." He looked through the band room, through the archway that led onto the stage, and asked, "Are those The Beatles that are on that record?" I said, "They are The Beatles. What do you think of them?" Well, it was lip reading because there was a hell of a din coming from the stage. His ears weren't accustomed to all that racket, though they'd soon get used to the sonic boom as he got to know them.

George Harrison: We used to do lunchtime dates. So we'd get up and go down to the Cavern and play from probably about 12 noon to about 2:00 p.m. It was very casual, you know. We'd have our tea and sandwiches and cigarettes onstage, sing a couple of tunes, and tell a few jokes. There was something that he [Brian Epstein] liked about all that, and he wanted to try and push us to bigger audiences.

Bill Harry: Now, if you read Brian Epstein's book, or know his story, in some ways he had to prove himself. I won't go into certain details about his life at the time, but he'd been put in as manager of his parents' record shop and I think he suddenly felt as if there was an amazing world around him. He saw there was a chance to get involved in it and maybe get some success. So he snuffed out that the most popular group was The Beatles locally. You know, he phoned me up and said, "This Beatles group, I'd be interested in seeing them. I notice in *Mersey Beat* they're at the Cavern. I've never been there. Can you fix me up to go?" So I phoned up the Cavern and said, "Mr. Brian Epstein of NEMS is coming down. Can you fix him up? You know, a big VIP thing?" Though it was only a shilling entrance, I wanted to fix it for him because he wanted to see them. So he went down. I think it was July or August 1961. It was at least three or four months before the famous Raymond Jones came into his store, asking for The Beatles' record.

It was a bit amazing later, because Brian was always an impeccable dresser — beautiful suits and everything. He started going down to the Cavern and emulating The Beatles. He was really into them — leather gear and all the rest of it! The people used to laugh at him, you know, because it wasn't really him. When he was in the suit, people were a bit awed by him, sort of like, "There's a guy with a few bob behind him, blah, blah, blah." But as soon as he started wearing all this leather, they were laughing a bit. He really did have the vision, though.

I admired Brian, what he did and what he thought. He said, "When I take over The Beatles, I'll get them the highest pay any group has ever had." After a while he announced to me proudly that he'd managed to get The Beatles a booking for 15 pounds. Nobody would believe it. Fifteen pounds! Nobody paid that for a group. Brian Kelly — everybody laughed. I had people on the phone to me, asking, "What's this rot you're saying about a promoter paying 15 pounds for The Beatles? No group is ever worth that! You must be joking!"

Alistair Taylor: One day Brian came to me and said, "Look, let's go and see this group." So we went down to the Cavern in our business suits. We went quietly in, paid our money, and sat toward the back. The Cavern was something else. It used to be a great jazz venue in Liverpool. I was very much a jazz fan and had visited the place many times. There was this very scruffy band onstage in black leather and black T-shirts. They were fooling about and they weren't very good musicians. But it was the most phenomenal experience I've ever gone through. They were incredible! They just had charisma. I don't know what it was. It was more than charisma. Lots of artists have charisma, but they had Ingredient X. You could literally feel the sound hitting you, pounding against your chest. One of the boys, Paul, announced they would play a number that he and John had written called "Hello Little Girl" which, of course, they never recorded. They gave it to The Fourmost, who later became one of our stable. When The Beatles came offstage, we had a brief meeting. We popped our heads into a tiny little cupboard where they retired to change. Actually they didn't bother to change. Brian said, "Hello, I'm Brian Epstein and this is my personal assistant.

Well, we [Epstein and Taylor] went for lunch, and that's when I did my famous turning down of two and a half percent of The Beatles. I was a very straight and fair guy over the years, really, but we were talking and Brian came out with this weird question: "Do you work for me, or do you work for NEMS?" I said I worked for him, so he said, "Well, we'll have to set up a separate company because we can't do the record shop and the furniture shop and all the other business. This will be full-time. Will you come with

me?" I said, "Of course I will. It'll be great!" He said, "Well, if you
do, I'll give you two and a half percent of The Beatles." I remember
looking at him and saying, "Oh, no, Brian, I couldn't take that
because it's going to cost you a lot of money to get them on the road
and we don't have any money to put into the company. It wouldn't
be fair to take two and a half percent." And that was it — end of
story. He said, "Oh, fine, well, you'll get a better salary and more."
So we signed the boys and nobody wanted to know about them.

Brian Epstein and Alistair Taylor arranged a meeting with The Beatles at the
NEMS Whitechapel store at 4:30 p.m. on December 3, 1961, "just for a
chat." In the intervening days the NEMS record store sold more than 100
copies of "My Bonnie" after Epstein arranged for the records to be sent
from Germany.

Bob Wooler: Brian came to the Cavern and was conquered by The
Beatles, and something was on his mind. Well, it came to light
what it was. The Beatles finished their lunchtime session, were
packing up, and I was playing my fadeout record, which was
Bobby Darin's "I'll Be There." The boys said, "We're going to see
this bloke at NEMS 'cause he's asked us to go across. He's talking
about signing us and being our manager. Will you come with us?"
The reason they asked me was because I'd been their friend and
buddy, as it were, and Brian was an unknown quantity. They'd met
some sharks in the business, you know. They'd been around since
1957. So I said, "Okay, are we going to the Grapes [a pub] first?"
Then I packed up my records and we went over to the Grapes and
had a few bevvies, so we were late for Brian's appointment.

That didn't trouble The Beatles, and it was good training for
Brian, because they would be late on many occasions for him.
Well, we got to the store, and it was a half-day closing because it
was Wednesday. In those quaint old days some of the city-center
shops closed for a half day midweek. Therefore the lights were off,
but there was this figure in the ground-floor sales department, and
it was Brian. He was hopping mad, but he was able to conceal his

annoyance. So in we went and they named themselves. We were all a little fidgety, and Brian wondered what I was doing there, so John said, "This is me dad." I'm not sure I took kindly to that.

Anyway, Brian said, "I'd like you to think of me doing management for you." They said, "What do you know about the business?" Of course, they were aware he had some record shops and that this was a way into the music business, though that was the sales side rather than production. But it was just a tentative meeting. There was a period of getting to know each other, and he followed them around and realized how difficult it could be getting them onstage on time. At the same time, once they were onstage, no one had any complaints about their performance. He asked my opinion of them because he realized I'd known them for about a year. He also asked Allan Williams, who advised him not to touch them "with a barge pole."

Brian Epstein: The first business meeting [their actual second meeting on December 6 at NEMS] we had was held at my store. It got off to a rather late start, and in retrospect it was actually rather amusing. John, George, and Peter arrived at the appointed time of four o'clock. After about half an hour, though, Paul still hadn't arrived. I was getting a little angry, since I considered this a very important meeting, so I asked one of the boys, George Harrison actually, to ring Paul. He came back and said that Paul had just gotten up and was in the bath. Well, this really made me angry, and I said, "How can he be late for such an important meeting?" George simply replied in a manner that proved to be very typical of the four of them, "Well, he's late, but he's very clean."

On December 10, 1961, The Beatles met Brian Epstein and Alistair Taylor at the Casbah Club in the basement of Pete Best's home. It was there that they agreed to sign a management contract with Epstein.

Alistair Taylor: I was asked by Brian if I would witness the first contract between The Beatles and him which, of course, I did. I signed it in five places. Funny enough, years later, when Brian wrote his book with Derek Taylor, the original photostatted contracts were reprinted. Although I signed it five times, there were only four signatures. So I witnessed a nonexistent signature, because Brian Epstein never did sign that contract, ever.

Clive Epstein: Well, obviously, as I was fairly closely connected with the record section in our store, Brian talked to me quite often about The Beatles. Also, we wanted to develop some type of reputation for the business in Merseyside. We started the promotions at ballrooms and theaters along with other Merseyside artists.

I always thought The Beatles were intriguing, but obviously it was difficult for me to accept what Brian said when he played their tapes and then announced that these guys were going to be bigger than Elvis Presley, who in those days was the giant of them all. I mean, I must be honest about this, I really took his remarks with a pinch of salt. Although I was involved with them on a business basis, I couldn't accept what Brian said because it seemed quite extraordinary.

I wasn't really surprised when Brian signed them because I think that he, at that particular stage of his life, was looking for something else. Although we had a successful chain of record and television shops, it wasn't really that creative. He was always looking for something a little more creative, you know, and I think this is the type of activity that excited him. I mean, as you know in his background, he went to drama school and this, that, and the other, but none of it was exciting enough. It wasn't creative enough for Brian. So, in grooming artists and managing them, he felt he was back in the creative world again after working in the family business. I'm sure he was right. It was creative work. It was quite a struggle, however, in those early days.

Brian Epstein: It was a decision by the five of us to change The Beatles' presentation. I encouraged them at first to get out of leather jackets and jeans. I wouldn't allow them to appear in jeans after a short time. After that stage I got them to wear sweaters onstage and then, very reluctantly, suits. The distinctive Beatle suits were actually their idea, which they'd seen in Germany. It was a French design from Pierre Cardin. I strongly agreed with their choice and, of course, it then became rather overworked in the media. Later they stopped wearing them because they became tired of them.

Bill Harry: Bert Kaempfert got a call from Brian Epstein, who'd found when he'd signed The Beatles that they'd already been con- tracted for three years with Polydor. Brian put the proposal to Bert Kaempfert: "What do I need to do to get you to release them from the contract?" He obviously thought he'd have to pay or whatever. So Bert said at the time that he wasn't sure. He liked the group, but his bosses were Polydor. So he went to Polydor and said, "I've had an inquiry about the group. What do we do?" They said, "Well, look, the lead singer's all we care about — Tony Sheridan. Blow the group." So Bert wrote to Brian, saying, "Yes, you can have The Beatles. We're not really interested. They'll keep Tony Sheridan." So he released The Beatles to Brian Epstein from their three-year contract for nothing. Absolutely nothing!

After Brian Epstein got the release from Bert Kaempfert, he approached the Liverpool representative of Decca Records. Through him he managed to get Mike Smith of the A&R department up to Liverpool to hear The Beatles at the Cavern. Smith thought The Beatles were tremendous, which made Epstein very excited. They secured an audition at Decca on New Year's Day, 1962, and at 11:00 a.m. they arrived at the studio in London. They taped several numbers and then returned to Liverpool to await the results.

Tony Barrow: I met The Beatles originally because I was a freelance record columnist at the *Liverpool Echo*. I'm a Liverpool man, but I'd long left Liverpool before The Beatles started to appear at the Cavern. I was working in London at Decca Records. Brian Epstein contacted, not Tony Barrow, sleeve writer at Decca Records, but Tony Barrow, record columnist of the *Liverpool Echo*, because he wanted me to write something about The Beatles in my column. He brought me an acetate when he came down and saw me at Decca, and the acetate was The Beatles at the Cavern Club. It was absolutely appalling. I mean, in terms of capturing the excitement of their Cavern Club sound, maybe it was okay, but in terms of showing what The Beatles were like, it was appalling. I kind of said so. I didn't do a "don't call us, we'll call you," because it wasn't my place to do so. I was strictly a sleeve note writer and had nothing to do with A&R or with signing the acts. I just wrote the notes on the backs of the album covers.

After Brian left, I made a call on the internal phone, not to the A&R department, but to the marketing people, because I was aware that Brian Epstein was a record retailer who had a record shop and maybe, just maybe, the sales people at Decca would be interested in giving one of their customers an audition. So that's what happened. I don't even remember what was on that acetate now. By all accounts, it would have to have been "Some Other Guy," which The Beatles never did record commercially. I was already doing a little moonlighting, as it were, because I was getting a full-time salary from Decca to write their sleeve notes, but I was also using their typewriter and carbon paper to write for the *Liverpool Echo*.

Dick Rowe: The young man that I had deal with The Beatles, Mike Smith, also auditioned Brian Poole [and the Tremoloes]. They came into London on New Year's Day. Both auditions were done on the same day, and Mike picked Brian Poole. Well, in fairness to Mike, he would have liked both of them, but you see, this isn't meant to blame anybody. I mean, it was my responsibility. Young people aren't too inclined to worry about the money — the cost of things. They don't put that first. It's enthusiasm that comes first. So when Mike said to me that he'd like both acts, I said to him, "No, Mike, it's impossible. They can't both be sensational. You choose the one that you think is right."

So he chose Brian Poole, and I can understand that because

I heard the auditions. The auditions by Brian Poole were better than The Beatles'. Another reason why Mike made that decision was that The Beatles were resident in Liverpool. Brian Poole lived only a mile away from Mike Smith, so he knew he could spend night and day with Brian Poole at no cost to the company, whereas Liverpool is a long way away. You've got to get on a train. You've got a hotel bill to pay. You don't know how long you're going to be up there. And London is so very strange about the north of England. There's sort of an expression that if you live in London, you really don't know anywhere north of Watford. So, you see, Liverpool could have been in Greenland to us then.

We hadn't said anything yet to Brian Epstein, who was then putting the pressure on Decca because now he had been to other companies. So when he realized we were being a bit indecisive, he really started to put the pressure on. And maybe because of this I don't think he and I really hit it off. He obviously believed in this group tremendously. So I went up to Liverpool to see The Beatles. I didn't even tell Mike Smith. I went there and it was — there's no other way of putting it — it was pissing with rain. It was falling down in buckets, and I went out to the Cavern and the place was crowded. You couldn't get in, and what with the rain outside, I was getting drenched. I thought, Oh, sod it, and I walked away. How could I have been so stupid? The very fact that I couldn't get in because it was so full should have struck me. But it didn't. I think the rain, and the fact that I was getting soaked, made me walk away from it. And that's how we made that cock up.

Alistair Taylor: Dick Rowe has taken so much [flak] by the media as "the idiot" who turned down The Beatles. But Dick Rowe listened. He was the one guy who sat down and listened, and he said no. There are people in the business turning down successful groups every day of the week. Okay, he made a mistake. Everyone talks about Brian and how he helped The Beatles become the biggest thing in the world. What people haven't thought about, and have quickly forgotten, are the Tommy Quicklys, The Rustics, the Mike

Haslams, The Fourmosts, and many more. You don't know any of these Epstein acts. They were zilch. They never got off the ground. So Brian had his failures, as well. He made some wrong decisions. So what the hell was wrong with Dick Rowe saying no? I asked to see one of the heads of A&R at Pye Records and they wouldn't even listen to "My Bonnie." I had a copy with me and they weren't even interested.

Dick Rowe: George Martin is not only taller than most of us, but he's also head and shoulders better than anybody else in his music ability. He was even better than Norrie Paramor [of EMI], and Norrie was as good an A&R man in England as we've ever had. George was only into a very specialized type of recording until he met or came across The Beatles. He wasn't considered a pop producer. We were the experts on pop and we all turned The Beatles down.

You see, when I heard the audition tapes and I heard their renditions of tunes like "Money" and "Twist and Shout," to me, they were the same as a number of English artists like Terry Dean and even Billy Fury. They were adequate, they were making adequate covers, but there was nothing really that startling about them. And, of course, for perhaps a year, everybody, particularly in the United States, confirmed this back to me, saying, "Well, they're never going to make it here." [Brian Epstein] couldn't even get Capitol to release [The Beatles'] product. It was put out on two very small labels and the records didn't sell at all. And though Brian put the pressure on, they couldn't get Capitol to release them, so they got Vee Jay [Records] to do it. Vee Jay and Swan had the first four singles. Lee Jollet, who was then a pretty important A&R man at Capitol, thought [the records] were terrible.

Eventually I told Brian that the people at Decca didn't like the boys' sound and that groups with guitars were on the way out. Brian replied, "You must be out of your mind. These boys are going to explode. I'm completely confident that one day they'll be bigger than Elvis Presley." I told Brian, "You have a good record business in Liverpool, Mr. Epstein. Stick to that."

On April 13, 1962, The Beatles were booked to open the brand-new Star-Club in Hamburg. When they arrived on April 11, Astrid Kirchherr gave them the news that Stuart Sutcliffe had died of a brain hemorrhage the day before.

Pete Best: Although Stu had left the band, we were still really good mates. He would come to Liverpool with Astrid occasionally to see us. Of course, when we were playing in Hamburg, we'd hang around a lot and he'd come to lots of the gigs. Unfortunately, when we went back to open the Star-Club in April 1962, we were expecting Astrid and Stu to meet us at the airport. John, myself, and Paul flew in. George was due to follow us out later because he had German measles. Only Astrid was at the airport, and it was only then, when we were getting off the plane and asked where Stu was, that Astrid turned around and told us he had died 48 hours beforehand of a brain hemorrhage. But, you know, the memories of him are good. And, as a guy, he was a lovely person. That was probably the first time I saw John physically break down and cry in front of someone. I think it showed the total admiration John had for Stu as a person and a friend. Paul and I were also deeply upset by the tragedy.

Astrid Kirchherr: I can't explain it. It's so hard. When you're so young, like we all were then, death is so far away that you never think about it. And when someone gets ill, you never, ever think of death. That is why it was like a dream for all of us. It was so unreal or unrealistic. Stuart was so sensitive. He liked beautiful things. We used to go out, which wasn't very often because I wasn't making much money and he only had his grant from college, and see ballet or classical concerts. He wrote stories and poems. He was very intelligent, very sensitive, with a wonderful sense of humor. He used to spend hours writing letters to John in Liverpool. He'd put down all his feelings, all his experiences, even put in illustrations, drawings, and pages of poetry. These letters ran to 20 pages or so. John's letters were just as long and deep. They were very close because they had exactly the same kind of humor, wit, and intelligence. They were so quick, and it was great listening to them. They were hilariously funny, both of them. To John, Stuart counted more than anything, and he felt he had to look after Stuart because he was so small and delicate. He really loved him as he would have loved a brother, if he'd had one.

Millie Sutcliffe: When Stuart died, [Eduardo] Paolozzi wrote me a letter in which he said that he'd noticed Stuart's health going down. He had a long talk with him one day and discovered that he was playing all those hours in the nightclubs and working like a slave at the art college during the day. So he gave him his option: one or the other, but not both! Now I remember Stuart telling me the ordeal of making a decision, the big decision. Oh, incidentally, he got a tremendous grant, a very generous one from the German government on Paolozzi's recommendation. He said, "It certainly puts Britain to shame, Mother, the pittance they gave me when I was 18." He wrote, telling me about this man Paolozzi: "Mother, he's so vibrant . . . brimming full of ideas. He's just wonderful." He really adored Paolozzi.

Horst Fascher: At the Star-Club I gave The Beatles all kinds of freedom. I said, "You can do what you want even onstage. Let the people have fun with you and have fun when you're playing." That's when they did all the crazy stuff. I was the guy who had the idea to open the Star-Club. I asked all the bands who played before at the Kaiserkeller and the Top Ten to go with me to the new club. Fortunately everyone said, "Sure! We've been working with you all these years. We'll go wherever you go!"

I was the one who was getting new acts, new bands, from Liverpool, and I was taking care of them through the night. I was like the manager. Don Arden was a British promoter who brought American acts to England. We could only afford to book these big American acts when they were touring England. That way we didn't have to pay all the fares and costs. It was much cheaper to bring them from England to Germany than all the way from America.

I met Don Arden one day by complete accident, and he asked me, "Are you interested in having these bands, as well?" I said, "Yes, we're very interested in having them." So he came one day to Hamburg and we made a deal that every act he brought to England would have to play the Star-Club in Hamburg. We could let the English bands participate with these big stars so they could see what the Americans were doing. The Beatles watched Little Richard, Fats Domino, Jerry Lee Lewis, and all those names very carefully to see what they were doing onstage. The Beatles were behind the curtains or backstage, taking in all the moves and performance tricks and trying to copy them. I think that had a lot to do with their success later.

Little Richard: Nobody knew [The Beatles] but their mothers. I thought they were a very good group when they performed with me at the Star-Club in Hamburg, but I never thought they were a hit group. I was offered 50 percent of them by Brian Epstein, and I didn't take it. I always thought Paul would make it, and we became good friends because he was a big fan of mine, but I didn't think the group would do it. They were singing my music and Chuck Berry's and some of Elvis's. They would sing "Love Me Do" every night, 'cause it was going to be their first record. It was really something else when they shook the world.

Don Arden: I was a partner in the Star-Club in Hamburg, and The Beatles opened it in 1962. We paid them $500 a week. And during that period of time, Brian Epstein would continually ask me to put them in my touring shows. The funny thing about that situation was that I had to ignore The Beatles because Epstein controlled them. It was a case of why should I help to promote a group I didn't own.

The Star-Club [held] roughly 850 to 1,000 people, depending on how we wanted to shift the tables around and lie to the police about capacity. The Beatles would start performing at about eight o'clock in the evening and go till four in the morning. They'd play as many sets as they could survive. It's very interesting to note that we booked the biggest stars in the world there. We used to have guest stars ranging from Ray Charles to The Everly Brothers. And no matter who we booked, whether it was Fats Domino, Jerry Lee Lewis, or Little Richard, The Beatles, I must admit, always did better than any of the them. We always felt that their success was because they had developed their own following, since they'd been [in Hamburg] for such a long time. I had heard around the clubs that right from the very first day they started appearing there they got instant notice.

Now, since I was an established promoter and agent in Britain, Brian Epstein knew me quite well. In fact, I was on the plane with them when they went down to EMI for their first recording session. Anyway, every time I would bring a star in to England and I had a tour going, Epstein would call and say he would like to take a venue in Liverpool. At first, when we didn't know him, we would charge him twice as much as anybody else in the hope that he would refuse, because in those days we always wanted to know who the hell we were dealing with. Eventually we got to know him, and he proved he could put on a good show.

What he did was he called me, as he always did about touring shows, and said, "I notice you've got Little Richard coming in. Would you give me the Little Richard show for Liverpool?" I said, "Sure, fine." I didn't travel continuously with these shows. I'd go for a few nights and go home. One Sunday night Little Richard, extremely annoyed, called me up at home and said, "Hey, man, who the hell's this act, The Beatles? This Epstein has billed them as big as me, and I don't like that and I'm not going on!" Then I realized what Epstein's game was. He wanted to use Richard to sell The Beatles at a big concert, and he took the biggest venue in town. It was the first time The Beatles had played a real big date.

[Epstein's] gotten a lot of credit. He did a good job, and nobody can ever take that away from him. However, it was discovered after his death that the deals he arranged for the boys, such as the recording contracts, were very small deals. He didn't understand what the group was worth. In other words, he understood that he was on to something big, he was becoming a personality, and he'd wallow in that glory, but he wouldn't let anybody talk to The Beatles. When it came to actually negotiating or renegotiating a recording contract, he never had the slightest idea. And when he died, I firmly believe The Beatles were on something like a ridiculous royalty of five percent on a worldwide basis. But that's something I think that could be forgiven because he had undying faith in this group, and he did predict to me and to my partner in Germany in the Star-Club that one day they were going to be as big as Elvis. And, of course, everybody laughed. Eighteen months later they were on the way to being the world's biggest attraction.

Klaus Voorman: The shows at the Star-Club were the same as always. Always the same songs. We heard them again and again, and it was always great. To me the fact that Paul started playing bass made it not the same kind of band as before. It was different. It wasn't the five people now. Stuart wasn't there, which was a little emotional, too. But for me it was a little of a letdown at first. They still only did copies or covers, which was basic hard rock and roll.

On May 8, 1962, George Martin, the A&R director of EMI's Parlophone Records label, got a telephone call in his office in London's Manchester Square from Syd Coleman, an old friend and the general manager of Ardmore and Beechwood, a music publishing subsidiary of EMI. Coleman had been told by Jim Foy, who worked downstairs from Coleman as a sound engineer cutting individual discs for customers in the HMV record shop in Oxford Street, about somebody who was looking for a recording contract. After listening to the man's demo disc, Coleman thought Martin would be interested in talking with him. Martin wasn't in his office when Coleman called, but his assistant, Judy Lockhart Smith, set up an appointment with the man. The next day Brian Epstein met George Martin.

George Martin: He [Brian Epstein] was a typical sort of young northern entrepreneur, if you know what I mean. He was well spoken and well mannered and obviously had a burning faith in these boys. He was determined that they were going to be successful no matter what I did with them. He just gave you that impression, and he was undoubtedly a tremendous influence in making them a hit. When Brian played me the disc in my office, I wasn't terribly knocked out by it. In fact, I thought it wasn't very good. But there was some undefinable quality of rawness. A kind, I suppose, that I hadn't heard before, so I thought it might be useful to investigate. Anyway, to be honest, I was looking for a new act. So I was ready for something, and I arranged for Brian to bring them down for a recording test. Now that wasn't a great decision, quite honestly, because I couldn't lose by it. It meant these poor fellows had to travel down from Liverpool and spend an afternoon with me in the studio, which I was quite prepared to do to find out how they ticked. And when we did meet on that occasion, well, it was just love at first sight. I thought they were super.

Norman Smith: It was just another band until they walked into the studio [on June 6, 1962]. In those days we had what was called an "artist's test," and everybody had to go through that no matter who they were. I mean, even if they were a name artist coming from another label, they had to take the test. The Beatles were in that category. And before they walked in, I thought to myself, Well, here comes another nothing group. But the moment they walked in I thought, Wowee, this ain't the usual type of group that comes in. There's something different about these boys. It wasn't only their hairstyle. There was some kind of aura when they walked in. Their equipment was another story, however.

Anyhow, I set them up in the usual way for an artist's test. By the way, George Martin wasn't there at first. A guy named Ron Richards, who was George Martin's assistant producer, was there. He eventually called George to come and have a look. As a recording engineer, I had gotten used to expecting groups to come in with nothing but tiny little box amplifiers no more than 18 inches square. We sort of stuck them on a chair and brought a microphone up to within two inches of it. We got the sound and separation that way. Well, [The Beatles] had just about the same sort of equipment. I can't even remember, to be honest, whether George Harrison and John Lennon shared the same amplifier. I've got a feeling that they did. But, anyway, Paul had something that looked like a bass speaker.

I set up the microphones and trotted upstairs to the control room and opened up the faders. I really couldn't believe what was going on. So I said I thought there must be something wrong with our mixer because there were so many extraneous noises, and that's putting it mildly. It was quite incredible. We had to do something about it before we began, so I went down with a soldering iron and tried to repair their very used gear. I even had to borrow some equipment out of our other studios and echo chambers. In those days we had echo chambers that were tiled rooms that had speakers and microphones. I had to use some of the speakers that were in the echo chambers to fix up Paul's bass-amp sound.

Anyway, we eventually found some sort of cleaner balance, which still wasn't very good. We did get something on tape, which didn't show us any sign of the writing ability yet to come. Certainly not from the instrumental side, at any rate. There was something, I think, in Paul's voice that I remember. Strangely enough, I was a great John Lennon fan from then on, as well as Paul's. I do remember Paul's voice sort of striking me. But there was nothing indicative about the songs that were to come. They played the old standards, old country-and-western things, and I think we had a couple of original pieces that didn't set the whole world alight. So, to sum it up, the artist's test The Beatles did was not impressive.

George Martin: They played through a lot of things they'd been doing in their repertoire. It wasn't a question of what they could do, because they hadn't written anything that was great at that time, but they had great personalities. They had a great way with them, and they charmed me a great deal. They knew I was the guy who made all the Peter Sellers records, and they were all fans of that sort of humor. Well, John, George, and Paul, that is. Pete Best, who was also part of the group, was very much the background boy. He didn't say much at all. He just looked moody and sullen in the corner. George, I suppose, was probably the most vociferous of the lot, but they were all very good.

Norman Smith: I don't think we were expecting anything, really. I don't think EMI was expecting anything exciting from them. It was solely because of their personalities. It was soon after the recording test that the powers that be got together and said, "Well, shall we or shan't we?" I was asked for my opinion and I gave it. I just had a feeling that simply because of the personalities and the humor that came through that they had to be something different. George Martin and I had a discussion about it, too. He felt the same way. And so they were signed.

Alistair Taylor: I'd seen Brian Epstein sitting and waiting for a phone call from George Martin, in tears, from sheer frustration and impatience. Brian could be a very emotional character.

George Martin: I was convinced I had a hit group on my hands if only I could get the right song. They'd played me all their stuff and I didn't think anything was any good. So I went around Tin Pan Alley looking for songs and my old friend Dick James came up with one called "How Do You Do It" that had been written by Mitch Murray.

Stephen James: George Martin used to produce my father [Dick James], who was a singer in the 1940s and 1950s. My father used to sing with quite a few English dance bands, and George produced many records by my father, including the famous one, "Robin Hood," which was used for the TV serial. Because of their long-term relationship, when my father went into music publishing and opened up Dick James Music in 1961, they continued to remain very closely in touch. In fact, we published for George Martin. At the time a new station was opening up on the BBC called Radio One. Until then it was called the Light Programme. It was moving from a sort of middle-of-the-road market into a pop market, so they wanted a new station identity theme. George Martin wrote that theme and we published it. So, therefore, we had a regular, ongoing relationship with George. When he brought this band down from Liverpool, The Beatles, and signed them, he felt he needed a commercial song for them. Among the batch we gave him to try with the boys was one called "How Do You Do It." The Beatles did go into the studio and record it, but they were never happy with it because they felt it was too "poppy"! It didn't give them the freedom to express themselves the way they wanted to. They really wanted to write their own songs, not from a greed point of view, but because they felt it depicted their musical direction [better].

George Martin: I listened to "How Do You Do It" and said, "Yep, that's a good song. That's a good commercial song. Give it to The Beatles and I'll have a number-one hit." So I sent it to The Beatles and said, "This is what you're going to record [when we get together again in September]."

On August 16, 1962, Pete Best was asked to leave The Beatles and was replaced by Ringo Starr.

George Martin: After the audition session, I decided that Pete Best's drumming wasn't good enough and it wasn't going to make my life very easy producing good records, so I pulled Brian Epstein aside and said, "Look, I appreciate the problem I'm giving you, but as far as personal appearances are concerned, there's no reason Pete shouldn't be part of The Beatles. As far as recording is concerned, though, Pete is out. I can get a very good session player in for the recordings, and that's the way we're going to do it." I learned later that the boys had been thinking of replacing him, anyway, so I guess my decision sealed it. I was actually surprised when they told me Pete had been replaced, because I thought he was the best-looking of the group and was a real asset in that sense.

Beryl Wooler: I'd been on holiday and when I came back I got the message that Brian would like to speak to me. He said, "Beryl, I was wondering, would you like to come up to see Ringo playing with The Beatles for the first time?" It hadn't been announced that Pete Best was no longer in the band. Rumors went around very quickly, and when we got to the gig that night, it was absolutely amazing. Some of the girls were crying. They wanted Pete back. "Who's Ringo?" they asked. It was really sad. Brian kept it quite light. He didn't want any issue about it. He said, "Well, you know we'd sooner have Ringo than Pete," and didn't give any explanation.

Mona Best: And you hear these people who say Pete was sacked from The Beatles because he couldn't play. Well, that's all rubbish as far as I'm concerned. When Pete was gotten rid of, I phoned up George Martin and said, "Did you have anything to do with Pete getting thrown out of the group?" He said, "I certainly did not, Mrs. Best." As musicians, he said, they were all pretty much the same and he didn't know who he might need as session drummers. He said he might need session musicians who played guitar, as well. But as far as Pete leaving the group, he had nothing to do with that.

There was a little resentment for the dirty trick they [The Beatles] played on Peter, which was only natural, but we treated them with respect whenever we saw them. When he was thrown out, Pete was sick, very sick. As he said, "To think how I had drummed those hours away in Germany. We all got into trouble together, we all went without food together, we lived in dirty, dingy apartments together, and just when we were going to get the golden apple in our hands, I'm the one who's booted out and

I get nothing." He was only young, so you can imagine how he felt. He cried. He was so depressed he almost took his life.

So I can't forgive The Beatles, because to get rid of Pete was quite unnecessary. It was so greedy and selfish in their outlook on life. They didn't appreciate what Pete had done for them, that all the fans from our club followed Peter because Pete was a real kind of James Dean idol. The girls loved him. He didn't realize what a following he had. And it was only after, when he went to other places and he was being mobbed, that he realized he had these fans.

Pete Best: There were a couple of things that happened when Joe Flannery came down and said, "You want to join my band, oops!" You know, that type of thing. That put a little bit of seed of doubt in me. Of course, that particular night when we played the Plaza in St. Helen's, I actually asked Brian. [He told me,] "Rest assured, my boy, nothing like that's going to happen. You dismiss it. I mean, there's no reason for it. You've been with them two years. You've been down to Abbey Road. There'll be no changes. You're along." And then all of a sudden, after being assured by Brian, our manager, and everything is put to bed and peaceful again, he calls me into the office, and bingo!

Ringo Starr: Well, I'd been playing with groups since about 1960, just playing, getting money, working. I met The Beatles in Germany when I was there with another group [Rory Storm and the Hurricanes], and we used to have 12 hours' work between the two groups. We got to know each other pretty well. We all came back to England, and their drummer was sick, so they asked me if I would sit in, just for a day or so, till he got better. I said yeah. Then I went with another group again and they got him back. Then he was sick again and they came and asked me again. So every time he was sick they used to come and ask me to sit in, which I used to love because they were a much better group than the one I was with.

I had this job at a holiday camp in England where you play for three months, which is supposedly the season, but there's never very much sun. Brian Epstein phoned me up on a Tuesday and said, "Would you like to join The Beatles?" I said, "Yeah, I'd love to join." Then he said, "Well, can you get here tonight?" I said, "I can't leave the other group just like that. I must give a bit of notice." So I said I'd be there Saturday. Then I arrived on Saturday and we had about two hours' rehearsal. We played that [very] night.

Pete Best: I'd known Ringo Starr through his performing in my mother's club, the Casbah, when he was with Rory Storm and the Hurricanes. I met him again in Germany because he was out there on the same tour, and when we came back from Liverpool, he was around the scene again. We "buddied" up and became great friends. Even though he took over my role in August 1962, I have absolutely no hatred for him.

On August 23, 1962, John Lennon married his girlfriend, Cynthia Powell, at a quiet ceremony in Liverpool at the Mount Pleasant registry office. The marriage was kept secret. Even the new drummer, Ringo Starr, wasn't told. Paul McCartney was the best man.

Cynthia Lennon: Aunt Mimi was very jealous and protective of John for a long time. I understood that because he had lost his mother and Mimi had become his mother. She had become a surrogate mother and she didn't want him to throw his life away. But you know, fate works in strange ways. If my mother hadn't gone to Canada to be a nanny for my cousin, then I wouldn't have had the freedom to move in with John, to the point where I wouldn't have become pregnant. It's a catalog of situations, because I got a bed-sit, my first bed-sit ever, and because we didn't have to sit in somebody's room or somebody's car or the back seat of the cinema. We had all the freedom going for us. No precautions. So that's what happened.

Julia Baird: They got married. They already had the baby on the way. You tell me what man immediately stays at home to look after the baby. Point him out. It's exactly the same situation. What he did do is insist that Cynthia stay at home with the baby, and I think she was the miracle girl in all this because she did. People say Cynthia was a mundane hometown girl, "mumsy," your average Mrs. Liverpool. That's a load of nonsense. Cynthia was a highly talented woman in her own right. A real artist. She painted, she drew, she sculpted, she designed. John, the macho man, said, "You stay with this child. I'm out touring. You stay here." She did tour occasionally with him. As you know, she went to America once. But John wasn't keen, and it wasn't to keep her out of the line, right? It was because he had a child and he wanted her to be with that child. I remember seeing Cynthia in the house in London with the hole in the kitchen floor. John was immediately off on tour and said, "There's enough rumpus going on in his [Julian's] life right now with the move. You stay here, and she stayed there. It's nothing to do with being hometown. It was because they were trying to do the best for that child. John was well aware he was already away for most of the time, that one of them had to stay with Julian. So it wasn't a matter of just abandonment and neglect. Yes, he did neglect Julian, but for reasons that most fathers neglect their children — time, business.

Sean O'Mahony: I never knew for a long time. It went on right through the first issue [of *Beatles Book Monthly*, first released in August 1963]. This is the funny thing. The Beatles' fans were marvelous. They always knew more than we did. At least some of them did. That is, in fact, how we used to find out where The Beatles were in London. Brian used to do everything to get them a flat and keep it private. Of course, we were always desperate to find out where they were so we could pop along with the cameras and have them say, "How did you find us?" How we usually found them was that the kids would ring up and say, "Is it true The Beatles are on Green Street?" We would say, "Which number in Green Street?" And they would say, "Number 20." We would say, "You've got it! You're very clever." Then we'd rush off to 20 Green Street. [The Beatles] were really desperate to get away from people. This is when Beatlemania really started going. But at the start we got all these phone calls and letters from fans and readers saying, "What about Cynthia?" We thought, Who's Cynthia? So I promptly got on to Brian and asked, "Who's Cynthia?" And so the big smoke screen went up. But we knew something was up.

Peter Jones: I went for the better part of a year knowing that John was married to Cynthia. During that time, there was an absolute denial of the fact as far as the press was concerned.

On September 4, 1962, The Beatles began recording "Love Me Do" at Abbey Road Studios in London, finishing it up on September 11 with session drummer Andy White instead of Ringo Starr.

George Martin: We had agreed to record what I considered the best of their songs, "Love Me Do," which I thought might have made a good B side. We listened to "How Do You Do It," and The Beatles said, "Well, okay. You really want us to record that?" I said yes, so we recorded it. John did the main voice and I think Paul sang occasionally on harmonies. I think it was a very good record. At the end of it I said, "Fine, great, super." They said, "Well, do you mind if we record one of our own?"

Paul McCartney: George Martin said to us that "Love Me Do" was all right, but if we wanted a hit record, then maybe we should consider "How Do You Do It," which had been written by a song-writer. We said, "We don't really like the song, George." He said, "I think you should do it." Then Brian Epstein gave us a warning. You know, we got the word from Brian. "Do It! It doesn't matter if you don't like it. Do it!" So we learned it and we did a demo recording, but we still didn't like the song for us. We were very conscious of our image, and as you know, we wanted to be different from all the rest. We didn't want to be like Cliff Richard and everyone else in England, because it was all changing then, too. We felt like we were the generation after Cliff.

George Martin: We recorded "How Do You Do It," and in deference to The Beatles, "Love Me Do." I reluctantly agreed to release "Love Me Do." It was a good song, but not a great song. The lyrics weren't exactly earth-shattering. It was a fairly simple song. Of course, it suited their style in those early days. The other key to it was John Lennon's blues harmonica. I should note that "Love Me Do" was always performed by John, even though it was Paul's song. I changed it and had Paul sing lead, not because it was Paul's song, but because I wanted the harmonica to flow in and overlap the voice. So suddenly John found himself without a song. I took it away from him. He wasn't very happy about that.

Norman Smith: It was very arduous, and again George Martin didn't start it off. It was Ron Richards, and it was very difficult. I don't really know why. Ringo had just joined them in the group and it was, maybe, not too easy for him. I personally think he did very well because it was a very easy drum pattern, anyway. But what followed was very interesting. We took them up into the control room, George and I, and we spoke to them about what was expected in terms of sound and such. We laid into them for quite some time about different things because George and I wanted to get them involved right from the start in the techniques of the recording studio and what would be expected from them in the future.

This went on for some time, and after, I remember something happened that epitomized what they were all about and what was forthcoming. George Martin said to them, "Well, you sat there very patiently listening to us and, you know, we've told you what we expect from you regarding technical and musical things and stuff. Is there anything at all that you want to say to us?" There was silence. They sort of looked at one another. I noticed a kind of a sparkle in their eyes. There was a mischievous thing going on. And then it was George Harrison, strangely enough, who broke the silence. He simply said to George Martin, "Yeah, I don't like your tie!" And that was that. Well, I looked at George Martin and he looked at me and, of course, we fell about laughing.

That really, I suppose, was not only the breaking of the ice, if there was any to break, but the indication of their humor. I think Liverpudlians have got a terrific sense of humor. I mean, it's absolutely amazing the things that happened on The Beatles' sessions. It's very difficult to recall actual instances, but there was always something funny that went on at all their sessions. You know, that great Liverpudlian humor came through, and it was a great beginning, even though it had been a long day. We probably recorded at least 17 takes. I don't think anything was expected. Nothing exciting, anyway.

Ken Townshend: Being from Buckinghamshire, I have a sarcastic sense of humor. But up in Liverpool it's even worse. I remember when I was moved up to be manager of technical operations, The Beatles all came in one day and stood in front of my desk, looking at me with very straight faces. John Lennon produced this roll of toilet paper and said to me, "Ken, we don't want to use this toilet paper anymore. It's too hard and shiny and it has 'EMI Limited' stamped on it. We don't think the staff should have to tolerate toilet paper like this!" From that day onward Abbey Road Studios has never had shiny, hard, EMI-labeled toilet paper. And the roll they gave me that day? I stuck it in my drawer and had it there for years and years. Later we had some kind of auction at the studios and I brought out this roll of toilet paper. I believe it fetched 100 pounds [sterling], which was given to a deaf school. I'd have to say it was a bit of a rip-off.

Norman Smith: The facts, or the fact, was that, yes, we did get a substitute drummer for the session. Ringo had only just joined the group when we attempted "Love Me Do," so we brought in a session drummer [Andy White]. That was the only title. After that it was always Ringo. He was a good drummer, anyway. He could have done it on "Love Me Do," but in those days he didn't have quite enough push.

On October 5, 1962, Parlophone Records released The Beatles' first single, "Love Me Do," with the B side, "P.S. I Love You." (Note: All release dates in this book refer to the British dates.)

George Martin: Oh, well, they [EMI executives] asked me what the name was, and I said The Beatles. They all sat around laughing. It was a silly name. Let's face it. They thought it was another of my Goon jokes, you know. They thought, He's come up with another comedy record and he's just spoofing us about it. Then, when I played it for them, they thought I had gone slightly mad. Nobody believed in it at all. I had to really fight within my own company to get the thing promoted.

Tony Barrow: I really didn't feel I could start publicizing an EMI act from behind a Decca desk, so I brought in Andrew [Loog] Oldham, who was later to become the manager of The Rolling Stones. This was late 1962 when the first Beatles single was coming out. Andrew, at the time, was a very young, ambitious publicist working in not only pop music but movies, too. Andrew had a new partner named Tony Calder. Tony had just left Decca's press office, and I was aware that Decca's press office had one of the finest mailing lists. I was pretty sure Tony would have taken a copy home with him, so I did this deal with Andrew where he took The Beatles round to see all the people. I mean, The Beatles went round to all the pop magazine editors' offices and actually saw these people. They trekked round Soho and Shaftsbury Avenue to the various pop weeklies and monthlies. Andy was the guy who took them round and introduced them to everybody, and I did the writing side of it. I did the very first press manuals, press releases, and so forth. It wasn't until the following year that I joined Brian [Epstein] full-time as the actual head of the new publicity and press division of NEMS.

Ringo Starr: I think when I heard "Love Me Do" on Radio Luxembourg one night it gave me the shivers. It only got to 40 or 50 [on the charts], but it was incredible that we had a record out and that it was on the radio. It was our first taste of success. For me that first record was more powerful than "Please Please Me" reaching the top of the British charts. Just the idea of being on a bit of plastic was really incredible after all those years of slogging it out in the clubs.

Philip Norman: I think "Love Me Do" sounds better in retrospect. It makes me think that perhaps our ears are more acute than they were then. I listened to "Love Me Do" when it came out and all I heard was a kind of thudding, thumping sort of loping tempo. It didn't seem very attractive. Now I listen to it and I listen for McCartney's voice and Lennon's voice and whether it's Andy White [on drums] or Ringo hitting the tambourine. When it first came out, we didn't have particularly good stereo equipment or radio reception. Now we have and it's extraordinary. The patterns and the levels — you can see it and hear it now! It's a rough sketch, but every element of the sketch is original. That's the difference. Even the bit where Lennon copies the harmonica from the Bruce Channel song "Hey Baby." It's still Lennon and everything is new and fresh in it.

Joe Flannery was a close assistant to Brian Epstein. He was doing a lot of the bookings in the early days for The Beatles because Brian didn't really have any experience in that area. One day he walked into a storeroom at the back of the NEMS store in Liverpool and saw all of these boxes of records. Brian had this little melody he used to sing when he went into that room. It went: "Here we go gathering dust in May." Those were all the unsold copies of "Love Me Do" sitting in his storeroom. Interestingly Dick Rowe, who has the great stigma of turning down The Beatles on Decca's behalf, said that he heard later that Brian had offered to buy 3,000 copies of any record Decca decided to record of The Beatles. Dick said that given the economics of the business, if he had known of Brian's offer, he would have signed them regardless of how they sounded because 3,000 copies would have provided Decca with a healthy profit.

Julia Baird: They made "Love Me Do," and I remember John running up the stairs with two records. We'd never seen demo discs before. One was "Love Me Do" and the other was "P.S. I Love You." They were flat on the reverse side, and the smell of acetate filled the room. We spent a lot of time looking at them. Then we all sat and listened to them together, with John there. I couldn't get over it because he played the harmonica all my life, and there it was on the record. He played it so beautifully in real life and he was only allowed to do a bit on the record. We all preferred "P.S. I Love You." Apparently there'd been a hoo-ha over which side was going to be the A side, and they'd decided on "Love Me Do." Then, within no time at all, it got to number 17 [on the charts]. We watched it crawl up the charts, and they said it was going to be played on the radio. John said it was being played on Radio Luxembourg on Friday night at 10:00 p.m. Every time Elvis Presley was on [the radio] there was a blackout. Terrible. You had to buy the record to actually hear it properly. And it was pretty much the same [with The Beatles]. It was all buzzing. But the school was buzzing, as well. When I went back on Monday, it was great. Then, after Christmas, "Please Please Me" was released, and the rest was like *poof.* It didn't stop.

Chapter Five

Thank Your Lucky Stars

On November 26, 1962, The Beatles went to Abbey Road Studios to record the follow-up single to "Love Me Do."

George Martin: As I've said, "Love Me Do" was about the best song I could find from The Beatles at that time, but it wasn't the one I needed to break through. In fact, we only got it to about number 17. I still had "How Do You Do It," which they didn't want to release. I had said, "Well, if you can give me a song that's as good as that one, we'll record it. Otherwise that's going to be your next record." They had said, "Give us a week." And they came back [for the November recording session] with a song I'd rejected previously because they'd done it too slowly. In fact, I told them they needed to speed the whole thing up, make it much more vibrant. This was "Please Please Me." Someone mentioned that it was originally inspired by Roy Orbison. So they played it to me again in the studio and I modified a little bit of an ending and so on. At the end of the session I was knocked out because it really was a great record. I said to them, "Gentlemen, you've got your first number-one hit." And they said, "Well, does that mean we don't have to have 'How Do You Do It'?" I said, "Fine, okay. I'll go along with you on that." So we released "Please Please Me" and, of course, it did become number one.

Stephen James: They recorded "Please Please Me," and I remember my father calling George to find out what had happened with "How Do You Do It." George gave him the sad news that although The Beatles had recorded it, unfortunately they didn't like it. They didn't feel their version was good and they didn't want to release it, which upset my father extremely. He was disappointed because he was just beginning and was finding it tough and any A side of a record would have been great at the time. [However,] George recommended my father to Brian Epstein, who wanted to find a regular music publisher for The Beatles' songs.

Brian met my father and played him the rough acetate of "Please Please Me," and my father hit the ceiling. Brian said,

"What do you think?" My father said, "I think it must be a number-one record. I think it's far better than 'How Do You Do It,' and if I could possibly publish it, I'll work on it personally and see what I can do." Brian said that the one thing he was unhappy about with the previous single was that they didn't get enough promotion on it. He felt that if my father was going to publish it, then he had to help with the promotion. So my father said, "Well, I'll phone a friend of mine right now, Philip Jones. He does a new but very important TV show on Saturday night called *Thank Your Lucky Stars*. If you can get your artists on there, you're pretty sure of a hit record the following week. So my father phoned Philip right there and played him "Please Please Me" over the telephone. He told Philip it was coming out that Friday [January 11, 1963]. Philip said, "Sounds good enough to be a hit. I'll book them two weeks Saturday!" Brian was a little taken aback with my father's very direct kind of promotion.

So The Beatles went on *Thank Your Lucky Stars,* and the breaks started from that moment on. That was the number-one show on television. It was very powerful in this country. Their record broke wide open and went to number one. It went to number one on the *New Musical Express* Chart, but in the industry trade paper, which was called *The Record Retailer* in those days, it only reached number two. Therefore, in Tim Rice's book on the charts, unfortunately, it shows that "From Me to You" was their first number one, not "Please Please Me," because it didn't make number one on the official trade chart. But it was their first big hit, and it led to a great relationship between my father, Brian Epstein, John Lennon, and Paul McCartney.

George Martin: I had "How Do You Do It" up my sleeve when Brian Epstein brought me his next line in the stable — Gerry and the Pacemakers. I said to Brian, "Okay, let them do 'How Do You Do It.'" Gerry did it and it became number one, too.

Billy J. Kramer (aka William Ashton): I was seriously considering working full-time for British Rail when I bumped into Brian

Epstein at a pub called the Grapes, near the Cavern. A little later he asked if he could manage me and gave me an offer I couldn't refuse. My band, The Coasters, were apprentices in different trades and didn't want to chance working full-time as musicians. So Brian suggested I join forces with a band called The Dakotas. We had a meeting in Brian's office, and The Dakotas weren't really into it at the time. I was wearing gold and pink lamé suits, and they didn't like the sort of image I portrayed. Brian said, "Well, that's not what Billy is going to do." So we rehearsed together at the Cavern, and John Lennon and Paul McCartney were there. They said we sounded really good. So we went back to Brian's office, and he asked The Dakotas what they thought. They said, "It sounds great." And Brian said, "If you decide to back Billy, you can make your own records with him." And together we were very successful.

One day I went into Brian's office, and he said John had an idea. I said, "What is it?" He said, "Why don't you call yourself Billy *J.* Kramer?" John was sitting there, and I said. "I think that's a great idea." Brian said, "John feels it's more flowing and American-sounding." And I said, "If anyone asks me what the *J* stands for, what shall I say?" John said, "Julian." I said, "You must be joking! It's a right puff's name." At that time, in Britain, it was sacrilege to be a pop star and be married and have kids. I sort of worked closely with The Beatles on numerous occasions and I'd met Cynthia and everything, but I wasn't aware that John was married and had a son named Julian. I still think it's a right puff's name, though!

The Dakotas were a very good band, very good musicians. I'd say they were the best in Liverpool. It was never announced publicly, but Brian definitely used to feel a bit worried about The Beatles' musical ability, not their songwriting ability, but their ability with their instruments. He even considered using The Dakotas on the backing tracks for The Beatles. But he never did, though there was concern at one time. But they came on in leaps and bounds once they became successful.

I never dreamed I'd get as far as making a record. When "Love Me Do" and " P.S. I Love You" came out, I was disappointed because I'd seen The Beatles do "Twist and Shout," "Money," you know, the Chuck Berry and Little Richard stuff. So when I heard their first single, I thought it was a bit timid. A lot of people say they prefer The Stones because they had a lot of balls. All I can say is that the first time I ever saw The Beatles live, which was at the Litherland Town Hall when they wore whatever they wanted, they made The Rolling Stones sound like a bloody squid.

Anyway, "Do You Want to Know a Secret" was given to me by Brian, and it was just John on tape singing, then apologizing for the fact that it was the quietest place he could find in the building to record it, which was a toilet. He even flushed the toilet at the end. So I learned the song and did it on numerous recording sessions, but it was "don't call us, we'll call you." One day, though, I tested with EMI and George Martin. Brian phoned me about a fortnight later and said, "EMI is going to release 'Do You Want to Know a Secret.'" I said, "Really," because I wasn't impressed with it. Then I said, "Don't you think we should wait for a better song?" But Brian said they were very pleased with it, and so they released it. There was nobody more shocked than me when it went to number one. A lot of people have said to me, "Did you get that song off The Beatles' first album, *Please Please Me*. But I recorded the track long before them. It took a long time to record because it was the first time I'd ever been in a studio. I couldn't make certain notes because I was so nervous and uptight. Maybe that's why, in his book, George Martin said I was a terrible singer.

Tony Barrow: Brian asked me to join him full-time and I actually turned the man down. I remember I got as far as saying to him, "Well, would there be a piece of the action? Would there be any part of The Beatles in it for me?" He replied, "Well, if there was, it would be a very small one." We didn't pursue that any further. I said to him, "Well, actually, Brian, I've got a very secure job at Decca Records. It's an internationally known company. I just recently brought my girlfriend down from Liverpool, got married, and we're going to start a family. No offense, but you're starting out with a band. Maybe they're going to be quite big, maybe they're going to be as big as you claim, as big as Elvis, but I'm going to stick with Decca." So he went off and put the same thing to Andrew [Loog] Oldham, who turned him down for the opposite reason. You see, Andrew didn't want to lose his independence. Andrew was already a totally independent publicist and didn't want to come in-house, as it were, and work for somebody. It was really after "Please Please Me," in the early part of 1963, that Brian came back and we went for a very good seafood lunch — I'm a sucker for Chablis and scallops. Over the brandy and coffee I eventually said yes, because by that time Brian had increased the money and leaving Decca meant I would double my salary overnight. Of course, security or no security, a newly married man can't ignore the doubling of his salary. But I have to tell you that the doubling of my salary meant I was to get something like 35 pounds a week.

On February 11, 1963, The Beatles recorded their first album, *Please Please Me*, in one day.

George Martin: After "Please Please Me," I told the boys to write me another song like it. The next one was "From Me to You," then "She Loves You," and then "I Want to Hold Your Hand." They couldn't put a foot wrong. It was absolutely marvelous. The first LP was recorded in one day. We needed to have things quickly. I was very conscious about that with "Please Please Me" being a number-one single. If I had an album to follow it very sharply, I would have a big album sale. I knew darn well we couldn't record an album of original songs. So the obvious thing to do was to record all the stuff they did in their live act. I'd already been to see them at the Cavern, so I knew their repertoire by this time. I just selected all the stuff I knew they could do at the drop of a hat. I got them down to the studio and said, "Right, we're going to record 'Roll over Beethoven,' we're going to record 'Money,' we're going to record 'Chains,' and so on." It was rather like a performance, actually. We started at ten in the morning, no, eleven, in deference to their long beauty sleep, and I think we finished about ten at night. We had a break for lunch and a break for tea and we recorded 12 songs. Norman Smith was at the controls and he got a good balance. It was knocked off like a live performance.

Norman Smith: What I tried to do was to create the live pop group on tape. Of course, there were predecessors before on wax where they had created the live sound, but I tried to get the sound of The Beatles singing and playing as they'd perform onstage. I thought if I didn't do it, I'd lose the excitement. In other words, I laid down the backing tracks first, then laid on the vocals. It was important to create their live sound as it happened, and I did get them exactly the way they performed onstage.

Paul McCartney: I wrote "I Saw Her Standing There" going home in a car one night, so I wasn't really thinking too much about it. The first two lines that came in the car that night were originally "She was just 17 and she'd never been a beauty queen." When I saw the lyric the next day and played it to John, we both realized it was a ridiculous line. So we thought of another line that rhymed with 17 and meant something. Eventually we got "You know what I mean," which means nothing at all, but it worked.

Paul McCartney wanted to record "Besame Mucho," which The Beatles had been performing in their live shows for years, but "A Taste of Honey" was chosen instead.

George Martin: When it came to recording the first album, [The Beatles] offered me various things they had, a lot of stuff other people had written. For example, Paul wanted to record "Falling in Love Again." You know, the Marlene Dietrich song. But I balked at that and he could never understand it. I mean, that's the cornier side of Paul's life, which occasionally emerges, but not very often.

Paul McCartney: We recorded the first Beatles album in a day. We did "Twist and Shout" last because if we'd done it first we couldn't have done any of the others. John's voice would have gone. One day for an album is pretty fast. Now it takes one day to switch on the machines, load the computer, find out where the on/off switch is. It takes forever to record one song now.

Norman Smith: John's voice was pretty shot. They had a whole tin of throat lozenges plus cartons of cigarettes on the piano. John had to do the last track ["Twist and Shout"] of 12 on that first album, so he swallowed two or three of the lozenges before we attacked it. It's not an easy number for any vocalist to sing, but we had to get it in one take. That not only meant John but the rest of the group and me as the sound engineer, because if I got anything wrong, then by God there was no way we'd have a go again. We started, I had everything crossed, and we got it in one take. I guess it [the whole session], not counting tea breaks and stoppages, worked out to no more than 15 minutes per title.

Peter Blake: The very first time I met The Beatles was at a rehearsal for a television program in 1963. It was the first one they did in London. The top of the bill was Billy Fury, and Tony Meehan and Jet Harris from The Shadows were on the bill, too. Billy Davis and The Beatles just sang the one opening song. I sat where the audience would have been all by myself and watched the show. After The Beatles did their song, they came into the seats and did an interview. They sat right in front of me, I suppose, because I was the only person sitting there and they were drawn toward me. I listened to the interview and they turned around, smiled, and waved.

The first time I really met The Beatles was probably the same year. A friend, Bob Freeman, who later did the cover photograph of *With the Beatles,* said they were playing at Luton, and we drove out to see them. We couldn't go backstage, but The Beatles said they'd meet us back in London at their hotel in Russell Square.

We drove back to town and went into the foyer. Ringo, George, and John were sitting around a table. We had coffee and sandwiches and only one person came up and said, "You're The Beatles, aren't you? Would you sign this for my daughter?" They were completely left alone.

John had never really spent time in London and wanted to go to the clubs. George was tired and went to bed, so John, Ringo, a friend named Joe Chelson, who was a painter, and I went on the town. We drove around in Joe's old Jeep. John, Ringo, and I were in the back. We went to a club called the Crazy Elephant and asked, "Can we come in?" The man at the door said, "Are you members?" We said no, but they were actually playing a Beatles song. So John said, "You're playing our song. You must let us in." The doorman said, "I don't know what that is. I don't know who you are. You can't come in." Then a voice came from inside the club and said, "It's all right. They're friends of mine. They can come in." We went in, and it was Paul, who was already there at the smartest club in town. He was completely at home and knew the town already. The evening went on and then we left without Paul and went to an all-night club where a couple of girls came up and said, "You're The Beatles, aren't you? Will you sign our things?" That was all quite early on.

Del Shannon: I probably had about 12 hits in England and I was doing a lot of touring there. All of a sudden The Beatles started to get hot. They had this big show at [Royal] Albert Hall in London and I was asked to be in it. The promoter told us we would close the show and then changed his mind and said The Beatles were too hot and he wanted them to close the show. He had a big fight with my manager.

In the end I closed the show and we did all right. It was very freaky meeting The Beatles. It was like meeting Dion. Dion was very New York and they were very Liverpool. They were very cocky, especially John, who was a scary guy. He was very frank, like Dion was, too! Meeting them was strange because they were hot and they had no collars on their shirts. They were really different and unique and they said what they felt. I sort of envied that because we couldn't be that way. We were from a different era where you didn't swear, you drank milk, and you looked very neat.

When "From Me to You" was number three on the British charts and I actually heard them do the piece and all the kids were going nuts, I decided to cover it. I never knew they would become so huge. Roy Orbison pegged them. He said, "These guys are going to be great and big." I thought they would be big in England with a couple of hits here. They had that little falsetto, and I said, "Hey, you guys are copying my falsetto, so I'll copy your record!"

Dezo Hoffman: I was a staff photographer on a London weekly, the *Record-Mirror*. One week we had an editorial meeting. We sat around discussing what we wanted to do the next day. I picked up a letter to the editor and a little snapshot fell out. In the snapshot were four boys with quite long hair. It struck me that the girl who wrote the letter was crying her heart out [about these boys]. I remember the letter had a lovely perfume on it. Anyway, that was my first introduction to The Beatles.

After the meeting, I asked the editor about doing a photo feature in Liverpool on these boys. He said it was too expensive to go to Liverpool. It took me three months to convince him to send me. When I arrived, I went to see Brian Epstein, and we had the most fantastic type of rapport straight away. Maybe that was because I didn't want to take the kind of pictures he expected, you know, the sort where people are shaking hands in the office. I wanted a picture with the background of Liverpool, so instead of taking one picture I stayed there for three days. And that's how The Beatles and I became friends.

The cover photo on the *Twist and Shout* EP was done [on March 25, 1963] when I was in Liverpool, long before the record was even thought of. I could have made them very sordid-looking because Liverpool was like that, but I never did. I never did anything of them that was sordid. I did a lot of pictures in a house, in a garden, that sort of thing. The Beatles and I clicked, and in that "jumping" picture [for *Twist and Shout*], I just wanted to show the boys' vitality, how they were full of life. I took about three rolls of film of the jump till I got it right. Each jump they did was better than the one before. They were the easiest boys to photograph.

On April 14, 1963, The Beatles went to see The Rolling Stones perform.

Bill Wyman: At the [railway] station hotel in Richmond we were playing away one evening in March 1963 when we looked up and saw four shadowy figures facing us in the audience. They weren't dancing, just standing there in their leather coats. We looked, turned away, then did a double take and whispered to each other, "That's the bloody Beatles!" They were standing there like clones, watching us. We chatted with them at the interval and then they stayed until we finished and we all went back to Mick [Jagger], Keith [Richards], and Brian [Jones's] flat. We stayed up all night rapping with them. They were going to do some big concert in London — Albert Hall or something — and they invited us. I think Keith and Brian went. They got attacked for the first time by kids and said, "Right, we've got to be more commercial now!" That's when we thought we should do more commercial material like the fast Chuck Berry stuff. Then we played a few smaller gigs with The Beatles in London. They headlined and we kind of opened for them in the very early days.

On May 10, 1963, George Harrison and Dick Rowe helped judge the talent of a "beat group" competition at Philharmonic Hall in Liverpool.

Dick Rowe: I was talking to George [Harrison] and told him how I'd really had my backside kicked over turning The Beatles down. He said I shouldn't worry about it too much and suggested I sign The Rolling Stones. I said, "The Rolling Who?" He told me I could see them at the railway hotel in Richmond. Well, I left him right on the spot, went down to London, picked up my wife, and drove to Richmond. I think it must have been the summer [in 1963]. We arrived at the back entrance of the hotel, and because of the low sun I had dark glasses on and had forgotten to bring my other glasses from the car, making it difficult to see.

Gradually I began to make out the room. I saw the group and then I noticed the room was full of young fellas. There wasn't a girl to be seen. The boys were standing in little groups of two or more, talking to each other. No one was dancing, just chatting and listening to the music. And all the time they were up and down on the balls of their feet to the rhythm. I asked my wife what the group looked like. I could hear them — it was a nice sort of earthy sound — but I wanted to know what they looked like. She said, "The lead singer's very good." I always stay for only 15 minutes when I go to see somebody at a club, for fear they may find out I'm there. So we left. The next morning I started chasing around to find out how to sign The Stones, and I found Andrew [Loog] Oldham, their manager. That was the start of The Rolling Stones with us [at Decca].

On May 18, 1963, The Beatles began another national tour, this time sharing the stage with American rock-and-roll legend Roy Orbison.

Roy Orbison: The crowds were really wild in Britain and all the way through, even in Australia. It didn't seem to be just the Beatle thing, though. I told them they should come to America. I was a roving correspondent while I was on tour for the *NME* [*New Musical Express*] in England and I was to report on how the tour was going. I told the boys to keep their hairstyle. It was short by English standards of that time. You would see guys with hair down to their waists in London, and then there was Screaming Lord Sutch. Anyway, I told them to keep their hairstyle for sure and to keep the clothes they were wearing and let it be known that they were English, then get on some big American television show, and it would work.

Derek Taylor: I was working on the *Daily Express* [in Manchester] as a theater critic and columnist when I made a point of getting front-row seats at the Odeon on May 31, 1963, to see Roy Orbison, Gerry and the Pacemakers, The Beatles, and others. Gerry and the Pacemakers closed the first half. They were sensational, so direct and with so much energy. It was the Mersey Sound, and the audience was shouting. So I thought, What must The Beatles be like if this is going on? Then we heard the opening bars of "From Me to You" and The Beatles crashed onstage, and life has never been the same from that very minute to this one. It was absolutely out of this world. From then on I was their devoted slave. I made up my mind that I had to join them somehow.

Freda Kelly: It [fan mail] came in sackfuls day after day. Two or more a day sometimes. I would look at all this mail, not just letters but packages and boxes, and I would close my eyes and think, Oh my, where are we going to put it all? What have I done to deserve this? Just because I decided to become the Beatles Fan Club person, do I need all this? I certainly never expected all of that. It was really overwhelming. We would put the sacks side by side and mark each one that came in the door — Monday, Tuesday, Wednesday — and eventually we would get through it. Then it just became too much.

Cynthia Lennon: They dreamed of being the "toppermost of the poppermost," but I don't think they really felt it would happen. They dreamed of it. It was fun for them. It was a joke for them. It was part of their humor, but really, deep down, what happened to them was unbelievable. If they hadn't met Brian [Epstein], who was a conservative, well-dressed, well-spoken man with a quest, I'm sure they wouldn't have gone anywhere. I don't think Brian has had the acclaim he should have had.

Paul McCartney: We were in a van up in Newcastle on tour [on June 26, 1963]. We were on our way back to the hotel and I got the idea for doing one of those answer-type songs where someone says,

"She loves you," and the other person says, "Yes" or "Yea, Yea." John and I thought it was a stupid thing, and it really was when you think about it, but at least we had the idea to write a song called "She Loves You." So then we just sat up in one of our hotel rooms for a few hours and wrote it.

On July 1, 1963, The Beatles recorded "She Loves You" at Abbey Road Studios.

George Martin: "She Loves You" was a brilliant song and certainly one of the most vital The Beatles had written so far. [It had] terrific atmosphere to it and was a great song performed live. It was the kind of song that not only aroused emotion when you first heard it, but with the way they actually sang and the way they shook their heads and so on, the young girls would be moved enormously by it. One of the interesting things about the song, of course, was the way it ended on a major sixth. I thought that was pretty corny. It was almost like Glenn Miller's orchestration, and I told them so. I told them I'd heard that so many times in my life and did they have to do that, but they'd never heard it before. They thought it was pretty smart and, of course, they stuck to their guns. And they were quite right, because it has become a hallmark hit.

Stephen James: Eventually, in August 1963, we started a company called Northern Songs, since they [The Beatles] were from the north of England, and specifically signed Lennon and McCartney to that company. At the same time we offered them something that was completely new to the industry, something that no one was doing at that time. We gave them equity in the company, as well, so they actually owned a piece of Northern Songs. That was never heard of in those days. It might be criticized now as not necessarily being generous, but it was extremely generous in 1963. Brian was so pleased with the way we were handling the promotion and everything that we also started another couple of companies with him in which he shared. One was called JAEP Music, for James and Epstein.

On August 3, 1963, The Beatles made their 292nd appearance at the Cavern Club. It was their last performance there.

Bob Wooler: During 1963 when [The Beatles] stormed the charts, we knew they weren't going to be at the Cavern much longer. Brian actually owed us three Beatle bookings because he had pulled them out three times for television. The last appearance was August 3, 1963. It was Saturday, a bank holiday, and there was an air of gloom, but the performance was fantastic. They played the way they had the first time before they'd recorded anything, and the fans loved that. The fans never jumped onstage or anything. It was such a marvelous scene. The audience respected the artists. It was my honor to introduce them at every Cavern show, which was very simple because they were an act that needed no introduction. I simply said, "It's The Beatles."

At the beginning of September 1963, "She Loves You" reached the number-one position on all British charts and stayed there for seven weeks. Fans started riots outside theaters, and the national papers began to discover firsthand the initial wave of Beatlemania.

George Harrison: Back in the Beatlemania days we were on the front page of most papers every day, and it became tiring because it was really a game. One game was to sell newspapers, so they put anybody in they thought would sell papers. The other game was to build people up into such a thing that it became ridiculous and there was nowhere left to go but to shoot them down. So this perpetual game went round and round. They put us up and they put us down until it went through so many changes that it didn't seem to matter because it didn't stop us from being "cute."

On September 10, 1963, The Beatles received the Top Vocal Group of the Year Award at the Variety Club luncheon. Afterward they went to a Rolling Stones rehearsal and wrote the song that would become The Stones' first hit.

Keith Richards: We liked "I Wanna Be Your Man." In fact, John and Paul came down to a rehearsal of ours and laid it on us. We hadn't heard their version. We just heard John and Paul on piano banging it out. We picked it up, and it was just one of those jams. They got enthusiastic. We got enthusiastic, and said, "Right, we'll cut it tomorrow," and that was it.

Keith Altham: In contrast to The Beatles, I think the "bad" image of The Stones developed gradually. Andrew [Loog Oldham, their manager] saw the virtue of it and began to exaggerate it and use it to his advantage. I don't think it was a deliberate attempt to start out right from the beginning and say, "The Beatles are a bunch of lads you can bring home to meet your mother, so we're going to make The Stones somebody you can't take to meet your mother." It simply began to slip that way, and Andrew began to realize it worked. You could draw attention to yourself just as easily, if not faster, by not behaving in a conventional manner. The Beatles, on the other hand, took a more orthodox route by becoming middle-of-the-road and family-oriented. Andrew understood intuitively that there was a postwar baby boom that you could sell to, so it didn't matter if you didn't appeal to all the mums and dads because you would appeal to all the kids that constituted a big segment of the population. It didn't matter, then, that the mums and dads didn't like the idea of a band urinating on a petrol pump. To me, and The Rolling Stones, it seemed absurd that the media made such a big thing about a bunch of guys leaving a pub late at night and relieving themselves in the forecourt of a petrol station while wars, famines, and other obscene activities were taking place around the world. The Rolling Stones were held up as the demons who were almost single-handedly going to undermine the moral and ethical values of a generation. It was just too absurd for words.

Peter Jones: I was in the very privileged position with both The Beatles and The Rolling Stones of writing their fan magazines, which they made money from, and working as a journalist at the *Record-Mirror*. So I had regular access to the groups that other writers couldn't get. But it was a difficult position for a journalist to be in because I was expected to gloss over any improprieties that I might have witnessed. It was decreed that The Beatles should be portrayed as incredibly lovable, amiable fellows, and if one of them, without mentioning any names, wanted to have a short orgy with three girls in the bathroom, then I didn't see it.

I think Brian Epstein was a very businesslike guy. He brought The Beatles into us at the *Record-Mirror,* and there was never a moment of relaxation. He did it all on a very straight business level, as if he was selling something he genuinely believed in, which he did! With Andrew [Loog Oldham] and The Rolling Stones the relationship was totally different because with Andrew it was a "wink, wink, nudge, nudge" kind of thing. He knew I knew that he was kidding. Andrew was pretty unscrupulous about getting his way with things. Brian, in a sense, was far too well bred. He was quite a gentleman, although very tough on percentages.

On October 31, 1963, The Beatles returned to London's Heathrow Airport after a short tour of Sweden. They were greeted by hundreds of screaming fans. The hysteria was witnessed by Ed Sullivan and his wife.

Derek Taylor: I began to ghostwrite a newspaper column for George [Harrison]. The Manchester *Daily Express* decided it would like to have a column written from within The Beatles. By then I'd met them at a backstage reception when they returned to Manchester in November 1963. I'd also met them in Southport. So, by the time I met them again in November, they still remembered me. George said, "We've got a new single, you know. It's called 'I Want to Hold Your Hand.'" He was his usual patient, methodical self, so when the time came for me to write the column, I picked George because he seemed to be a painstaking man with an instinctive news sense, and he turned out to be an extremely good subject for ghostwriting. Once he rang me when he was on holiday in Dublin and said, "I've just been visited by the *Daily Mirror*, and as a loyal *Daily Express* journalist, I thought I'd better ring and tell you they found us in Ireland. Since I work for you, I don't want you to be stranded." He wasn't a good collaborator with the press in later times. He wasn't good on the road because he couldn't bother with the hassle. He was never known as the *diplomatic* Beatle but, in fact, he was terribly helpful with the column. Paul was the diplomatic Beatle.

On November 4, 1963, The Beatles made their triumphant appearance at the Royal Command Variety Performance at the Prince of Wales Theatre in London. The charity event was attended by the show business establishment, minor society, and the musical trade people, all hoping to get a glimpse of the Queen Mother, Princess Margaret, and Lord Snowden. In their performance John Lennon introduced "Twist and Shout" with a remark that was to be echoed around the world: "For our last number I'd like to ask your help. Will the people in the cheaper seats clap your hands, and the rest, if you'll just rattle your jewelry?"

Paul McCartney: I think the whole bit really started when we did the Palladium show and then later when we were asked to do the Royal Command Variety Performance, where we met the Queen Mother and she started clapping.

Clive Epstein: I think the time when it really hit me was when the *Daily Mail* developed the four boys' fringes and so forth and slapped it all over the front page. Then, when they had their Royal Command Variety Performance in 1963, it was at that particular stage that I realized this was probably the biggest event in entertainment since goodness knows when. I mean, I'm quite sure there hadn't been anything similar since, maybe, Rudolph Valentino.

On November 22, 1963, The Beatles released their second album, *With the Beatles*. It had been recorded mostly in July, with additional work in September and October.

George Martin: When The Beatles started to get really big in Britain, and in some parts of Europe, I felt they should get a shot at the States, or at least a release of their recordings. I was constantly told that Capitol Records, our company in the U.S., had turned The Beatles down. I got increasingly frustrated because our American counterparts had always been slightly superior, saying, "Well, of course you don't really know about rock and roll in England. We are the fountainhead of rock and roll and we should know about it." Every time a record was rejected by them, I told myself they must be right. By the third time I knew damn well they weren't right and I got increasingly hard about it. The Beatles records issued [in the United States] on the Swan and Vee Jay labels were getting more and more prominent. So, by the time "I Want to Hold Your Hand" came along, Capitol realized they had to get behind it before the dam burst. The pressure was too great, and that's really what contributed to the enormous success of The Beatles in America — with men wearing silly Beatle wigs on Fifth Avenue and that kind of thing. It was fun, though. It was incredible to watch. And so this breakthrough of "I Want to Hold Your Hand" was enormously significant, not just for The Beatles and me but for the whole record industry and indeed the economy of Britain.

Stephen James: America was always frustrating because, as you know, up until then no British acts had broken in America. It was very unusual for the Americans to take any notice of British acts. At that time Britain was inundated with very successful American acts, and middle-of-the-road music was the main scene. Although we had some successful British artists like David Whitfield, Dicky Valentine, and Shirley Bassey, it was impossible for them to succeed in America because they were too much like the very good and successful American artists. So the novelty of a group of four guys with slightly different haircuts and different outfits who actually answered back was quite revolutionary. They were always making fairly cryptic and humorous comments that impressed the press. They created a buzz, as it were. But it took a long time to break The Beatles [in the United States].

At the beginning of their career we didn't have any representation for Dick James Music in the States because until then we didn't have any reason. So for the first one or two titles we subpublished. We gave the songs to an American publisher to handle, and to be honest, it was normal in those days for publishers to get local artists to record the songs rather than promote a British act singing them. It was unheard of for a British act to break in America, so publishers gave "Please Please Me" and "From Me to You" to local artists to record.

It came to the point where Brian and my father felt this was wrong, and we decided to open up our own company, take on our own promotion, and employ indies only to promote Beatle records as opposed to using cover artists. The first one we worked on was "She Loves You," and it started to work. Our American company, Dick James Inc., was opened in 1964 for that purpose.

Tony Barrow: The idea for a [plastic] flexi-disc to be given away to fan club members was unique. Somebody somewhere in the world is going to shout at me, "No, I thought of it before," but as far as I'm aware, it was unique at the time. The membership of the Beatles Fan Club had increased enormously and a whole staff had been taken on. On paper the secretary's name was Anne Collingham but, in fact, she didn't exist. Anne Collingham was a staff of full-time clerks answering fan mail. I was very well aware of the impersonal nature of this and that "the Beatle people" weren't getting very close to The Beatles. I saw a chance to do a good PR ploy and do something a bit special for Christmas that had never been done before. I hit on this idea of a flexi-disc [recording]. *Reader's Digest* and many others used it on a huge level. But at the time it was fairly unique, and copies of those records can now fetch a lot of money.

The disc became an annual thing, of course, and I remember that The Beatles asked me to write a script for them during the first year or two. It was almost like a Linus blanket. They were far better ad-libbing, so they sent it up, using bits of script purely as Goon-style humor. Basically the digressions from the script were far funnier than sticking to it.

The editing in those days was pretty primitive. For the first Christmas recording I sat down with a guy named Paul Linton, the boss of Linton Records, who turned out the discs for us. Paul and I went through a 30- or 40-minute tape of Beatle chatter with a pair of scissors and snipped out great chunks of actual Beatles' recordings done in the studio. We pruned it down to six or seven minutes and put the rest of it in the waste bin. One reason for editing it was to get rid of quite a number of sick jokes and a number of expletives.

On November 29, 1963, The Beatles released "I Want to Hold Your Hand." In America Capitol Records finally gave into demand and released it on December 26.

George Martin: In January 1964 The Beatles were in Paris appearing at the Olympia. I had flown over because there was a request from the Germans to have a version of "I Want to Hold Your Hand" and "She Loves You" sung in German, which The Beatles thought was nonsense since they'd sung in English in Hamburg for years. So I explained to them very carefully that in Germany nothing ever sold in the English language, which was true at that time. I said, "Look, chaps, if we do want to have German sales, let's go along with them. Let's see what they can do." So they sent over their A&R guy, Otto Demmler, to prepare the translation of the lyrics, which weren't terribly subtle.

The boys were having their troubles with the French technicians, who insisted on sabotaging them and pulling out their plugs in the middle of the show. There were actually punch-ups backstage. So I don't think The Beatles were too fond of people other than the English at that time. In fact, on the recording day they didn't turn up. I waited at the studio with Otto Demmler for an hour, then rang their hotel. Neil Aspinall [The Beatles' assistant] answered and said, "I'm sorry, but they asked me to tell you they're not coming." I said, "You mean to tell me they're telling you to tell me? They're not telling me themselves?" He said, "That's right." I said, "I'm coming right over and I'm going to say 'hello' to everybody."

So I rushed to the George V [Hotel], and they were all having tea in the center of the room. It was rather like the Mad Hatter's tea party. Jane Asher [Paul McCartney's girlfriend] was Alice in Wonderland, with her long golden hair, and was pouring tea. As soon as I entered the room, they exploded in all directions. They ran behind couches, and one put a lampshade on his head to hide. They just did "Goon things" and a chorus of "Sorry, George. Sorry, George" from behind the sofa. Of course, you couldn't be angry with them for long, so I told them to apologize to Otto Demmler, and they did. Then they went back to the studio and did the recording.

And, of course, The Beatles were right. The German version didn't sell any more. In fact, it sold rather less than later issues in the original language. The next day Brian Epstein rang me up in the early hours of the morning and said he was sorry to wake me but that he had terrific news. He said, "We are number one in America. 'I Want to Hold Your Hand' has gone straight to number one." It was the very first record that actually reached a million sales before release. Of course, I put on my clothes and went around to the George V and we all had a great party. It was a terrific time for all of us.

At the end of the session for the two German songs on January 29, The Beatles recorded what would be their next single, "Can't Buy Me Love."

George Martin: As an example of my role, when The Beatles first sang "Can't Buy Me Love" to me, they started singing *da da da da,* and that was the beginning of the song. So I told them we needed a tag for the ending and beginning. I took the first few lines of the actual chorus and changed the ending and said, "Right, let's just have these lines, and by altering the end of the second phrase, we can get back into the verse pretty quickly." They said, "Hey, that's not a bad idea. Okay, we'll do it that way." So that, in fact, is the way it was done.

Dave Dexter: There was a day in either late 1962 or very early 1963 when I received the usual tall box of sample 45s from [EMI in] London. All three labels — Parlophone, HMV, and Columbia — were there. In that batch of samples there must have been, oh, I think 18 singles. One ["Love Me Do"] was by The Beatles, and I didn't care for it at all because of the harmonica sound. I didn't care for that harmonica because I had grown up listening to the old blues records and blues harmonica players, so I nixed the record instantly. I told EMI to peddle it somewhere else. So EMI placed the record with Vee Jay, which was in Chicago at that time. Vee Jay issued the record and a second Beatles record ["Please Please Me"], but neither sold and neither was a success. Then, for The Beatles' third single ["She Loves You"], EMI leased the rights to Swan Records in Philadelphia, but Swan couldn't give it away. I don't think they sold more than a couple hundred copies, which is fewer than you send out to the radio stations for promotion.

So The Beatles were pretty well stone-cold dead in the U.S. marketplace. This was August 1963. I went out on a long trip to pick up masters all over Europe. I went up as far as Helsinki and down to Rome and all over and wound up in London at EMI headquarters. The A&R man there — Tony Palmer — insisted I listen to a new record that was a smash by a group that was beginning to sell a lot of records in the United Kingdom. I said, "Okay, who is it?" He said, "It's The Beatles." I said, "Oh, forget it. They've died on two American labels. We don't have any interest in them." Tony said, "Please listen to it." So I did, and as he put the needle down and the first four bars of the record were played, I knew it was going to be a hit. The record was "I Want to Hold Your Hand."

John Burgess: We never anticipated anything being released in America quite frankly. I used to regard England as the world, and if I got a hit here, I was delighted. If it went round the rest of the world, that was the cream on the cake, and America was a far-off land where records occasionally happened. So I never thought too much about the rejection we got. EMI started to put it right. I think George [Martin] was the one who started the whole thing off when EMI put a guy out there and he took all the product with him. His name was Roland Rennie, a British guy from EMI who lived in New York. All the product was channeled through him. He licensed the first three Beatle records to Swan and Vee Jay and not to Capitol, who didn't want them. Then once the Beatles did happen in America, Capitol insisted on hearing everything. We did have British hits before in America and around the world, like Laurie London's "He's Got the Whole World in His Hands." I was in the studio with Norman Newell, who produced that record and who would have known how big it was.

Norman Newell: I was happy for George [Martin] and his enormous success with The Beatles, but what I wasn't happy about, what I thought was so tragic at the time, was that if two or three people could sing together, everybody signed them. Every single record company signed them regardless even if they were any good or not, and you were afraid, though I wasn't because it wasn't my world, but most producers and record people were afraid to turn anything down. Everybody who had turned The Beatles down suffered for it all their lives. It's not a crime not to believe in something. Everybody hasn't got the same taste.

Louise Harrison: My mother had sent *Please Please Me,* the first album, to me [in Illinois], and I was playing it when the dry-cleaning man came to pick up the dry cleaning. He asked, "Oh, what's that music?" I said, "That's my younger brother. He's in a band." So he sat and listened to the whole album, then asked if he could come back to hear it again. He told me he was a member of a band called The Four Vests and that his name was Gabe.

So he came back with all of the guys in his band, and they started coming over almost every week to listen to the album. At the end of the summer I told Gabe that George was coming over with my other brother, Peter, to visit me. So he asked, "Oh, can we come over and meet them?" I said sure. By this time *Please Please Me* had been at number one in England for almost a year, but no one had heard of The Beatles over here.

Gabe was doing a show at a little place called El Dorado, a tiny village in southern Illinois. He asked George and Pete if they would like to come along to this show. So we went down to this big dance hall. I guess there were 300 to 500 people there. The band was playing and nobody was listening to them. I thought it must be awful to play in a band when nobody even applauds. Later the lead guitar player said to my brother Pete, "Do you think George would play a song with us?" Pete said, "Well, if you actually put the guitar in his hand, he might not be able to resist."

So the guitar player told George, "Hey, I've got to go out back for a minute. Can you take over?" George got up onstage with the band, but he didn't know many of their songs. The band knew some Chuck Berry and Elvis Presley songs, though. So they started playing, and people in the room started pounding on the tables, stamping their feet on the floor, applauding, and screaming! They played through the songs a couple of times. Finally George got off the stage, and a person came over and said to Gabe, "You'd be a fool if you didn't take on that young fella that's trying out for you." Later somebody else came over and said [to George], "You know, with the right kind of people looking out for you, you could really go places, son."

Paul White: I guess I was the first international A&R man for an EMI company to show interest in The Beatles. I worked for Capitol [in Canada] and I was getting samples of every 45 released in England. I'd had success in the late 1950s and early 1960s with Cliff Richard, who had enormous popularity in Canada, but not in the States.

Tommy Steele was Britain's king of rock and roll, and if you listen to Tommy Steele records today, you wonder why they would even call it rock and roll. For EMI Cliff had filled the American-style gap quite admirably by being England's Elvis, but the company still wasn't into the world of rock and roll.

So, after hours, I'd sit in my office and go through all these 45s that came from England. Most of them were pretty boring and basic, a lot of skiffle-sounding bands. One evening, as I was getting bored again listening to all these 45s, "Love Me Do" slipped out of its sleeve and plonked down onto the turntable. I thought, My God, that's different! I only thought it was different because, although the guys were definitely singing a simple lyric, they seemed to be happy doing it, compared to the guys on the other 500 records I'd heard that week. So I put them [The Beatles] on the "must listen to again" pile. When I listened to it again, I thought, I've definitely got to release this record, so I contacted EMI in London. The guy there said, "Oh, yeah, that record is just going crazy on the charts over here." In fact, they didn't think it was going to last. They thought The Beatles would be a one-hit wonder.

I released the record about a month and a half after the English did and it fell right to the bottom. Well, it didn't even fall. It didn't get on to any charts. Some of the rural Canadian stations that would take a chance on something played "Love Me Do," and in the end I think the sales result after six months was about 140 copies. By that time I had The Beatles' second single, "Please Please Me," and liked that even more than "Love Me Do." When I released that one, it became a zinc record and sold about 180 copies. Then I went with the third record, which was called "From Me to You," a record I really liked. So, you see, I still thought these guys were amazing. But "From Me to You" probably sold 240. The president of the company finally said to me, "Why are you releasing these records? They're all stiffs!" I said, "Quite frankly, I like them."

Well, by this time The Beatles were breaking all records in England, and everything had gone completely crazy over there. But no Canadian radio station really took a chance except for

CFPL in London, Ontario. They were the first to really chart a Beatles record, and a fan club was started here [in Canada], as well. So, in 1963, this whole Beatles invasion started building and then I released "She Loves You," which went absolutely crazy. Then, when I released The Beatles' first album, it became such a fast seller that we had to literally press it on weekends. So by the time The Beatles arrived in the States to do Ed Sullivan's show and Carnegie Hall, everybody in Canada knew who they were.

Red Robinson: Why did The Beatles become so successful in North America? I've always used the analogy that what they really did was bring rock and roll back to the shores of America. After the 1958 disc jockey convention in Miami Beach, where there was a lot of graft and payola, America went soft, musically, pop music that is. We had Bobby this, Bobby that, Bobby Vinton, Bobby Rydell, Bobby Vee. Bobby, Bobby, Bobby. And it was pretty, but it really wasn't rock and roll. It was a form of commercialized ear candy. All The Beatles and other British groups did is recognize the tremendous amount of great music that America had. They recognized rockabilly artists like Carl Perkins, who were doing their own music. Because if you look at the early Beatles recordings, they were new to that next generation, the mid-1960s generation. But people like myself who had been around playing rock and roll since 1954 on radio knew these were redos of old songs. How many people think "Twist and Shout" was originally done by The Beatles and not the Isley Brothers? Same with "Shout" with Joey Dee when the twist came in. So what The Beatles did was bring rock and roll back and say to North America, "You've been sitting on your hands listening to this cotton-candy music. Let's rock and roll again." And that's really what happened, I think. When The Beatles came along, it was the rebirth of rock and roll.

Brian Epstein: I don't know about music, but I know, or I think I know, about hit songs, hit numbers, hit sounds. George Martin is The Beatles' and many of my other artists' recording manager and, fortunately, we get on extremely well. We work very closely on what is recorded. Once the titles are decided upon the rest is left to him. I sit in on a lot of recording sessions and so on, and I'll say what I think about various records and what sides should be issued, but he makes the recordings. I'm not a technical person. The great pleasure for me is when a record comes into the hit parade or hits number one. That's a great feeling. It's a simple thing really, but it's a great feeling. Because you've been right. The artist was right and you were right and the recording manager was right and the song was right. It was put over in the right way and it proves that all one's work has been worthwhile.

Paul McCartney: If I went away and wrote a song, it was daft sitting around and waiting for the other to help come up with ideas. It was a lot easier to complete it on my own. So if I got stuck coming up with the middle eight bars of a song I was writing, I'd give it to John and ask for ideas and he'd finish it off for me. A real fifty-fifty arrangement. That's what happened with a lot of our songs.

Norman Smith: We were always very conscious, both The Beatles and myself, that we weren't coming out with the kind of sound we would like to come out with. You see, the thing is that we were always basing our sounds on certain American records, and each time they came into a session with me, they would say, "Norm, have you heard so-an-so American record? Have you heard the bass sound or the drum sound or whatever?" Of course, I was very aware of that and so we were always striving for that kind of development in terms of sounds. Eventually it led to EMI getting more tracks and certain electronic developments. It was the start of the recording development at Abbey Road. All I can say is that we were striving to emulate the American records at that time and certainly the Americans set standards for us.

Sid Bernstein: I was a student at the New School for Social Research [in New York City]. One of the courses required us to read an

English newspaper, and I began reading one in October 1962. I noticed The Beatles mentioned in October, November, December, and then January 1963, and as a promoter, I thought, I must bring that group here. So I contacted Brian Epstein early in 1963 and we made a date over the phone for the following year, February 12, 1964. It was a handshake over the phone. Brian was one of the few people in this business I can remember doing a deal without it being altered beyond recognition. He was that kind of man.

We made the deal for $6,500 for two shows after he told me he was getting top dollar in England — equivalent to $2,000 a show. I topped that by saying $6,500 for two shows, meaning $3,250 per show. He said, "Wait till I tell the guys at lunch." I said, "I'd like to bring them to Carnegie Hall." And he said, "Oh my, wait till I tell the boys." Then he told me, "If our group doesn't mean anything by the end of this year [1963], don't hold me to the deal." Well, of course, that fall Ed Sullivan booked them right around my dates. He bought them for February 9, 1964, just three days before the date we had booked, and then he bought them for February 16, four days later. That practically ensured my dates, because anything on *Sullivan* twice in a row was tantamount to being a superstar.

Ed Sullivan: For years we visited London, and on one of our visits to England in late 1963 we couldn't believe all the commotion at Heathrow Airport when we arrived. Mrs. Sullivan and I were literally besieged by thousands of youngsters. I asked them what celebrity was arriving. Was it a member of the royal family? I asked some people who worked at the airport, and they told us these hundreds of teenagers were awaiting The Beatles. And as I was always on the lookout for new acts for my program, I decided The Beatles would be a good TV attraction, and also a great news story for our show. So I contacted their manager, Brian Epstein, and agreed to pay them a fee of $10,000 for three shows plus five round-trip airplane tickets and all their expenses for room and board while in America.

Paul White: It was Brian Epstein who just kept hammering away at EMI to get their American affiliate to release The Beatles' records. Of course, the A&R guy in Hollywood was a jazz man named Dave Dexter, who couldn't see pop records, anyway, so he continually turned them down. There are famous memos back and forth in which he said, "This group is no good for our market." And replies from Epstein saying, "Then what is good for your market? Please give me an example?" We all know American Top 40 in those days was bland white artists, and that's the way the American record companies wanted it then. There were the Fabians and ordinary types of things that didn't offend anybody, so that was the kind of trouble Epstein had. He actually got nowhere until, of course, "She Loves You" really forced EMI to say, "Look, this is so huge and the album sales are so huge. They're going to do *The Ed Sullivan Show* and Ed isn't an idiot!" So finally Capitol released "I Want to Hold Your Hand."

Chapter Six

What Will You Do When the Bubble Bursts?

On February 7, 1964, all four Beatles, George Martin, Brian Epstein, and others in their entourage, including American producer Phil Spector, boarded Pan American flight 101. The Beatles were nervous that their appearances in America would flop.

George Harrison: I remember Phil [Spector] was so paranoid about flying that he canceled his flight and booked on the same flight as us because he thought we were winners and he wouldn't crash.

Ronnie Spector: The Beatles were on their way to the States the first time and we, The Ronettes, were just wrapping up a tour in Europe, but they weren't on the tour with us. We just knew them as friends. We were flying back, so Phil [Spector] made us return a day earlier than The Beatles did because he didn't want us with them all that time on the airplane. But he came back on the plane with The Beatles, and it freaked us out. We got home the day before and we were watching television and all this Beatlemania was starting up. They had it on the news. And they were talking about people getting off the plane [in New York City] with The Beatles. Then they said, "There's Phil Spector." So I freaked because here was the man who told us not to travel with The Beatles and here he was stepping off the plane with them. I know why he did that. It was because of my relationship with John Lennon at the time.

Murray Kaufman: I remember in October '63 a fella by the name of Bud Helliwell, who was a promotion man, bringing me a record called "She Loves You." At the time I had what was called my record-review board contest where I'd play five records. They were the best of the day's releases, and people would vote on them. The Beatles came in third. The records that beat them out were "Coney Island Baby" by The Excellents and one by The Four Seasons. Regardless of that, because of the hype that was given to me about this group from England, I played their record for about two and a half weeks, and nothing. No reaction. Absolutely nothing.

At Christmas there was still no Beatle invasion, no Beatle records. So a couple of weeks into January I took my usual vacation and went to Florida. When I hit Florida, every radio station I turned to was playing "I Want to Hold Your Hand." It sounded like an English version of The Everly Brothers because of the thirds in harmony. Beatlemania had begun. Then I received a call from Joel Chaseman, who was program director at WINS. He said, "Murray, you've got to come back to New York." I said, "Wrong. I'm on my vacation. I'm wiped out. I need this." He said, "You don't understand. The Beatles are coming." I said, "Fine. Get an exterminator." Then he sort of insisted and put my job on the line. WINS was going to be the only station to broadcast The Beatles' arrival live. They were going to send me out with an engineer and a newsman.

So I came back to New York, went out as a very ticked-off Murray the K to the international arrivals building at Kennedy Airport, and was up front where the radio people were when The Beatles walked in. I told the engineer to turn my mike on, and I was just going to let the [radio audience] hear anything, but I got wrapped up in the fact that here were four guys who had such a completely different approach than any so-called superstars or record people before. Their sense of humor was so commensurate with mine. I began to love it and got caught up with all the excitement.

Cliff Richard: When I arrived in America in 1960, it was three or four years after Elvis had started and even a couple of years after Ricky Nelson, Bobby Darin, and others had made it big, so my band and I got a tremendous reaction to our performances and stage show night after night. We literally stopped the show and I thought, Wow! Fantastic! We've made it here! But, of course, if the machinery isn't working on all levels, then you're going nowhere fast. So stopping a show in Denver or Dallas means nothing if they know nothing of you in Cleveland or Chicago. It is such a large country. So with all the ups and downs, we lost incentive and motivation and we left mainly because we didn't get the national recognition that you have to have, at least at that time, because America already had what we were offering and I wasn't different enough. Now what happened with The Beatles was that they were the first real group where there was no one single individual who was the center of attention, the so-called rock idol. Suddenly you had a four-piece band that played their own instruments and so they came in on another wave and were the first as Elvis was the first of his generation of pop stars. Of course, their irreverent wit helped them, and America was ready for them.

Sid Bernstein:. By the time the end of 1963 rolled around, The Beatles were a household word in America, and my long-shot guess turned out to be a very important one for me. We sold out in one day. There had never been a one-day sellout in the history of concerts up to that time. Twenty thousand people were outside Carnegie Hall, which is a 2,870-seater, hoping for a chance to see them, find a ticket, buy a ticket from a scalper. It was history in New York. History in the world.

Paul White: It [the press conference in the Pan American lounge of John F. Kennedy Airport in New York City] was so controlled you literally had to have a stand-up picture of yourself to get into the press conference. They were an elite, hand-picked group that was going to ask questions, and they were given a certain amount of time. Now The Beatles, once you started to ask them questions, would ramble off and be very funny, hysterically funny, and everyone had a jolly good time. Their humor was marvelous.

George Harrison: They started asking us funny questions, so we just started answering them with stupid answers.

Reporter: Are you all bald under those wigs?
John Lennon: I'm bald.
George Harrison: And deaf and dumb, too!

John: We're all bald, yes.

Reporter: What do you think your music does for these people?

Paul McCartney: Ah, well.

Ringo Starr: Pleases them, I think.

George: It must do, 'cause they're buying the records.

Reporter: Have you heard about the "Stamp Out the Beatles" campaign in Detroit?

Paul: First off, we're bringing out the "Stamp Out Detroit" campaign.

Reporter: Seriously, what are you going to do about it?

Paul: About what?

Ringo: How big are they?

Reporter: Why does it excite them so much?

Paul: We don't know, really.

John: If we knew, we'd form another group and become managers.

Reporter: Someone says you guys are nothing but a bunch of British Elvis Presleys.

John: He must be blind.

Ringo: [mocking Elvis's gestures] It's not true. It's not true.

Reporter: Are you in favor of the lunacy you create?

John: No, it's great fun. We like lunatics. It's healthy.

Reporter: Would you sing a song?

Beatles: No!

John: We need money first.

Reporter: How much money do you intend to take out of America?

John: About a half a crown, two dollars. It depends on the tax.

Reporter: Do you ever get haircuts?

George: I had one yesterday. [He laughs.]

Ringo: That's no lie.

George: Honest, that's the truth.

Reporter: I think he missed.

George: No, he didn't.

Ringo: You should have seen him the day before.

Reporter: Why do you sing like Americans but speak with English accents?

Paul: That is English, actually.

George: It's not English. It's Liverpudlian, yah see!

Paul: The Liverpool accent. The way you say some of the words. You say *grass* instead of saying *graaaasss*. So the Liverpudlian accent sounds a bit American.

Reporter: When are you going to retire?

Ringo: We're going to keep going as long as we can.

George: When we get fed up with it. We're still enjoying it now, and as long as we enjoy it, we'll do it, because we enjoyed it before we made any money.

Reporter: What do you think of Beethoven?

Ringo: Great! Especially his poems. [He laughs.]

Murray Kaufman: I used to wear a lot of hats that either were straw or Russian style. George [Harrison] said [upon arrival in America], "Hey, I love your hat." I said, "Hey, you can have it. You came over on the plane with some friends of mine." Now this is all live. George said, "Who's that?" And I told them who my friends were and that I was Murray the K. Well, they just stopped. So The Beatles invited me over to the Plaza [Hotel]. There were about 4,000 or 5,000 people at the airport to greet them. There was something in the air. We had lost President Kennedy, and the kids seemed to sense we were missing something in America, something The Beatles were ready to give to us. It was something new. It was something different. We were a country that was ready for a change in attitude, and that's what The Beatles had. I was impressed, as were a lot of people. Not so much with their music, because how the heck can you compare the music from *Sgt. Pepper* to "She Loves You" and "I Want to Hold Your Hand"? It was their attitude that really attracted and created this tremendous Beatlemania excitement.

So I went to the Plaza. And as Tom Wolfe wrote in his book, "Murray the K walked into their room and he never left." I was very intimidated, because when I went out there, when The Beatles came onto the floor, there was Edwin Newman and all the other disc jockeys. And John Chancellor was waiting to get in to interview them. The entire wing where their suite was [located was] completely blocked off with security.

That night I did my broadcast via beeper phone right from their suite. They had a suite in which there was a two-bedroom suite or a three-bedroom suite because Cynthia Lennon, who was married to John at the time, was there. Brian [Epstein] had his own suite someplace else, and The Beatles didn't leave their rooms. They weren't looking for gals. What impressed me about them was that they were very disciplined, very together. They had to take care of business and to do what they had to do and try to enjoy as much of it as they could.

They asked me, "Look, Murray, would you mind acting as our host while we're here?" I said okay and took them to the Playboy Club for dinner. A woman reporter for the [*New York*] *Post* came over and asked them if they would make a comment about the Playboy Club. Paul's great line was, "Well, you can print for your readers that the Playboy Club and The Beatles are just good friends." Of course, it was that sense of humor that really attracted me. George was writing a column for one of the English papers, and he did three days of talking about me and the kind of disc jockey I was and the fact that they didn't have anything like me England.

The one thing about The Beatles was that they always looked at the crowd as the entertainers and themselves as the audience. They were the observers. They really enjoyed what was going on. In fact, during concerts, John and Paul made bets on which side of the stadium would break through the barriers first. They'd root for each side to do it. The Beatles selected me [at the Plaza]. I didn't select them. They selected you. You never selected them.

Louise Harrison: George had booked me into The Beatles' hotel in New York and left a message saying to come up and see him. So I headed up to the room, and there was a big mob of people and security guards everywhere. I tried to edge my way past this crowd nice and politely, and one of the security guards said to me,

"Where are you going?" He put his arm out to block the way, so I said, "I'm going down to see my brother." And everybody started to giggle and laugh. He said, "Do you have any idea how many times that's been tried today? Get back there, lady." So I tried to figure out what to do. I didn't have anything with my name on it because, of course, my name wasn't Harrison back then. It was Caldwell. So there was nothing to prove that I was a Harrison. Finally I remembered I had a picture in my billfold of me and Peter and George when they visited me in Illinois. I showed the security guard this picture and he said, "Yeah, that looks like one of those guys." Then they went down, knocked on the door, and George came out and down the corridor. We hugged, he spun me around, and everything was okay. Then all the people who'd been laughing and making fun of me started cheering me.

Sid Bernstein: When they arrived, I met them at the Plaza Hotel, which was their first check-in place. There was a little party given by Capitol Records. We took pictures and we exchanged some laughs and information. I found Paul warm and very kind. I found John kind of satirical and very clever. Ringo was rather quiet, funny but quiet. And George was very serious, very somber, meditative, which he became and still is today. I liked them so much individually. I had a chance to talk to each one and adored them all. Each one was someone special. Every time I put on a show with them, my wife was pregnant with a child. We have six. One time Ringo said, "Hey, if we play for Sid enough times, he'll have two baseball teams." They'd always ask where my wife was and I'd say, "She's home pregnant and afraid to come to the concert."

Ed Sullivan: The Beatles first appeared on our show on February 9, 1964, and I have never seen any scenes to compare with the bedlam that was occasioned by their debut. Broadway was jammed with people for almost eight blocks. They screamed, yelled, and stopped traffic. It was indescribable. And on that same bill with them were the comedian Frank Gorshin, Tessy O'Shay, and the youngsters from the Broadway hit of the day, *Oliver!* There has never been anything like it in show business, and the New York City police were very happy it didn't and wouldn't happen again.

Murray Kaufman: I called a meeting in The Beatles' suite with Brian Epstein and told Brian, "You better cancel your plane reservations and get the special train because we're going to have a snowstorm." And it was prophetic because we did take a train to Washington. We had a lot of fun. We arrived at Union Station and over 10,000 kids were there. They broke through the barricades and came rushing out. We were crushed against the locomotive of the train, and I said to myself, "I'm going to die with four kids with long haircuts from Liverpool." George, who was right next to me, turned and said with a big, silly grin on his face, "Isn't it fun?" I'm dying and he says, "Isn't it fun?" We did the show at the Washington Coliseum with The Righteous Brothers, Jay and the Americans, and Tommy Rowe. I broadcast my entire show from The Beatles' dressing room.

Louise Harrison: After New York, we all went to Washington. While we were there we were invited to the British ambassador's place. I remember going up this huge staircase with all these pictures of grand old people, and Ringo making some really comical remarks. The ambassador was Sir David Ormsby-Gore. He and his wife, Lady Ormsby-Gore, were very gracious and sweet. We went to a building next door where they were having a big charity ball and they asked if the boys would pick out some of the raffle tickets for prizes. I was sitting at the back of this place with Lady Ormsby-Gore, and the guys were up there at the front. The next thing I knew Ringo was all upset and angry, shooting for the door, and calling a cab. And off he went. Apparently some kid, a college student or someone, had a pair of scissors and had cut a chunk out of Ringo's hair. So he was very upset. But the rest of The Beatles stayed and did the public thing that they had to do.

David Ormsby-Gore: I think The Beatles are great. I think they're a riot. They've given me more work to do than I've had at any time since the queen of England was here seven years ago.

Reporter: One wit said The Beatles were the British payment for the Skybolt. Do you think there's any validity in that?

David Ormsby-Gore: No, I don't think they're payment for the Skybolt. Let's say they're the British payment for all that Spam you sent us during the war.

On February 11, 1964, The Beatles were interviewed by the press in Washington, D.C.

Reporter: Here I am surrounded by Beatles and I don't feel a thing. Fellas, how does it feel to be in the United States?

Ringo Starr: It's great. We're having a really nice time . . . all very nice.

Reporter: What have you seen that you like best about our country?

John Lennon: You! [He laughs.]

Reporter: Thank you very much. Under advisement, do you have any plans or arrangements to meet the [Lyndon] Johnson girls?

John: No. We heard they might come.

George Harrison: I didn't know they were in the show!

Reporter: Are they coming to your show tonight?

Ringo: We don't know.

Paul McCartney: We're not sure, but if they do, yeah, we'd like to meet them.

Reporter: You and the snow came to Washington at the same time today. Which do you think will have the greatest impact?

John: The snow!

George: Will the snow last longer?

Other Beatles: Yeah!

Reporter: What has struck you the most so far?

Ringo: When we first came in, you know, in the airport, we never expected that. Nothing like that. It was great.

Reporter: You mean the crowds?

Beatles: Yeah.

Reporter: Despite the snow, the crowds were big here in Washington?

John: Yeah, a great crowd, even though half of them thought we were coming by air and the other half by train.

Reporter: So why do you think you're so popular all of a sudden?

John: I don't know. It must be the weather.

Paul: No idea at all, really.

Reporter: Do you think it's your singing?

Paul: I don't know. I doubt it. It could be a lot of things.

Reporter: Where did you get the idea for the haircuts?

George: Where did you get the idea for yours?

Paul: We didn't. It was just a thing. It's just something we liked. We enjoy wearing our hair this way. So it's developed this way.

John: Yes, and it costs more money to keep it short than to keep it long, Don't you think?

Reporter: Where do you go from here?

Ringo: Back to New York tomorrow.

George: Then we go to Miami on the weekend for the next Sullivan show and then we go home.

Reporter: Are you still number one in Europe?

John: Europe is a lot of countries, really

Beatles: We're number one in America, Finland, Denmark, Hong Kong, Australia, Sweden.

Reporter: And you haven't any idea why?

John: When a record is released in a foreign country, it was released at home, maybe a year before. So it seems so distant.

George: It's very unusual because they've been out in England for over a year. "Please Please Me" is a hit over here now, but it's over a year old. It's funny.

Reporter: You think of your records as funny records?

Beatles: No! No! We mean funny, peculiar.

Reporter: Do you feel they're musical?

John: Obviously they're musical. It's music, isn't it? Instruments make music.

Paul: (mock singing) Um, bum, um.

John: That's musical, too!

Reporter: All right then, what do you call it?

Paul: We try not to define it because we get so many wrong classifications of it. We just call it . . . music.

Reporter: Have a good time in America.

Beatles: Thank you, and look after yourself.

Dave Dexter: There were all kinds of stories, and they still float around. I understand that there are now more than 100 books that have been written about The Beatles and how Capitol Records really promoted them in the beginning. Well, the truth is Capitol Records didn't do anything with The Beatles. The record ["I Want to Hold Your Hand"] came out on December 26, 1963, in America. Our sales and promotion staff didn't know whether to take me [seriously], since I had constantly cried, "Wolf," so many times before. I'd tell them how big a hit something was somewhere in Europe or whatever, and they didn't want any more imported records to sell. They were happy enough to be selling The Beach Boys, Nat King Cole, and a few others. So without any promotion The Beatles were an absolute phenomenon. By New Year's [1964] the orders for "I Want to Hold Your Hand" were in the millions, and there had been no promotion that first week! The only thing I can remember was that the old Huntley-Brinkley news hour showed a little short about how hysterical Beatle fans were over in England. That might have caused a little stir, but by the first week of 1964, we were hiring RCA Victor and other record labels to press [discs]. Later, when The Beatles were in Florida, I called them to see if they liked the sound of the Capitol issue — we changed some of the sound characteristics from the British Parlophone record — and they assured me the sound was even better, [that it had] a hotter sound and a little more volume.

Murray Kaufman: It was ridiculous. The PA systems weren't really what they are today, so you never got to hear what The Beatles were doing. I think it wasn't their music as much as it was their actual presence, and the fact that the songs, when they started, were at least recognizable. You have to realize they had paid their dues. They had gone around Europe and played these dumps in Hamburg and Liverpool. So to receive this kind of ovation from the United States, which had always been the leader in music, was quite a thrill. And they just went along with it. In Florida they were able to take a few days off for a vacation, but it got so bad that they wanted to go out. We were on the beach and saw that The Coasters were at some little dump in Miami, and that's where they wanted to go. In order for us to get out of the hotel, we went down through the kitchen and got into a refrigerated meat truck. Then the cars met us about eight or nine blocks away. We were freezing in that meat truck! But we had to escape the crowd. It was that bad. There were 10,000 people outside the hotel constantly.

Cynthia Lennon: It was a dream come true, to be in a position like that, where everyone wanted your music. Not mine. I was on the periphery, observing all that was going on. But for The Beatles it was unbelievable. Arriving in America at that age with that response, the reception, the mounted police, and the Plaza Hotel, was really mind-blowing. We did have some very hairy moments, however. There was an occasion in Florida that I will never forget. We went from New York to Miami for a few days. This off-duty policeman who was looking after us, our security guard, invited us to dinner at his home to get us away from the lunacy. We ended up getting into a meat van with many hooks, no meat in it, just a lot of very sharp hooks. This cop got in the front of it and drove off at an incredible speed. We slammed about from the back to the front and side to side. How we survived it, I don't know.

Dezo Hoffman: During The Beatles' visit to Miami, John [Lennon] gave me a very good reason not to follow them any longer. It was quite a silly argument. I took a picture of him being taught how to water ski. He had no hair on his forehead [because it was blown back]. John was terribly vain. That was his only fault. I was annoyed that he [yelled at me] in front of everyone. He treated me like a five-year-old. So I just turned my back and left. I never saw them again.

Murray Kaufman: The Beatles had an unbelievable appetite for music. If I brought them one, I must have brought them about 400 albums. They were into Motown. They were the ones who told me about an artist I'd never heard of in my life. Because of them, I was the first jock to play Bob Dylan on AM radio. Later, at a club called the Ad Lib — which at that time was the only club in London The Beatles could go to where people didn't bother them — they introduced me to Mick Jagger. They asked me if I would bring The Stones over and do for them what I did for The Beatles.

George Harrison: We had heard that our records were selling well in America, but it wasn't until we stepped off the plane in New York that we truly understood what was going on. Seeing thousands of kids there to meet us made us realize how popular we were there. We thought we could go shopping for records and things, but we couldn't. Some people gave us records, though. I know our sound was new and the American people were ready for something new. We looked funny and different with our hair. You really can't pinpoint one particular thing. People called our music, or our sound, the "Liverpool Sound." But we didn't like the term, because the only reason it was called the Liverpool Sound was because the British press was looking for a name it could peg us with. They didn't think it was rock and roll and they didn't think it was American rhythm and blues, so they called it the Liverpool Sound. We didn't believe our sound was different enough as a sound. As far as we were concerned, we began performing American rock-and-roll and rhythm-and-blues material and our songs incorporated those elements. That's really what happened.

When The Beatles arrived back in London from their first visit to the United States, they were besieged at the airport by the British press.

Reporter: What was it [America] like?
Ringo Starr: We never expected anything like this.
Reporter: Any complaints?

George Harrison: They don't have soft jelly babies in the States but hard ones like bullets and they hurt.

Reporter: Did you have time to take in anything properly?

George: Oh, yeah, I don't know. I think I enjoyed the sun the most of all. You know, healthy.

Reporter: You're the healthy one of the four, I see.

George: No, no. But the sun was sort of.

Reporter: Very healthy.

George: Yeah, very healthy.

Reporter: What did you like about the trip, Ringo?

Ringo: Oh, I just loved all of it, especially the trip to Miami. The sun, you know. I didn't know what it meant till I went over there.

Reporter: Don't you get it up in Liverpool?

Ringo: No, they're finished up there, you know. Cut it out.

Reporter: Did you ever have a chance, John, to just get away on your own without anybody recognizing you?

John Lennon: Yes, we borrowed a couple of millionaires' houses, you know.

Reporter: You could afford to buy a couple of millionaires' houses, couldn't you?

Beatles: No, not yet.

Paul McCartney: John could.

John: We'd sooner borrow them. It's cheaper.

Reporter: John, are you a millionaire?

John: No! That's another lousy rumor. Wish it were true!

Reporter: Is Brian Epstein a millionaire?

John: No, not even he's one.

Reporter: Well, then, where does all the money go?

John: Well, a lot of it goes to Her Majesty.

George: She's a millionaire!

Brian Epstein: Obviously I thought about America in connection with The Beatles for a long time because I was always quite sure, really, that The Beatles would make it big over there. We were all rather unsure, however, about it because we seemed to be issuing the records and nothing much was happening. I went over the first time to have a look around and see why the records were having no success and to try to get a sense of the American market. I also took with me one of my other artists, Billy J. Kramer, to do some promotional work, which I thought would be a good idea. And both worked quite well actually. As far as seeing what was the matter, I think it was very simple. My answer to the boys when I got back was that I didn't think we had yet produced a record that was right for the American market. I did think, after having listened to a lot of American music and getting a sense of what was popular over there, that "I Want to Hold your Hand," which was just about to be released, was the right one. Plus [there was] the fact that a lot of information had filtered through from the British press from the Royal Command and Palladium shows and the scenes in London and Beatlemania in general. There was great interest, and it was just the right moment for the issue of "I Want to Hold Your Hand." I can't say I timed it for that moment, but it was right. Going over for those two Ed Sullivan shows couldn't have been more right, too.

Gene Pitney: The Beatles and I were working comparable tours in England. In other words, in the beginning, I'd have a tour at the same time they did. We were both put out by a guy named Arthur Howes. Arthur had a very good deal because he ended up having the next three Beatle tours of England, not knowing what was going to happen to them. I did a lot of television shows with The Beatles, as well. One of the things that comes back to me is sitting in a room at a birthday party for Ethel Merman, believe it or not. The Beatles had just come back from New York and they had filmed a television special, or someone had done something about them in America, and it was being shown in England. They sat sitting cross-legged in front of the television set watching themselves. I mean, they were really just four giggly kids watching themselves on television, not really knowing at that point what more was to come.

On February 28, 1964, the brother of Paul McCartney's girlfriend Jane, Peter Asher, released a new single with his musical partner, Gordon Waller. It was written by Paul, but the record stated that it was composed by John Lennon and Paul McCartney.

Peter Asher: We didn't know what we were going to record. Paul had been playing this song to us. It was a piece they weren't recording, or it wasn't finished. It didn't have a bridge, so when we were given a record deal, I asked him to finish that song ["A World Without Love"], and he did. At the time Paul lived with our family on Wimpole Street in London and was going out with my sister, Jane, so I certainly knew him well. He would sing different songs to me all the time.

On March 2, 1964, The Beatles started work on their first film, *A Hard Day's Night.*

Victor Spinetti: The Beatles were marvelous to work with. They had seen me in a play in London called *Oh! What a Lovely War* and asked me to be in their film [*A Hard Day's Night*]. I think we had an instant rapport because we came from similar circumstances. I was from a small mining area in south Wales, not far from Liverpool. One day on the set of *A Hard Day's Night* I said I had to leave early because my sister, Genina, was getting engaged and as an engagement present I was giving her and her fiancé a weekend in London. We were going to go to a nightclub and to a show and all the things they wouldn't do once they were married and settled down. That was my present to them. I went to the nightclub to meet her and her fiancé and, can you believe it, in 1964, when The Beatles couldn't go anywhere, they all turned up. I didn't ask them to because I wouldn't have wanted to importune them in any way, but they all turned up to wish my sister luck on her engagement. And they all had a dance with her and said, "I hope you'll be very happy." My sister remained very calm throughout the whole evening, maintained her composure, and as soon as they left, she exploded with an "Ahhhhh!" That's the kind of people The Beatles were and why we remain friends to this day.

Richard Lester: The deal was that if we got it [*A Hard Day's Night*] into the cinemas before the beginning of July [1964], then they would make it because they, the music department of United Artists, felt The Beatles probably wouldn't last the summer. We are talking about Britain, of course. So we started shooting in February. We had to make the film, cut it, dub it, and all of it in a very short period. We had to do it quickly so that the company wasn't left with a film about some has-beens.

We set out to make the film that best captured what was going on around us. The week we began shooting, The Beatles went and did *The Ed Sullivan Show,* and we provided a bit of material to take with them. By the time they came back, it was fairly obvious we were going to be all right. It still didn't alter the fact that on the first run of the picture, one of the [United Artists] executives said, "Fine, but we're going to have to redub it! We're going to have to postsync them because nobody in America will understand their voices."

Alun Owen, Walter Shenson, and I went to Paris where The Beatles were doing an Olympia concert at the beginning of 1964 with Silvie Vartan. We watched them in their hotel room at the George V behaving in a way that was extraordinary. In other words, they were prisoners. They had come to Paris and they saw the car that took them there, they saw the backstage of the Olympia, they went to their hotel room and stayed there and sandwiches were brought up. In essence, a screenplay began to form in our minds because we were watching it happen. And since we had already decided we wanted to make a documentary film, or a film that was going to be a fictionalized documentary, all we were doing was just trying to keep our eyes open.

Walter Shenson: I was an American living in London and felt The Beatles' music was typical copycat stuff. Elvis Presley had been doing it and The Beach Boys and so forth. I didn't recognize the nuances and the brilliance of The Beatles until I got to know them and work with them. United Artists approached me when they apparently found that the contract between Capitol Records and The Beatles didn't cover movie soundtracks. They wanted to cash in on the Beatle craze, so the movie was just an excuse to release an album. They didn't give me much of a budget because they didn't expect The Beatles to last through the year. That's why it was black-and-white. It was very low-budget. In retrospect I think it wouldn't have looked as good or had the same impact if it had been shot in color.

When we first met with Brian Epstein, we were afraid he was going to want too much of the profits to make it worth doing. We thought we would have to give him at least 25 percent of net profits. He came to us and said, "I'm sorry, but I'm going to have to insist on getting seven and half percent of net profits." We were obviously stunned, but overjoyed. Eventually, when the movie was such a hit, we voluntarily changed the percentage back up to 20 percent just to be fair. After the first day of shooting, I looked at the rushes and my wife said, "Can they act?" I said, "I don't know. But I do know you can't take your eyes off them."

Richard Lester: Someone has stated that The Beatles were extremely fortunate and therefore had to be extremely clever in that they were always well served by the people they chose to associate themselves with. Rightly or wrongly, Dick James at the time was the right music publisher for them. George Martin was absolutely the right producer for them. Brian Epstein was the right manager, and so on. And I was the right film director for them. I chose them. They chose me. They'd seen a short film of mine [*The Running, Jumping and Standing Still Film*]. They knew I'd made a pop film [*It's Trad, Dad!*] before that. They knew I could play a bit of piano and that I would understand them musically.

By accident, I happened to know who they were and they knew I was a kind of surrealist gag man. It all came together and it worked. We didn't set out to change the world. I don't think any good work is conceived with the objective of saying, "This is the film that's going to alter mankind." Films are mirrors. Films reflect the times. I had a marvelous image in front of me to reflect, and that is, or was, their energy and their originality. And whatever I had came because I was an enthusiast of Buster Keaton's work and of French cinema in the late 1950s. It just gelled. We didn't work it out.

When we went to the George V [Hotel in Paris in January 1964], they were playing at the Olympia and we all stayed on the hotel floor with them. The film wrote itself in front of us. We just took out all the X-rated bits! There was nothing written. There was nothing planned. But what was clear for both Alun Owen and myself was that for the first part of the film they would be under duress and ordered about in low-ceilinged places. [There would be] trains, cars, small rooms, and at a certain point they had to say, "We have had enough! We are going to break away. We want to get out!" And the film suddenly went into something that opened out.

Walter Shenson: When The Beatles [John Lennon and Paul McCartney] originally wrote the new songs for *A Hard Day's Night,* they wrote one extra song that Dick Lester and I couldn't find a place for in the movie. It's on the soundtrack album. It's called "I'll Cry Instead." All Beatle fans, and those who have had the album all these years, are very familiar with that song, but we never used it in the movie. Since the synchronization rights — the rights to go with the movie — are mine, I decided I was going to put it in the movie. Obviously I wasn't going to tamper with Dick Lester's picture. So we put it on as a little prologue. It's sort of an overture to the movie. Then I had some visuals made. We took about 300 stills. A lot of them had never been seen before. There were publicity shots and production stills from *A Hard Day's Night.* Some graphic artists in Hollywood arranged these stills into a collage and edited them to the beat of "I'll Cry Instead."

We were calling the picture "The Beatles Movie." We didn't have a title. Our distributors were calling from New York and begging us to come up with a title because they didn't know how to publicize it. I said we would keep calling it "The Beatles Movie" until we came up with a title. Originally I thought the title of one of the six or seven songs would lend itself. But neither I nor Dick Lester nor The Beatles themselves felt that any of those songs would make a good title. Then one day, while we were filming, I had lunch with John Lennon, who asked me, "Have you ever heard Ringo misuse the English language?" I asked him to give me an example and he said, "Well, when we work hard on a recording session that lasts until four or five in the morning, the next day Ringo's apt to say something like, 'Wow. That was a hard day's night!'" It struck me that it was kind of a catchy phrase. So I said to John, "Why don't we call the movie *A Hard Day's Night* and get them off our backs about the title?" John said, "Why not?" Then we asked the other Beatles and Dick Lester and they all said it was pretty good.

Now it dawned on me that I didn't have a song called "A Hard Day's Night," and I wouldn't be much of a producer if I let a picture go out without a title song, so I asked John one evening, "Can you and Paul write a song called 'A Hard Day's Night'?" He said, "Oh, God, we've already written all the songs!" But I told him we needed it. He said, "Does the song have to reflect the story?" I told him it didn't, and he said he'd do the best he could. That was at ten o'clock at night. At eight-thirty the next morning John and Paul called me into their dressing room at the studio. On the back of a matchbook cover they had the lyrics of "A Hard Day's Night." The two of them then took out their guitars and played this song, which became a number-one song when it came out. I couldn't believe the genius of these two writers who could write a hit song on demand.

Dick Lester [later] made a picture called *How I Won the War* with John Lennon. I don't think the picture was successful, though it was a very interesting movie. John was a very special person. I honestly feel that Ringo has a [movie] career. He's made some movies, and given the right role, he has an actor's ability. People ask me, "Were The Beatles good actors?" And I say, "The Beatles were better than good actors. They were brilliant at being themselves." Peter Sellers once said to me, "The hardest thing for me to do is to be Peter Sellers. I can hide behind an accent or some makeup or a costume and be anybody you ask me to be, but God, there is no Peter Sellers." But The Beatles had that incredible self-assurance of being themselves. When you see *A Hard Day's Night*, George Harrison is brilliant being George Harrison, especially in the scene where he walks by mistake into that shop with the shirts. It's a classic scene. Dick directed it beautifully. Alun Owen's screenplay, which got an Oscar nomination, did a great job. But it took a George Harrison to make that thing come alive. He was cool. He understood the humor in the thing.

Victor Spinetti: The set of *A Hard Day's Night* was chaos because nobody really knew what they'd gotten into. Walter Shenson went to the American movie companies and said, "I'm doing a movie with The Beatles." And they said, "Who?" But The Beatles had a ball. Dick Lester had five cameras running all the time because The Beatles would never stick to the script. You never knew what they were going to say or do. They had to cut so many scenes. Honestly, if you could get all of the outtakes, you'd have another film because they shot enough to make *Gone with the Wind*.

They sent each other up all the time. They'd say things like, "Paul, you're the prettiest. You get out of the car first." As the lunatic director, I'd walk up to them and say, "You're late. You should have been at rehearsals ages ago." John would say, "You're not a television director. You're Victor Spinetti acting as a television director." They were always sending people up, and because the cameras kept rolling the whole time, the essence of The Beatles was caught, and that's the magic of that film.

People have asked me what we spoke about on the set of the movies [*A Hard Day's Night* and *Help!*], and I tell them that we talked about everything from [Marcel] Proust to [Pablo] Picasso. You'd never have conversations like that on a normal movie set, but The Beatles were curious and wanted to learn everything. They weren't just interested in being the best [music] group in the world. They also wanted to know what we were all about and why we were all here on this planet. Once you start asking those kind of questions, you have to start writing about the truth.

Phil Collins: In *A Hard Day's Night* there's a boy who walks with Ringo along the river. People think that was me, but they're wrong. I'm in the end with all the kids screaming at The Beatles. It was a bizarre experience. I was at a stage school, and we all got sent down there — about 80 or 100 of us — to the Scala Theatre in the West End of London on March 31 to scream at The Beatles. And we got paid for it! We sat there and we didn't have to be told to scream, because there they were — The Beatles! It was 1964 and they were the band everyone wanted to be. So, yeah, I was there, and I got a check at the end of the day.

In 1963, 1964, I was already into school groups playing early Motown, so I was already bitten by the music bug. I was playing drums by the age of five. I would set up my drums in the living room with my mother and father, brother and sister, and play along to music on the television. I'd play to groups like Joe Brown and the Brothers, which was the very first record I bought, and Cliff Richard and the Shadows. So I was well hooked before The Beatles, but it was The Beatles who gave us the direction. They were a group. Before then it was all dance bands, so they gave us the reason to do it. You could get three or four people together and form a band, and as long as your hair was the right length and your trousers were tight, you were okay. The Beatles started it all for many musicians.

Victor Spinetti: I was in a car with The Beatles on the way to shooting for *A Hard Day's Night,* and we couldn't move because of all the crowds of kids in the street. Some of the girls grabbed the back bumper of the car and were dragged along. They scuffed their legs, but they didn't care because it was The Beatles' car that did it. George was the first to get out of the car, and a girl grabbed him and pulled some of his hair out. Well, the blood started rolling down his face. It was an extraordinary time.

Carl Perkins: It was 1964 and it was the first time I went to England. A promoter kept calling my agent in Nashville, and I really couldn't believe it. There had to be something wrong. He wanted the wrong guy over there. They didn't know me in England! But he kept calling. And one day he called Nashville, got me on the phone, and said, "Carl, Chuck Berry's going and he's never been. Chuck wants you to go with him." I think that's what really made me go to England the first time. So I said, "Okay, the money's better than I'm getting around home."

I went over there, and Chuck and I had a great tour. For about three weeks we toured and the places were packed everywhere. Every night I saw a crowd reaction like I hadn't seen in many years. It was just really thrilling for me to walk out there and [see] the kids holding up signs that said "The King of Rockabilly" and "We Love You, Carl." It just really filled me up, man, every night.

At the end of the tour the promoter told me I was invited to a party, but he didn't tell me who or where. So I said, "Well, I'm leaving to go back home tomorrow, but I'll go for a little while." As it turned out, it was John, Paul, George, and Ringo. The Beatles were giving the party for me and Chuck. I don't think Chuck went, but I will always be grateful and happy that I did go. I wound up at three o'clock in the morning with the four Beatles, who sat on a couch. I sat on the floor, as I usually do with a rhythm guitar. They asked me how I kicked off "Honey Don't" or "Right String Baby, Wrong Yo Yo." I said, "Hey, man, where'd you guys hear these old songs?" They said, "Man, we got all your old songs and records!"

The Beatles and The Rolling Stones sort of saved rockabilly when it could have been lost forever. It was really in danger of dying a fast death in the early 1960s, and as I've said before, they put a nice new suit on it and they never strayed from its basic simplicity. They just made it a lot more sophisticated.

That night The Beatles invited me to Abbey Road Studios. They said, "Could you come? We're recording tomorrow night." Which was basically that night because, you got to remember, it was three in the morning. I said, "Sure." So I called home and told my wife I would be a day late, but to tell our kids, "I'm going to the studio to watch them little long-haired boys called The Beatles record." I didn't know they were going to cut three of my songs that night. I did play on some of the stuff that night with them, but none of the stuff I played on has ever come out. It really gave me, as we say in Tennessee, a new lease on life. I came back across that ocean to my little place in Tennessee with a great feeling. It's very easy for me to go back to that frame of mind.

Derek Taylor: I was still on the *Daily Express,* and Brian Epstein's personal assistant at the time — Barry Leonard — said that Brian had liked an interview I had done with him and wanted to thank me. So I went to Brian's office and he asked me if I knew any authors. I said, "I don't know any authors. I only know journalists." Then he said, "Well, I've had an offer for an autobiography. Do you know anybody who could help me write one?" I said that maybe I could. So we went off and did it.

It was a hack job. I regret it wasn't done better, but there was no time. I was still writing it on the road. I was literally writing it like Charles Dickens, but not as well. They were taking pages off the typewriter for serialization in Australia. The chapter, "Beatlemania," was written mainly from *Daily Telegram* clippings, a paper I don't like. Serialization began in June 1964, and I'd only started the taping of the interviews in April of that year. So you can imagine things went very quickly — April, May, June — it was a quick time of life. We did it on reel-to-reel tape, on a little amateur tape machine, in Torquay [England] in four to five days. Then his secretaries, Barbara Bennett and Diana Vera, transcribed it and finally, with the help of those little pills we took in those days but don't now, we typed it out and embellished it a little. There is "journalese" in it. You can read the *Daily Express* all over it really. Actually, had I left in all he said, not that there are any grim secrets or dark areas, it would have been even more vivid.

It's a shame. He was much more frank, for instance, about some of the disc jockeys in England than I let him be. Everybody had to be lovely then. There were one or two other villains. Wild horses wouldn't drag their names out of me, but there were little descriptions like "short, fat, balding, stocky, pudgy, vulgar, flashy," and other words describing people in that bitter period. In the end Dick Rowe, who none of the preceding adjectives apply to, was rather left alone. History has judged him more harshly than he deserves to be judged.

The NEMS people were honest and loyal. There wasn't a rotten person in that organization. Brian had a very good sense of people, although he treated us like an old miller from Victorian times. Brian was a dreadful employer. I fell out with him many times. I was a very unsuitable appointment because I still was very much an entrepreneurial journalist. That's all I really knew about was communicating. I didn't have tact or diplomacy, and Brian had been trained in retail in a pretty strict Jewish hierarchical retail environment. He knew where the lines were to be drawn, and I knew no such thing. We had rows all the time about all manner of things. In Australia I booked John on a TV program to be interviewed about his book [*In His Own Write*]. There was an awful row in front of the head of BOAC, with Brian screaming at me at lunch, "Nobody books The Beatles for engagements except me, Derek! How dare you?" He apologized, but it was a good out for me. I was really knackered.

On July 6, 1964, the film *A Hard Day's Night* was premiered at the London Pavilion Cinema. The album and single were released on July 10. During August and September of 1964, The Beatles returned to North America for their first major tour there.

John Lennon: You want to know about our acting in the film? Well, it is as good as anybody who makes it but can't act, you know.

Paul McCartney: As you all know, we are not actors. We're, first of all, singers and then, sort of, musicians, but last of all, we're actors. So we didn't really know how to act, but lots of people on the film helped us with it. The real actors, like Wilfrid Brambell and Norman Rossington, who were in the film, helped us with it and told us one or two things to do.

Bob Bonis: Comparing the first American tours of The Beatles and The Rolling Stones, I'd have to say that The Beatles were much more of a problem because of the kids. Hotels really didn't want us because of all the kids we would attract. I remember once with The Stones that we returned to our hotel and found that all our things had been moved to another hotel while we were out! But it wasn't because of the bands. It was the kids. And they were much worse in the case of The Beatles. There were more kids trying to sneak in, and in the hotels we had to take over a whole floor and have guards watching at the exits and the elevators. The whole show was bigger with The Beatles. They had about 65 people, including 10 press that Brian Epstein charged $1,000 a week just to be on the tour.

Keith Richards: To us The Beatles were always the door opener. Somebody knocks on the door, like the gasman, and gets in and gets his foot in the door. He's the salesman. That's what, to us, was the parallel. They were the ones the people would open the door to. If we knocked on the door first, forget it, they would just put the other chain on. So it was like using The Beatles as a door opener and then using the difference between us, as soon as we could, so that we could make it apparent. In actual fact they weren't any different. They were really the same kind of blokes as we were, and they'd proved they were that way. The way that they were projected meant we had to make a difference between ourselves and them, which wasn't that difficult. So, in a way, we were encouraged, especially by Andrew [Loog Oldham], to be a little more outrageous than we even felt. Since then it's become a well-known scam.

Bill Wyman: There was always an impression created by the media that we were against each other. It was always The Rolling Stones versus The Beatles. They always tried to build a war between us as the two top bands in England. But it wasn't true. We were quite good mates, and they liked our music and we liked theirs. Besides, it was completely opposite music. So there was room for both bands.

Reporter: Do you ever get frightened when kids start to get too close?

Paul McCartney: No, not really. There's enough police around and enough people around all the time.

Reporter: What was it like being in an ambulance?

Paul: We all had a laugh in the back. They put other people in to disguise it. There were about seven sailors. They were all screaming and laughing. It was just to hide our heads, you know. Because nobody knew we were in the ambulance.

Reporter: What's the most interesting kind of decoy that has been used in trying to get out of a place?

Paul: That was probably one of them actually — the ambulance. There is a story that we dressed up as policemen once. It's not really true, 'cause all we did was put policemen's hats on and posed for a photograph. But everybody thought we'd dressed up as policemen, so we just played along with it. It's easier to go along with something than to deny it. I think last night the ambulance thing was pretty different.

Reporter: How did this thing where people throw jelly beans at you get started?

Paul: It started because of a magazine article in a pop magazine whereby John had been sent some jelly babies. The ones in England are soft and they're shaped like little babies. John was eating some and the magazine made up a bit and said that George pinched some of

John's and John said, "Don't pinch mine." And it got around and in the end people kept sending them in to George saying, "Well, you won't have to take John's now, George." It just got ridiculous in the end, we got millions every day. Then these people started throwing them.

Reporter: Should entertainers like yourselves get involved with politics?

Paul: Well, it depends on the entertainer. The only reason we never get involved in politics is because we don't know anything about it. I mean, probably if we knew and were interested in politics, then we'd take sides. But we just don't happen to know a lot about the policies of the parties in England, and we know even less about them here. I just know that I don't like the look of [Barry] Goldwater and the things he says. But that doesn't mean he's no good. It's just that I'm personally not very keen on Goldwater at the moment. But I still don't know what his policies are.

Reporter: Do you prefer performing live in concert to radio or television?

Paul: We like each of the different media in a different way. It's best when we can do a tour like this, then we can go back and do some TV, radio, and film. That's the big point about it — the variety. As long as we keep getting changes, then it all seems fresh. If we were stuck on TV for a year or so, or stuck in films for a couple of years, we'd be right to the eyeball, wild and screaming and things. In earlier days, when we were doing tours, we used to have to build the whole thing, really, like the accepted kind of act where we'd have to do jokes and play the whole thing up.

Reporter: In our country [the United States] every psychologist has tried to come up with the answer to what it is The Beatles have that make these teenagers react as they do. Do you have any idea what it is you have?

Paul: We've been asked this millions of times, of course, because everybody wants to know. I don't ever think there'll be a psychiatrist or psychoanalyst who will be able to work it out just by saying it's one thing and by putting his finger on one thing. Because if it was one thing, then we'd know it.

Reporter: Will there be a Beatles film this year or next year?

Paul: I think it'll be a comedy because I don't think we could do anything else. We enjoy doing comedies. So I'm sure it'll probably be the same kind of thing. We would definitely want to make it different from the last [*A Hard Day's Night*]. So there will be changes made. There's going to be some changes made, boys.

Reporter: How do you pick the songs that you perform?

John Lennon: We pick the most popular ones in the States over the last couple of months. You see, our hit records come out a little different here, and our history has developed later here, as well. On this American tour we've missed out a lot of our early hits. Sorry about that!

Reporter: John, people are constantly asking what you like, but what do you dislike?

John: I hate people throwing things at us while we're performing. The jelly babies in England are soft, but here they're called jelly beans and they damn well hurt. Sometimes the fans, if we can call them fans, throw cans and pens. Many times we come off the stage and it looks like we've gone through a war zone, which I guess it is when you come to think of it. And you've a problem carrying on singing and laughing with things hitting you all the time. It does take the pleasure out of it. Now you know why we run off quickly.

Reporter: Do you ever get homesick when on a long tour like this?

John: Oh, yeah, you get homesick all right. Every other day I miss seeing the Mrs. and my young son. The others, as well. But we have a great and wild time, and look at all these gifts [we get]. Some of them are really unusual. The other day I got a bra with "I Love John" embroidered across it. I never saw the person who gave it to me. I didn't keep it, though, because it really didn't fit. I must have received thousands of stuffed toys. My little boy at home will like some of them.

Reporter: Do you ever forget the lyrics to the songs?

John: Yeah, I'm the one who often does that. Paul is very good, but I'm always forgetting the words. It's almost a sure thing, and Paul and

George are always ready. In Germany, when we covered a lot of other people's material, I would never have a problem, but when we started performing just our material, I suddenly went blank and I didn't know where I was singing or playing or anything. They've all got to sort of tell me what's happening.

Reporter: I guess the jelly beans and such don't help.

John: Yeah, you can't play if they keep hitting you. You know, you keep stopping 'cause it's natural. You sort of duck and you stop playing. But it's been quite good [lately]. It's stopped now. So I suppose we should stop talking about it.

Reporter: John, a little off topic here. Do you have any feelings about the Cold War?

John: I feel it will never end. Someone always wants to be on top. Some country, some power, has to be in control. If everybody was all rich and happy and each country had all they wanted, they'd still want the next bit. I don't think there'll ever be any solution. It's sad, but history repeats itself all the time.

Reporter: Do you ever get tired of the same questions at press conferences?

John: Not really, because even though sometimes they do know the answer, they want to hear from us rather than from a story they've heard or read. Our two favorites, of course, are "What are you going to do when the bubble bursts?" The other one is "What are you going to do with all the money you're making?" Reporters want to sort of confirm something and see you say it. I really like to hear how a story changes over a short time. It's like a chain letter. In the end no one knows its origins.

Reporter: If you got two weeks off, what would you do, Ringo?

Ringo Starr: No idea.

Reporter: What would you like to do if you had that much time off?

Ringo: In England I'd know what to do and where to go, but here [in the United States] I don't know what to do.

Reporter: Well, even in England, could you get away from the crowds and get away from the people and really enjoy yourself?

Ringo: Well, it's not like this all the time. It's only when we do a tour. When we're off, people don't know where we are half the time. We get away, you see. It's only touring that you get the big crowds.

Reporter: I notice you guys like to watch telly quite a bit. Does this relax you, or does it take your mind off the program coming up?

Ringo: We all know we've got another show, but we just love telly. I love it. I'd turn it on even if the test card is on.

Reporter: What kind of a television show do you prefer — western shoot 'em up, science fiction?

Ringo: Any, as long as I'm enjoying it. I never like those sort of draggy shows that don't work.

Reporter: Ringo, there are millions and millions of young girls all over the world who'd like to become Mrs. Ringo Starr. Have you thought of getting married, having a family, and settling down?

Ringo: No, not yet. It would be impossible. We're moving around too much. It wouldn't be fair to any one girl to get married.

Reporter: Someone said George was wanting to pull out of the group. Was this a complete fallacy, a rumor, was it true, or did he ever mention it to you?

Ringo: No, well, when we first arrived in America, it was John who was leaving. The next week it was me who was leaving. And now it's got to George. Next week it will be Paul. Believe me, it's a bunch of rubbish. They just make it up. Someone starts it and it goes round like that.

Reporter: Ringo, in your personal opinion, what is the best record The Beatles have ever recorded?

Ringo: Um, "A Hard Day's Night," I think. I like a few of them. "You Can't Do That." I like most of them.

Reporter: How do you like the movie [*A Hard Day's Night*]?

Ringo: It's not bad. It's okay.

Reporter: Are you pleased with your performance?

Ringo: Yeah, I think so. We all went to see it on the Saturday before we had the premiere in London. About 10 of us, meaning the four of us and managers and that, and we didn't like it too much because we pulled ourselves to bits and things like that. But when we went with an audience, they were sort of laughing at the jokes and it made it a lot better, so I like it now.

Reporter: When you're on the stage with the rest of the boys and you're beating away at the drums, how in heaven, with 30,000 screaming fans, can you hear the others?

Ringo: I hardly ever hear them.

Reporter: Can you hear them singing?

Ringo: No, not very often.

Reporter: Well, how do they know how to follow your beat or keep any semblance of order?

Ringo: Well, I sort of watch their mouths and actions and I get something back from the guitars and bass, if I'm lucky, which gives me a rough idea of what's happening.

Reporter: On your tour, what so far has been the greatest thing that happened to you?

Ringo: I don't know. A lot of things have happened. The crowds, especially. It's marvelous. I can't explain it. It just knocks me out.

Reporter: Who looks after all your fan mail?

Ringo: Well, we have clubs in each or most cities, and they sort of get the bulk of it. We do a couple, and the toys get shipped back to England. We send some to hospitals and things like that.

Reporter: How often do you get your hair trimmed?

Ringo: There's no set time. Could be a month or two months.

Reporter: Do you have a particular barber you use?

Ringo: No, anyone with a pair of scissors sometimes.

Reporter: Are you getting tired of the hotels, crowds, and living out of a suitcase?

Ringo: Sometimes it gets to be a bit of a drag. You want to put something on and it's been crushed to bits. But I'm having a good time.

Reporter: Paul, along with John, you've written a lot of songs. Do you know how many?

Paul McCartney: How many songs? Well, we've written a lot that have never been published. Before we got "Love Me Do" published we'd written over 100 songs, of which about three have been used.

They're not very good songs. That's mainly why [they haven't been published]. Since then we've written at least 50.

Reporter: If you had some time off, where would you go?

Paul: No idea.

Reporter: Do you have any hobbies — fishing, hunting, anything?

Paul: Fishing or hunting? No, not really!

Reporter: Where would you go?

Paul: Just go to someplace quiet [that had] something to do. You can get away to places that are quiet. You can go to the Sahara Desert, but there's nothing much happening there, you know.

Reporter: Is there any chance in the next five years of your taking a bride?

Paul: Of taking a what?

Reporter: A bride.

Paul: A bride! Oh, I thought you said a bribe. There's every chance, you know, because it's never been any other way. If I want to get married, then I'll get married.

Reporter: What have you enjoyed more than anything else on this North American tour so far?

Paul: The audiences and playing, the actual playing, and second, meeting the people, and third, press conferences.

Bill Medley: I still don't know how we, The Righteous Brothers, ended up on the tour, but we did. Right before we left town, there was this guy who asked us if we would do this TV show called *Shindig,* but we weren't really interested. And then we went on The Beatles tour and it was so difficult. Singing before The Beatles for 35 minutes, all we heard were young girls yelling, "We want The Beatles!" It was real difficult. It just wasn't fair. They had other acts on there who weren't advertised. It was just The Beatles. That was it. So we left the tour about three-quarters of the way through, came home, and did *Shindig,* which really helped our careers. We also went out with The Rolling Stones on their first tour and, yes, the same thing that happened with The Beatles happened with The Stones.

Reporter: You have a couple of great telegrams there. Could you read them?

Derek Taylor: Yes, one was from a girl who wanted to buy Ringo's tonsils after he had them out, and the other was from an enterprising businessman with less taste than ingenuity, who wanted to buy, in bulk, Beatle bath water. That's water a Beatle has said to have bathed in. Although, of course, like James Dean's car, it could be anyone's bath water or anybody's car and then he would market it in bottles labeled "Beatle Bath Water" and we would get a handsome royalty.

Reporter: You get these requests by the hundreds?

Derek: Every day when I wake up I'm bombarded with questions and requests. The phone rings the first thing every morning with "I know this may sound strange, but I would like to meet The . . ." And I know the word *Beatles* is coming. In the end you think that life is just a great explosion of fire and thunder and wind and everywhere the echo of the word *Beatles*. The world will know that one day there will be no Beatles, but I can't see that for a long time.

Reporter: Who decides how much money The Beatles will be paid per performance?

Derek: Brian Epstein.

Reporter: What's the most The Beatles have been paid?

Derek: Well, I think it must have been the Kansas City concert. Fifty thousand pounds or $150,000, which is an extraordinary amount. The first offer was $100,000.

Reporter: You've traveled with them for a while now. What are they like personally?

Derek: Nice, good. They're extremely amiable, rude, aggressive, friendly, marvelous companions, and very sharp. Too much for any person to cope with. And they have a sort of collective appeal and they're great individuals. The only reason that would take me away from my four kids for these weeks on end is The Beatles! And I think the hearse is ready and calling for us so I must go!

John Rowlands: The dressing room was decked out to make The Beatles feel they were eating in a ballroom at a hotel. There was a carpet on the floor and there were a lot of drapes and we all ate English food. They had some specially prepared for them in an attempt to try to cut out the hotel crap, I guess. Rice pudding for dessert, that kind of thing. Backstage there were police everywhere because, although they weren't seen out front, they didn't know how to gauge this type of crowd. This was only at the beginning of the British Invasion. It was brand-new for these hockey halls to suddenly have 18,000 screaming kids in them, so the police ringed the stage and backstage in case anything happened.

Jay Nelson: I was chosen to introduce The Beatles at one of their shows, and I was thrilled. It's something I will never forget, ever! I walked out onstage to introduce the guys, and all I could see was flash-bulbs going off all over the place — thousands of flashbulbs — and when I started speaking into the mike, I couldn't hear myself because the screams were so loud. They screamed their heads off when they brought out Ringo's drum. If I couldn't hear my own voice, then how did The Beatles hear themselves? It would have been impossible. The whole experience was unreal.

Ronnie Hawkins: I was playing over at the Le Coq D'Or Tavern in Toronto when The Beatles first came into town. The Bill Black Combo was opening up for them on the tour, and since Bill was Elvis Presley's former bassist from his Sun Record days and he was an old friend of mine, I hooked up with him at The Beatles' press conference. The Beatles, specifically John and Ringo, decided to join us for a postshow jam session. It didn't happen, though, because Ringo called us and said they just couldn't get out of their hotel rooms. All of us were upset, especially John and Ringo.

Red Robinson: Well, it's an incredible story. The promoter, who was based out of Toronto, came into town [Vancouver]. He used to put on the teenage fairs where you went in and saw the new clothes and fashions and stuff that was big then. He said, "We've got The Beatles coming in." Well, excitement was crazy and we didn't have an indoor place big enough. So they went to Empire Stadium. Thank God the weather allowed it. I mean, it was Beatlemania just as you see in the movies or just as you hear on the audio tapes from that era. "Beatle time is 3:21," et cetera. They really captured the imagination of the new generation of young people.

So the crowd was basically made up of 80 percent of kids from 13 to 16 years, and it was the screaming, the crying, and trying to rush the stage. The Beatles only performed about 19 or 20 minutes at Empire Stadium. I had assigned one of my disc jockeys to MC the show, but he got sick just before it, so I did the assignment myself. As funny and odd as it sounds, some of the other disc jockeys wouldn't stand up on that stage in front of 25,000 people and do that. It was nerve-racking and it scared the hell out of me, but I'd done it for Elvis Presley in 1957 in the same stadium. So I went and did it and it really got out of control. In 1957 they did the same thing to Elvis. The kids pushed forward to the stage, and Elvis ended up doing only about 22 minutes.

With The Beatles it was even worse in 1964. The chief of police said, "Look, you've got to get up there, interrupt the show, and tell them if they don't back away from the stage, somebody is going to get hurt." People who don't understand that concern must look at some of those soccer game riots in England. It was very similar. They were going to crush each other. Not meaning to, but just the frenzy of the moment. So I said to the chief of police, "Gee, you know, Chief, in show business you don't inter-rupt an act while they're performing." Then Brian Epstein said to me, "Red, go up there at the end of this song and break in on The Beatles." I said "Okay." Can you imagine my position?

I went up and stood in the little area at the back of the stage. When the song finished and the crowd was screaming, I walked out to the microphone. As I was going by John Lennon, who was on my left, he said, "What the fuck are you doing on a Beatles stage?" So I went over to him before I went to the mike and said, "John, I apologize for this, but your manager, Brian Epstein, and the chief of police told me to come up and make this announcement for their safety." John said, "Oh, that's okay." So I went and did it. You can see in one of the photographs taken that John has his hand on his forehead, like he was wiping the sweat away, and out of the corner of his mouth he's saying those words. Paul McCartney is saying, "What the hell is going on here?" They played another song and then McCartney said what I had said again, and you can hear it on a bootleg recording — "If you don't stop, we're going to have to leave." I guess I'm one of the few people in our business in front of a crowd of 25,000 that ever had John Lennon say, "Get the fuck off our stage." True story.

Reporter: Do you have nicknames that you call each other?

John Lennon: I call George, Ray Coleman.

George Harrison: I call Ringo, Dave, but apart from that we don't.

Paul McCartney: We're lying, of course.

Reporter: Are you concerned about the rumors going around that The Rolling Stones are now more important than The Beatles?

John: Is it worrying us? No.

Paul: It doesn't worry us because we get these rumors every so often. I mean, Dave Clark was supposed to be bigger than us a couple of months ago.

George: Every couple of months there's someone.

Female Reporter: Paul, are you the only unmarried Beatle, or are you the only married Beatle?

Paul: No! You're really mixed up. John is the only married one, and all the rest of us are unmarried and single and free and everything.

Female Reporter: And you're available?

Paul: Yes.

George: Hello.

Female Reporter: Hi, you're not married?

George: No, I'm George.

Reporter: Did you write "Ringo's Theme"?

George: No, did you?

Female Reporter: It's beautiful.

George: You haven't been reading the little bits of paper, have you? The ones that say who wrote "Ringo's Theme"?

Paul: It was John and I who wrote "Ringo's Theme."

Female Reporter: It's a beautiful piece of music.

Paul: Thank you.

John: Thank you.

Female Reporter: And you're the married one, right?

John: (laughing) Yeah, that's me.

Female Reporter: What does your wife think about your traveling away all the time?

John: (with a mock accent) Well, she don't like it much, but she doesn't mind it too much because it makes a lot of money for her.

John: Hey, it's Ringo.

Female Reporter: Oh, hi, Ringo. Where are you from?

Ringo Starr: Most likely the place we're going to play tonight.

John: Whatever it's called.

Ringo: Have a crisp.

Female Reporter: Do you always eat on the run like this? With all these people around, don't you get indigestion?

Ringo: Well, we usually eat in the room, but seeing the hotel doesn't have our room for us, then we have to eat here, you see.

John: That was unfortunate, though.

Ringo: Yeah.

Female Reporter: Do all the teenagers, the mobs you always have around you, do they bother you?

Ringo: No, never. Maybe it might when I get old, but not yet.

Reporter: I'd like your impression of a new American singing group, The Cockroaches. Have you heard them yet?

John: I haven't heard them, but it's already happened a hundred times in England. Sorry, Cockroaches.

On November 27, 1964, The Beatles released the single "I Feel Fine/She's a Woman." On December 4 they released the album *Beatles for Sale*.

George Martin: When we chose the cover songs The Beatles recorded for the *Beatles for Sale* album, they just picked the ones they liked playing. I guess they weren't quite so prolific at that time, so they thought, Let's do these ones. We've always fancied them.

On February 11, 1965, Ringo Starr married Maureen Cox, and the next day reporters converged on him.

Reporter: Ringo, what do you have to say to all the teenage girls who broke into tears yesterday when they heard the news?

Ringo Starr: I don't think there were that many actually. Everything seemed to go fine. It's only sort of you, only a few who are going off the edge.

Reporter: Where did you propose?

Ringo: In the Ad-Lib Club. [There is loud laughter from the crowd.]

Reporter: Was this in the early hours of the morning?

Ringo: No, well, about two o'clock in the morning.

Reporter: You weren't on bended knee?

Ringo: No, I didn't. Sorry about that.

Reporter: What or how did the honeymoon location leak out?

Ringo: I don't know. I'm trying to find the fella. [He laughs.] Does anyone know? [There is no response from the crowd.] No! Liars! [More laughter.]

Reporter: Is there any place in the world where you feel you and Maureen can go when you want to be alone with her and walk outside freely?

Ringo: I have no idea . . . only Vietnam. [More laughter.]

Chapter Seven

Eight Arms to Hold You

Ringo Starr: The best thing about this group is that we all work everything out between us. It doesn't matter who's playing what. If someone thinks of something, then we'll try it. If I'm playing drums and someone says, "Try that bit, or do something there," I'll try. If John is playing the guitar and someone wants him to do something, he'll try it. When we're performing, if it's a great crowd, then you'll go potty trying to give them all you've got. But if they're a bit dull, then you just play in a very ordinary way.

On February 22, 1965, The Beatles flew to the Bahamas via New York to begin filming their second movie, *Help!*

Victor Spinetti: After *A Hard Day's Night*, I was in a Broadway play called *Oh! What a Lovely War* in New York. Teenage girls showed up at the performances, and as soon as I walked on, they'd start screaming. We'd have to stop the play and explain that it was a serious play and that if they would be quiet I would talk to them about The Beatles after the show. It became a regular part of the play. So, after the show, I'd come out and talk to the girls about The Beatles. They'd say [in a crying voice], "What's John like?" Or "What's Paul like?" Eventually they formed the Victor Spinetti Fan Club.

When we were on our way to the Bahamas to shoot *Help!*, we had a refueling stopover in New York and there were all these screaming kids shouting at the plane. We didn't really take notice until an American official walked onto the plane and said, "Is there a Victor Spinetti on the plane?" John [Lennon] just looked at me and said, "They're deporting you." The official said, "The members of your fan club are waiting to see you." All The Beatles looked at me and said, "Your fan club?" So they all came and stood at the door of the plane with me as the girls continued to scream, "Victor!" As a result of that, each of The Beatles became members of the Victor Spinetti Fan Club.

When they started making *Help!*, they got someone to write a story, but The Beatles didn't like it much. *Help!* was a straitjacket of a film for The Beatles. *A Hard Day's Night* was basically the truth about them coming to London. In *Help!* they had to act out parts and weren't really happy about it. The first day of shooting for *Help!* was almost the end of the film and The Beatles. We were on a yacht and I was the mad scientist trying to cut the ring off Ringo's finger. Ringo escapes me and dives off the yacht 30 feet into the sea. They had a bunch of people watching the area for sharks. So Dick Lester said, "Let's do another shot." They dried Ringo off, and he was shivering because it was out of season and bloody cold. We did another take and then another and after the third take Dick said, "Let's do another." Ringo said, "Do we have to do it again?" Dick said, "Well, I'd like another one. Why?" Ringo said, "Because I can't swim." Dick Lester went white and said, "Why on earth didn't you tell me?" Ringo said, "Well, I didn't like to say."

What they had onstage was the gift of truth. When you listen to any of their songs, they don't sound as if they're lying. They sound as if they're telling the truth. If you remember the time in which they appeared, pop stars were never seen taking a drink or smoking a cigarette. The Beatles were real, and when they appeared onstage it was as if they were actually singing about the truth.

At the height of their fame the favorite thing to do was to go round to Ringo's basement flat in Portman Square and have fish and chips, and bread and butter, and a pot of tea and sit around talking and watching television. I said to them, "Do you realize that onstage you have the gift of truth?" John said, "Well, I'm no martyr. I'm only a musician." But they could speak directly to the young across any barrier. I was with them once when they were standing on a balcony in Salzburg and there were thousands of Austrian kids in the square below. The Beatles each put combs on their lips so that they looked like Adolf Hitler and started speaking in German like Hitler. And those thousands of kids laughed right back. The Beatles were plugged right into the kids, and that's why some countries banned their records and why Apple was doomed to fail from the beginning because countries and big business don't like people who have that kind of power speaking about the truth.

Roger McGuinn: It was still pretty crazy when we were hanging out with The Beatles. It was like going to see the president or something. You had to get down in the limousine, and there were screaming girls on either side. Then the guards would open the gates and you'd drive into the estate and they'd close them again and everybody would be pressed up against the fence. It was that kind of a situation. Guys would be patrolling around the house. Craziness. But once you got in there, it was kind of normal. They had a common bond within the group, a unity that kept them together. It was just like a spirit that they had. I remember asking George about religion. I said, "What do you think about God?" He said, "Well, we don't know about that." He was answering personally, but he answered for the four of 'em, because that was his spirit. That was the common mentality they all had. That was a protective device they had and that kept them together for as long as it did. I guess that eroded eventually, but they really had a tremendous run for a pop group under that kind of pressure.

Norman Smith: There were always hundreds of teenagers, mostly girls, around Abbey Road Studios. Abbey Road wasn't a very popular place, in terms of the local residents, and having all these teenage girls outside added to [the neighbors'] annoyance and the unpopularity of the studio location. The Beatles added to this. At one particular session I couldn't believe what happened. I went down into the studio from the control room and I thought I heard a noise. We had a little room that we called a "trap room," which housed all the percussion equipment — bongos, congas, and stuff like that. I opened this door and there were two girls in this little room. How the hell did they get in there? I don't know. The moment I opened the door, of course, they rushed out into the studio toward Paul and John The only way I could get them out was to grab them by their hair and literally push them out. They were kicking and screaming and scratching. It's something I'll never forget. Eventually I handed them over to the porter at the entrance, and he took over from there. But how they got there I'll never know. They must have gotten in through the roof.

On April 9, 1965, The Beatles released the single "Ticket to Ride."

Reporter: Where were you when Ringo got married? You were out of town?

Paul McCartney: Yeah. I was on holiday in Tunisia.

Reporter: And you got a telegram?

Paul: Yes. I couldn't understand it, though. Because the international operator, the Tunisian operator, read it over the phone. It was supposed to say, "Rich wed early this morning." But the way he read it, it came out, "Request early tea." So I thought Brian Epstein was sending me a telegram requesting early tea for just a bit of a joke. Then I got the telegram the next morning saying, "Rich wed early this morning." So I still didn't quite get it. I eventually picked up a newspaper and found out that he was married. To my great delight.

Reporter: You were really surprised?

Paul: Yeah. Not surprised, shocked, or anything. It was just a drag I wasn't there, because I would have enjoyed it.

Murray Kaufman: George [Harrison] was a very nitty-gritty person. When you said something to George, he'd say, "Okay, now, what do you mean?" He wants to be very specific. He's very up-front. He's very truthful. He will not allow something to go by that he doesn't know exactly. He got interested in the sitar on the set of *Help!* and the sitar led him into learning more about it. The more he learned about it, the more he learned about Indian philosophy. And he found a way of life and he really got into that. Therefore, his life followed that pattern. That's what his interest was and that's where his psyche went. That's where his whole attitude about life and people and about what he was going to do was affected. He was the one, of course, who inspired the guys to go to the guru, Maharishi Yogi.

Derek Taylor: After I stopped working for Brian Epstein, I hoped I could escape the madness, so my wife and I moved to America and I started working for Bob Eubanks. I said to him, "What do you want me to do?" He said, "Well, the first thing I want you to do is go to the Bahamas and interview The Beatles." That's how people get themselves into trouble. I know now when I see other people who've got themselves into deep water that they haven't thought it through.

Being on the set of *Help!* was like any other film. It was extremely long and tedious. I've never enjoyed being on film sets. I think it's easier if you have a function. Murray the K was there. He managed to get himself a little job as a tribesman. It was always fun being around Murray. In fact, I look on Murray the K with enormous fondness. He's so much a part of this stormy novel we've lived in and are still living in. A rather sensitive man, a rather sweet man, and a damn good broadcaster.

On June, 12, 1965, a storm of controversy was unleashed with the announcement that The Beatles were to be made Members of the British Empire. This outraged existing members of the order and a number returned their medals. One was Hector Dupuis, a member of the Canadian House of Commons, who claimed that it placed him on the same level as "a vulgar nincompoop!"

Reporter: What do you say about Mr. Dupuis turning in his medal?
George Harrison: If Mr. Dupuis doesn't want the medal, he had better give it to us. Then we can give it to our manager, Brian Epstein. M.B.E. really stands for Mr. Brian Epstein.
Reporter: Why do you think you got the medal?
John Lennon: I reckon we got it for exports, and the citation should have said that. Look, if someone had got an award for exporting millions of dollars' worth of fertilizer or machine tools, everyone would have applauded. So, why should they knock us?

On June 14, 1965, The Beatles began recording "Yesterday," which would be included on the album *Help!*

George Martin: I thought it ["Yesterday"] was a super tune, and I kept saying to Paul, "You've got to write a great lyric for this because it's a great tune." We'd been calling it "Scrambled Eggs" because it fit it so well, and Paul was looking for a single word that would fit the phrase [*da, da, da*], and he came up with "Yesterday." I objected to it actually. I said, "The only problem is there's a pretty well-known song called 'Yesterdays,' in the plural. It's still very vivid in my memory." He said, "People don't know about that, do they?" He hadn't heard of it. So he went ahead with "Yesterday" and, of course, nowadays you never hear the other one.

When Paul played it to the group, Ringo started tapping away on drums and we thought, What will we do with it? It wasn't a three-guitars-and-drums kind of song. I said, "Put down guitar and voice just to begin with, Paul, and then we'll see what we can do with it." Which we did. I told him there was nothing else we could do, that we couldn't put heavy drums or even a heavy bass guitar on it. I said, "What about having a string accompaniment, you know, fairly tastefully done?" Paul said, "Yuk! I don't want any of that Mantovani rubbish. I don't want any of that syrupy stuff." Then I thought back to my classical days, and I said, "Well, what about a string quartet then?"

He dug that. He thought it was neat. At that time he was living with the Ashers, who were classical music people, and I guess that rubbed off on him, too. So we sat down and together we wrote the score. I mean, obviously, I wrote it, but I had him with me when I was writing. He would say, "Can we have the cellos doing this bit?" And I'd say, "Sure, why not?" Or "No, that's out of their range." He devised the cello line, which I think is one of the best parts of it. So it was kind of a collaborative experience. We spent an afternoon mapping it out and I went away and wrote it. We booked the string players, and that was it. Later on the other boys came round and said, "Marvelous, super." I did discuss with Brian whether we should call it a Paul McCartney record. He said, "No, it's The Beatles." In the end we all agreed that it should be listed as The Beatles. It would have made him stick out too much otherwise.

Paul McCartney: It's funny and awkward talking about songwriting and the creative process. You don't sit around with people and discuss it. It just comes out of nowhere, sort of out of the blue. It comes through your own layers of personality, your own mindset and your musical background. From your basic children's melody to classical to ragtime to Tin Pan Alley and from jazz lines all the way to Chuck Berry and Little Richard. My brain will filter out all that I don't like. Sometimes it just arrives at my doorstep, appearing right before my eyes, like the day I literally fell out of bed and the line "Scrambled eggs, oh, baby, I love your legs" just came out of nowhere. Eventually, and really quite a long time after, it became "Yesterday."

George Martin: I think one of the basic challenges of the producer is to get inside the mind of someone and find out really what they're driving at, what they're trying to achieve, and then help them to achieve it if you think it's the right thing to achieve. The majority of people I work with aren't incredibly articulate when it comes to knowing what they want. So consequently you've got to live with them and find out their weaknesses and their strengths and amplify the strengths and try to get rid of the weaknesses. When I started in the record business way back in 1950, there was no such thing as a record producer. All that person did was to troubleshoot, make sure the engineer did a good job, and make sure the artist was happy. So gradually the producer evolved into being something a little bit more creative. He had to become a force in his own right and become a partner with the musicians.

I was talking to a famous artist recently that I'm thinking of recording again, and he said to me, "Well, you know what I'm looking for is a collaborator." And I said, "I know. That's exactly what we are." As a producer, I don't actually write the songs with the artists. I help the artists put them together and suggest what key they're going to go with and that kind of thing. The role has changed in that respect. I think nowadays, too, since the rise of the completely independent producer, he's become something of a manipulator, as well, which I'm not sure is a good thing. He's become a businessman, and there are an awful lot of people now producing records. When I started in the business, there were probably about 10 people in England who could call themselves record producers. Now, about every one in three persons I meet is a record producer.

Norman Smith: George Martin undoubtedly influenced The Beatles in terms of recording responsibility. He has a tremendous way of doing this. I mean, of relaxing people, but at the same time being somewhat of a disciplinarian. There is, obviously, a certain amount of discipline required. That was the initial area, I think, in which he had an influence. After that, musically, he demonstrated the use of orchestration and the arrangement of a song. You don't just sit down and twang out the chords and let it come out willy-nilly, you know. He would try to get it in some sort of order, with some kind of musical interest. And, of course, with the vocal harmonies he undoubtedly played a part in that. Having said that, Paul most certainly had, whether he knew it or not, a very natural ear for harmonies. I mean, perhaps he couldn't tell you the actual technical symbol of a chord in those days, but he certainly knew the notes that went into that chord to make it up. So there was this combination, a natural coming together in that respect.

On June 24, 1965, John Lennon's second book, *A Spaniard in the Works*, was published.

John Lennon: All my life I never quite got into spelling and writing, mainly because, I found out later, I was probably dyslexic. So I developed a weird style of writing and humor to cover it up, as all people who have dyslexia do. I would write out little stories, actually type them and keep them in a book. I can only do it very slowly and the stories would be quite short, mainly because I couldn't bother writing long pieces. I had little patience. If the words were spelt incorrectly, it was really irrelevant. As long as they made people laugh, then that was great. It was the story and the sounds the story made. Many people have said that my writing reminds them of James Joyce, who I had never read. So I got a copy of *Finnegans Wake*, and after reading a few chapters, I thought it was great and felt a sudden kinship. I could see what people were saying. But my style does come about because of my visual handicap. When I was a kid, I liked *Alice in Wonderland* and the poems that came from *Jabberwocky*, and I loved the drawings of Robert Searle. I wanted to be a combination of Lewis Carroll and Robert Searle. I'm always asked why I kill people off in my book, which isn't necessarily true, but it's a quick way of ending them. I suppose it was showing some hidden feelings inside. I like the sketches.

On July 29, 1965, The Beatles' second film, *Help!*, had its royal premiere in London, England. The album *Help!* was released on August 6.

Walter Shenson: I don't think The Beatles were as pleased with *Help!*, but I never felt that at any point that they weren't happy in the making of the film. I think they liked making the movie. It was fun. We went to the Bahamas on location. We went to the Austrian Alps. I like to think that we, the film crew, the director, we were their family. They had that other family on the road, but they could come back and feel comfortable with us. We protected them from the outside world. It was a nine-to-five job, unlike the world of rock and roll concertizing, and we were a very nice unit.

I think they liked *A Hard Day's Night*, as everybody did, and probably were let down with the response to *Help!* not being as big as it was for *A Hard Day's Night*. However, if there hadn't been *A Hard Day's Night*, I think *Help!* would have knocked everybody out. Personally I think Richard Lester did a brilliant job with *Help!* Every time I see that movie I find something more in it. It works on many levels. There's some brilliant satirical humor in that movie. It looks beautiful, the color's great, the locations are good, the camera work . . . David Watkin is a marvelous cameraman. I think it's a knockout of a movie.

As far as how the single was released using the title "Eight Arms to Hold You," somebody jumped the gun. The same problem existed with *Help!* as with *A Hard Day's Night*. We started the movie without a title. This time the working title was "Beatles #2." We just didn't know what to call it, and someone came up with an idea that seemed to feel pretty good, which was "Eight Arms to Hold You." After we thought about it, we felt it sounded corny. The one thing that The Beatles weren't was corny, and I think rightly so, they rejected the title and I was delighted that they did. I think it was Dick Lester's wife who suggested we call it *Help!*, which was the title of one of the songs they had written for it. So that's how *Help!* came about. But somebody jumped the gun. I guess the word got out, or in their eagerness, United Artists wanted to start publicizing the picture with a title.

Brian Epstein's job had a lot to do with keeping those boys happy. I know that because after two pictures Brian said to me, "I want to thank you for making my life easier during the course of the making of these two movies. I didn't know who you were before we started. I was frightened to death that I was going to get complaints from The Beatles, either as a group or individually, that I had set them up with this terrible guy from Hollywood. I was anticipating having to be on the set all the time to keep the peace, but I have never been around. They like you. They come home and don't call me and say they have a problem with our producer or that this director I picked out is an ogre or something like that. That's terribly important to me and I want to thank you." I loved him for it because nobody usually tells you the nice things. They always complain. Brian was busy keeping The Beatles happy.

Richard Lester: A third film was contracted at one time and they talked about doing it. It was to be based on a Richard Condon book that The Beatles owned. Joe Orton wrote a screenplay for them, which I then acquired the rights to. In fact, we were due to start work on a Monday morning in this [London] office. It was our driver who found Joe Orton's dead body, so that never happened. The Beatles went off and things happened and *Let It Be* became their third film. So, from a contractual point of view, they were no longer obligated to make a film.

On August 15, 1965, The Beatles kicked off their North American tour at Shea Stadium in New York City. Ed Sullivan introduced them.

Sid Bernstein: The biggest gross in the history of the world was achieved by The Beatles — $304,000. If I wanted to charge higher prices, we could have done a million-dollar gate. I just wanted to keep it within reach of youngsters. So I charged $4, $4.50, and $5. Had I charged double that, or three times that, I would have gotten it and retired and you fellows would have had to fly to Hawaii or Tahiti to find me for this interview. I met John [Lennon] once on the street, by accident, some years later. He was with a friend. We met by accident on 91st and Madison Avenue [in New York City]. He asked me for a good place to eat, knowing I was into food. Then he said, "Shea . . . weren't those the days, Sid? Wasn't that the one?" I said, "Yeah . . . those were the days." That still rings in my ears.

Murray Kaufman: Well, first of all the stage was set up around second base at Shea Stadium. I remember Brian Epstein had insisted that Sid Bernstein, who was promoting this, keep the top ticket price at $5. This was, in Brian's mind, to ensure the fact that everyone could get in and that it would be a complete sellout. Of course, they could have gotten $10 or $12.

    If ever there was hysteria, Shea Stadium, I think, personified the word. You had a mixture of executives and children of rich people who used all kinds of influence to get good seats. Well, the time came for The Beatles to be introduced and they came on. And from the time that they came on, I felt that it was a combination of a snake pit and *General Hospital* all going on at the same time. First of all, nobody heard them. It was absolutely impossible. You might have heard two or three words at the most.

I was very close to the stage and I couldn't hear them. So I figured, Okay, I'm going to go back to my dressing room. I went under the stands, and it was as if I were in a disaster area. The New York police and special police were carrying girls out in dead faints, others in hysteria, screaming and thrashing around. There must have been over 300 or 400. There were ambulances there — just absolute excitement. Under the stands was this emergency disaster area, and a cop said to me, "Listen, we're running out of space. Can we use your dressing room?" I said, "Sure. Do you want me to scrub?" It was that kind of a scene. Then I got on a helicopter and got the hell out and went back to the Warwick Hotel.

I've often said to myself that I was glad [Bob] Precht had the kind of sensitive mikes onstage that could pick up the music and at least make a film out of The Beatles at Shea. If you ever speak to anyone about a Beatles concert, they never say, "Gee, didn't they do this song great or wasn't this song sensational?" All they talk about are the scenes around them or the fact that they didn't hear The Beatles or that they couldn't see because someone was jumping up and all that. The fact that they are amid this scene with everybody getting off gives them the freedom to do what they do.

Dick Clark: You know, it's an amazing thing. Over the years I've talked to thousands of recording artists about who influenced them when they were kids. Then, when we began to prepare the early days of The Beatles story for a motion picture called *The Birth of the Beatles* and I began the research, I realized they had been influenced by people like The Everly Brothers, Buddy Holly, and The Shirelles. All of sudden The Beatles became an influence on yet another generation of musicians to follow. So the big wheel turns. The Beatles obviously have to be among the top-listed artists of all time in influence on other people, to say nothing of affecting our lives. They were a unique experience. They, and the English artists in general, shipped back to America what we sent them to begin with. And it was all new to that audience. It's strange when you stop to consider that they borrowed the look of The Everly Brothers, much of the harmonies and the sounds and then the music of Chuck Berry, Little Richard, and Fats Domino, shipped it over with a slight Liverpudlian accent and a little longer hair, and it was all brand-new again. We were just ready for that.

Bob Bonis: I went with The Beatles when they went to visit Elvis Presley on August 27, 1965. I remember that he gave them each a replica gun as a present. I didn't stay for very long because I didn't want to get in their way, but they were there for hours while I waited for them back at their rented house. They were really nervous before they met him. Mal Evans, their roadie, was some kind of heavy-duty officer in the Elvis Presley Fan Club of England. He was a nervous wreck, and when it was time to go over to Elvis's house, he couldn't even walk. He had to be carried over.

On October 12, 1965, The Beatles began recording material for what would become the album *Rubber Soul.*

George Martin: Even through the *Rubber Soul* sessions my main role was that of tidying up the basic unit of three guitars and drums, and the occasional keyboard. In fact, in those days, if there was a keyboard used, it was generally me who played it. It was later on that John and Paul did much more. So in the early days, as I've described in *Can't Buy Me Love,* I just did a little bit of manipulation to get a slightly more concise arrangement. In *Rubber Soul* I was responsible, generally, for the solos. I don't mean that I would write George's solo necessarily, although sometimes that did happen, but I would say, "Right, we need a solo here." Or "We need a line here. How about this?" For example, in the song "In My Life" I played the harpsichord solo. There was a gap in the song. I said, "We need a solo here." They went away and had their tea, and I thought it would be rather nice to have something fairly quaint or fairly Baroque in this piece. So while they were out at tea, I wrote something, like a Bach invention, and played it, then recorded it. I played it back to them when they returned, and they said, "That's great. That's fantastic. We don't need more. That's it." So we left it like that. Later on, when we came to do the middle bit of "Michelle," I actually wrote that. It isn't terribly difficult. All I did was take the basic chord sequence of the "Michelle" song and almost inverted it. Then I played it with George. I gave George the notes to play on his guitar and then played it on electric piano with John. That's the actual sound on it. So those are the kinds of things I did, which weren't orchestration. They were just manipulation of the resources we had at the time.

Paul McCartney: "Michelle" was a joke really. A French tune that you may hear at a party and you'd parody it to death until you realize that maybe you have something. Then you put words to it, and boom, it's a song.

John Lennon: When we began to record, everything was very polite. The engineers and George Martin did their job and we did ours. They set up the equipment and we just performed for them. When we were finished, they would invite us into the control room to listen, and we really didn't have much to say, even though we were asked our opinion of everything. By the time we got to recording *Rubber Soul,* which was a title that Paul came up with — a good little pun, too! — we started to get involved with the recording process, both technically and musically. Paul always wanted to get more bass into the sound, like Motown did. We were getting better all around. We really learned a lot about the whole thing on the recording sessions of *Rubber Soul.*

Norman Smith: The change, by the time they recorded *Rubber Soul,* was that it was taking so much longer to put down each song. I also noticed there were musical clashes coming in. What I mean by that is it seems that Paul wanted to go one way and John wasn't maybe too keen. There was a certain turbulence that I didn't like. It wasn't in the songs themselves. Certain things came up when we were recording. Things didn't seem eye-to-eye between John and Paul. I suppose I didn't know more than that. John wanted to go into a deeper message or psychological type of thing, and Paul still wanted to keep in the middle of the road. I guess that's what I sussed out.

George Martin: John wrote "Norwegian Wood" while we were on holiday in St. Moritz. John, Cyn [Cynthia Powell Lennon], Judy [Martin], and I went for a skiing holiday, although none of us had ever skied before except Judy. It was a lot of fun, though we were constantly pursued by photographers. Finally I managed to make an arrangement with them where we agreed to do a photo session in return for leaving us alone. And they did, so it turned out all right. The four of us shared a suite in the Palace Hotel, and though there were plenty of stories in the press about the wild parties and all of the nightclubbing we were doing, the truth was quite the opposite. After our days of skiing, we were so tired all we could manage was to go back to our rooms and play Monopoly and have hot cocoa. John, meanwhile, used part of the time to write "Norwegian Wood," which was a very personal song. The lyrics go "I once had a girl or should I say she once had me." Now Cyn married John when she was already pregnant with Julian, and I've often wondered how much of that was in the lyric. The song told a sort of bitter little story but a charming one, as well. It also used a different sound, which was typical of The Beatles continually wanting to have new sounds on every record. For the first time George [Harrison] was playing sitar, which he was struggling with at that stage, but it added just the right touch to the song.

Norman Smith: Of course, he [John Lennon] always told us he hated his voice. It was like saying English people don't like tea. I guess he really didn't know what his voice had because his voice was probably one of the easiest voices to record. Paul had a cutting voice that would get through without necessarily being a different sound. John's voice had a "sound," a different sound that nobody else, in my view, for my ears, had ever done. I learned later in my "Hurricane Smith" days that nobody else could reproduce it. John had one of those voices that was inimitable. His personality was similarly unique. He was a Jekyll and Hyde. He could be one of the sweetest guys you ever met, but he could also be one of the most terrible monsters. One of the most horrible. You'd better please John, otherwise forget it. In the beginning he didn't give me a hard time, but he certainly gave Eppy [Brian Epstein] a hard time. John was very rude to Eppy, very rude. I don't know why, because Eppy always showed to me that he was for them. There was only one group that he was interested in and that he would give his life for and that was The Beatles and maybe himself.

Rubber Soul did have a different sound. I think that was partially because they kept saying to me, "Haven't you heard that latest American disc? It has an amazing sound to it." The Americans seemed to be ahead of us in those days. And I had to admit that it was an amazing bass sound, but what could I do about it? I could get a great bass drum sound, but then the stylus would jump across the disc and I'd get hell from EMI. So I had to record within certain limits, but at the same time I knew exactly what they were talking about.

The Beatles and myself, and for that matter all the other engineers, I suppose, were screaming for more sophisticated equipment, more flexible equipment, that could give better definition. We had, by the time of *Rubber Soul,* gone from the early days of only having one track on which to record to two tracks. By the time we recorded *Rubber Soul,* I think we had eight tracks which, of course, was a luxury. So we got to fill up eight tracks. Well, that doesn't take too much doing. And, because of the extra tracks, *Rubber Soul* did take longer to record. One took that much more trouble about hearing an individual instrument over an individual track. And instead of having just two pairs of ears, the sound engineer and the producer, listening to the performance, you had the rest of the group sitting up there while the other member was playing his part. So this was what started to take so much time.

Obviously I didn't want to give up The Beatles, but George Martin meantime had left EMI and formed his own company. Fortunately EMI invited me to be a producer and to replace George. So I had to go out and find my own artists to record. In the meantime The Beatles had a new album coming up and an agent phoned me for a group called Pink Floyd. I had only just started as replacement producer at EMI and the agent said, "Listen, I've got this group. Would you come along and look at them?" I said yes and went to see them. Pink Floyd was into sounds and lights. I was very impressed and thought, Well, how the hell can I sell this group to EMI after The Beatles with their melodic songs? Fortunately I did and began to record Pink Floyd. Paul was in another studio at the time when I was doing this first Floyd session. The door opened, and who should walk in but Paul McCartney. He gave me the best sales talk you've ever heard in your life, which really broke the ice for me with Pink Floyd, because I was nervous at the time.

The Beatles received their Member of the British Empire medals on October 26, 1965. Outside Buckingham Palace on October 26, 1965, thousands of fans screamed and The Beatles spoke with the press.

Paul McCartney: We've played many palaces, including 'Frisco's Cow Palace, but never this one before. It's a keen pad and I liked the staff. I thought they'd be dukes and things, but they were just fellas.

Reporter: What about the queen?

Paul: She's lovely, great. She was very friendly. She was just like a mum to us.

Reporter: How did you know what to do during the ceremony?

Paul: The man shouted out, "George Harrison, John Lennon, Paul McCartney, and Ringo Starr." "Starr" was the cue for us to walk forward, left foot first. It was just like a show.

Ringo Starr: And we bowed and walked to the queen and we walked back and bowed, then we walked away.

John Lennon: Left foot forward. We were drilled beforehand by some big guardsman fella, and every time he was reading out the names and he got to Ringo Starr, he kept cracking up.

Ringo: Nice man.

Paul: There were only a few people there. Nobody was trying to get to us. They were all friendly, though.

John: All the people waited for us. We signed all the autographs for people waiting to get their M.B.E.'s or O.B.E.'s.

Paul: They were all very nice, you know. Though there was one fella who said, "I want it for my daughter. I don't know what she sees in you."

George Harrison: Really?

Paul: Yeah.

George: Did he say that?

Paul: Yeah.

Reporter: What did the queen ask you?

John: She said to me, "Have you been working hard lately?" And I couldn't think what we had been doing, so I said, "No, we've been having a holiday." But I forgot that we have been recording. I couldn't remember that.

Paul: And then she said to me, "Have you been together long?" I said, "Yes." It was a joke. I said, "Yes, many years." And Ringo said 40 years.

Ringo: The old songs with the same name.

Paul: And she laughed. We all had a little laugh.

George: She just said, "It's a pleasure to give this to you." That's what she said. She actually said it to everyone. Then she put John's on and said, "Have you been working hard?"

John: I must have looked shattered.

Ringo: And I was just butting in when she spoke to everyone else. And then she said, "Did you start it all?" I said, "No, they did."

Paul: And then he said, "I'm the little one."

Ringo: I joined last and said, "I'm the little fellow, 'cause I am."

John: Isn't that cute?

Ringo: Look at him. He's smiling.
Reporter: What will you do with your medals?
Paul: What you normally do with medals. Put them in a box.

On December 3, 1965, The Beatles released the album *Rubber Soul* as well as the single "We Can Work It Out/Day Tripper."

Stephen James: Paul McCartney didn't want radio play too long before the release of a Beatles record because he didn't want people to get tired of it before they could buy it, which is, of course, very clever. Therefore, he made it a rule that no promotion manager, either from EMI or myself, could take the records around to the BBC until a week or maximum 10 days before the release. The moment you took the record in, you see, they would put it on immediately. So we weren't allowed to take the records around, even though we had copies. It was a matter of saying, "Hey, you'll never believe it, but the next Beatle record is great! Unfortunately I can't let you hear it."

On March 25, 1966, The Beatles shot the controversial "Butcher Block" photograph that would be used on the American release called *Yesterday and Today*.

Bob Whitaker: It was the spring of 1966, and I felt The Beatles needed a new approach with their image. I wanted to do a real experiment with them. People will jump to the wrong conclusions about it being sick, but the whole thing was based on simplicity, linking four very real people with something real. I got George to pretend to knock some nails into John's head and took some sausages along to get some other kinds of pictures. They turned out well. I also created some strange shots with dolls and eyes. I dressed them up in white smocks as butchers, and it was decided to use those pictures. The use of the camera as a means of creating situations worked very well with them.

The original cover concept never really materialized. It was meant to be a double-folded album cover where the front showed the four Beatles holding sausages, which would have stood for an umbilical cord. Therefore, each of The Beatles would be linked to a woman by means of these sausages. Now this woman was going to be inside the double-album cover and there was going to be people blowing trumpets announcing the birth of The Beatles and all kinds of surreal, far-out images.

I was completely surprised when they used the picture of the butcher smocks and the meat pieces for the American LP. Paul was asked about the pictures and said, "Very tasty meat." George said, "We won't come to any more of your sick picture sessions, Bob." John said, "Oh, we don't mind doing anything." And Ringo said, "We haven't done pictures like *this* before." Speculation circulated in the media that The Beatles were asked by Capitol in America for a picture for their new "filler" album between *Rubber Soul* and *Revolver,* and The Beatles thought they would play a little joke on them by sending this special print for the album *Yesterday and Today.* Whether it was public reaction, or whether Capitol found out about the prank, isn't known, but the cover was replaced very quickly in the States.

George Harrison: When the American company released albums like *Yesterday and Today,* we didn't have anything to do with them. They always used to put out more albums in the States than we actually had. In England we'd put 14 tracks on a record and in America they'd put out about 10. Plus, we'd release singles in England and we would never include them on our next album. So if we put out two singles and two albums, they'd convert them to three albums by keeping the extra tracks. So they were different over here. We started to put our foot down when it came to albums like *Rubber Soul, Revolver, Sgt. Pepper,* and all those because it was important that they be the same songs in the States.

John Lennon: We would carefully sequence the material, you know, the songs, and have it just the way we felt it should sound for an album. We would put a lot of thought and work into the process and then we'd come over to America . . . and hear what they had done and it would drive us crazy!

On April 6, 1966, The Beatles began work on what would become the album Revolver.

George Martin: With the new sounds on *Revolver* it was basically an attempt to get more color into our records. I mean, The Beatles were always looking for new sounds and they were always looking to a new horizon. And it was a continually happy journey, even though it was also a continual strain to try to provide new things for them. They were always wanting to try new instruments, and new sounds. They didn't know much about instruments, though, which put the pressure on me. They needed someone to translate for them. I was there, so it worked very well. I had a foot in both camps. I knew what they were trying to get and I knew how to get it, and I became the official interpreter.

A classic instance was when we were overdubbing some saxophones on a John Lennon song. John did a lick on the guitar and I said, "I think it might be a good idea to imitate that with the saxists, so I'll get them to do it." I wrote out the bits, gave it to the saxists, and said, "Copy these notes down, please, boys." John was listening and said, "George, you've got it wrong. You're saying A and a G and an F, and it's not. It's an E flat." I said, "Well, it is for you, John, but for them they're different notes because they're playing in different keys." He said, "That's bloody stupid, isn't it?" I said, "Well, of course it is, but that's the way the thing works. I mean, the instruments are in different keys." I had to explain to him that a saxophone was in either B flat or E flat, and when you played particular notes on it, they sounded different from the guitar. He couldn't understand that at all. He thought it was quite crazy. Obviously that was the beginning of his understanding.

Donovan Leitch: Paul and I had a close relationship in the 1960s for brief periods, and I have nothing but respect for that man's writing talent. I can write a song every five minutes if we get going, and Paul can, as well. And that was the breakup really with The Beatles, I think. Because Paul is so creative. Honestly, if he just tinkles the piano, there's another song. Paul needed, at that time, somebody like me, who could sit around and jam with him. The Beatles didn't jam at that time. They made records. Every time they got together the tape was rolling. So that's what I did for Paul in those few months we were together.

I had a flat in Maida Vale, and Paul came around one day. He pulled up in his 1966 Astin Martin, left the doors wide open, and parked, with a tape blaring, in the middle of the road at an angle so that the traffic was held up. That was the power we had then. He came up and said, "I've got this new song. It's called 'All in the Tungy.'" He started playing his guitar, and it was "Eleanor Rigby" before he got all the words together. He was chunking away and said, "Isn't this a great song?" Then we heard *dring-dring*. I said, "It's a fantastic song. You've got to cut that."

We opened the door and it was a policeman. The policeman said, very politely, "Mr. McCartney?" Paul said yes. The policeman said, "Could I ask you to move your car because we have a little problem in the street?" Paul said, "Oh, certainly." And he went down and moved the car and parked it. And that was what was happening then. The whole town knew who they were, and they could do anything they wanted. But Paul needed to jam and that's what we did. And on that particular day he said he had another song. It was called "Yellow Submarine." He played it for me and said, "There's just one line I haven't got." So I said, "Let's go into the other room." We did and I came out with "Sky of blue and sea of green" — my only contribution to The Beatles' lyrics. So Paul and I had a productive little relationship there for a while.

Geoff Emerick: I'd been engineering about three months up until the time when Norman [Smith] wanted to become a producer. I'd always worked with Norman as his second engineer, tape operator. Then George Martin asked me, "Would I do The Beatles?" I didn't know whether to say yes or no, but I said yes. "Tomorrow Never Knows" was the first track that was cut for *Revolver*. At the time the multitrack machine was remote from the control room in the studio. It was in another room in the building. I always remember the staff at Abbey Road gathering outside the room, listening to these backward loops and things that went on that track because no one had ever heard anything like it before. Looking back on it now, it's commonplace.

Paul McCartney: It was quite unusual and funny from the beginning with "Tomorrow Never Knows." John had this idea with the lyrics because he had just read *The Tibetan Book of the Dead*, and he was duly impressed, dead impressed with it. He decided he'd write a song inspired by it, but there was a problem. We only had one verse to work with. We worked very hard to stretch it to two verses. We racked our brains but couldn't come up with any more words because we felt it already said everything we wanted to say in the two verses. So we had to make it longer somehow and make it different, as well. I had an idea to use something I had been experimenting with at home on my tape player where I would put a piece of tape over the record head and saturate the tape with all kinds of sounds. I was listening to [Karlheinz] Stockhausen, the experimental modern composer, at the time, and these saturated loops were inspired by his work. So I brought some of these recordings into the studio. We made loops of them and we tried mixing them into the song, and it turned out great. It was vaguely my idea to create that weird stuff in the song.

George Martin: At that time they'd all gotten their own Grundig tape recorders, and I think it was Paul who found out that by removing the erase head and putting a loop of tape on it, you could actually play a short phrase that would saturate itself. It went round and round and overdubbed itself until the point of saturation, and that made a funny sound. When you played it back, it was cute to listen to. It was what we call Musique Concrète.

So they all vied with each other. They each went home and made these funny little loops and they would bring various tape loops in for me to hear. They recorded them at different speeds, you know, one and seven-eighth [inches per second], three and three-quarters, seven and a half, and 15.

With "Tomorrow Never Knows" I selected eight of them and put them all on different machines. We had people all around the building connected to our control panel with these silly loops held up with bits of pencil to keep the tension going eternally. I then decided the best way to do it was to put them all through a mixer. So all the eight tracks of these loops came into our mixer and it was like an organ. By bringing up any one track you could have any loop at any time. With a 24-track machine that's a fairly common technique, but we didn't have that so it meant that when we were mixing it that was the actual performance. We had everybody on the mixer. Apart from the engineer, who was Geoff Emerick, we had Paul on a couple of faders and John on another, I was on the pan pots. We would all make a concerted mix and just do our own thing. When we felt like the seagull sound should appear, we'd put that fader up and so on. We did many mixes and then decided which was the best one.

Paul McCartney: The only similar thing between "Eleanor Rigby" and "Yesterday" is that we used strings on both recordings. Apart from that similarity there is nothing else remotely the same to me. I think they're completely different kinds of tunes. I also think that I sang "Yesterday" a lot better than "Eleanor Rigby." It sounds terrible. Listen to it. It's pretty bad.

George Martin: On the song "Yellow Submarine" we were embarking on the sound-picture thing. I mean, "Yellow Submarine" was almost a Goon record, with John actually in the studio using a PA mike and an amplifier. He used them for the captain's commands and the boat sounds.

Alan Civil: George Martin, their musical director, rang me up and said, "The Beatles want a change of image from the guitars and rock." They had tried a string quartet and various other things and now they wanted something classical such as a horn. So he asked me to do the session. I didn't know what I was in for and it started well after midnight. The reason being that all these fans, girls, used to plague the studios. They had to become secretive about the sessions, which took place between twelve and one o'clock in the morning. They had already recorded the guitars, bass, and voice. Paul McCartney, who seemed to be in charge, said, "Look, I want the horn to play something here."

There was nothing written at all and I had to improvise something. I played various things, and Paul didn't know much about the possibilities of register and that sort of thing. So naturally I played him a sort of hornistic classical line and he said, "How high can you play?" I said, "Well, you know, it gets more expensive as you get higher. It gets physically impossible unless you've got a lot of money." We eventually worked something out, but the problem was that the tuning of the guitars was right in the cracks. It wasn't in B major and it wasn't in B flat. It was right in the middle. This, of course, really throws you out on the horn. I think they had a method of raising or lowering the pitch in this case, but it made the horn part for me a very, very awkward key, purely because these fellas just tuned their instruments to themselves and not to an A on the piano.

What was intriguing about it was that there were pirated records within days of this session, with people stealing the same tune, the little horn motif. The other funny thing is that I've played in symphony orchestras pretty well all my life, chamber music and all, but that piece "For No One," and playing with The Beatles, does me more good when I go to my local pub. They say, "This fella, he played with Otto Klemperer, [Sir Thomas] Beecham, and [Leopold] Stokowski." But The Beatles are above them all. It's very, very interesting, that.

Les Condon: Apparently they felt something extra was needed on the song "Got to Get You into My Life." That's why we were there. As far as the arrangement goes, well, they hadn't anything written down, so we just listened to what they had and got an idea of what they wanted. Most of it went right the first time. We jotted down some voicings, but eventually everybody chipped in and the credit must be evenly divided. I suggested something for the trumpets for the ending and we dubbed it on with three trumpets. I didn't think it was quite strong enough, so we dubbed it on with three trumpets again. You'll really be hearing six trumpets in that coda. It was the most relaxing session I've ever been on. The Beatles all seemed like very nice fellows and, you know what, they kept asking *us* things!

George Martin: It's a funny thing, but John never liked his voice. I don't know why, because I always said he had the greatest of voices, but I guess it's the same problem you have when you wake up in the morning and you shave yourself and you look at your face and say, "What an awful face." He was always wanting to distort it, always wanting me to do things to it, to ADT it or double-track it or whatever. "Don't give me that thing again, George," he'd say. "Give me another one." He was always wanting something different.

Geoff Emerick: Around the time of *Revolver* we first tried ADT, automatic double tracking, which gave Lennon his sound on some things. We also tried altering the speed of the tape machine and making it sort of phasey. We used to do that on guitars, as well. In those days it was the first time anyone had heard of doing that. We were sort of pioneering in different ways.

Klaus Voorman: Well, it came out of the blue. I wasn't doing any art in those days. I was playing music in bands, and suddenly John [Lennon] called me and said, "Look, Klaus, if you have any idea for our next album cover [*Revolver*], scribble it down and let us see it. And if it's something we like, you might get the gig." So I did sketches and I had 10 or 15 suggestions, ideas, but I already liked this one with the hair. I went to the studio, which was always a good idea while they were recording the work, because you needed time to do the cover as much as they needed time to finish the LP. I showed it to them and they all jumped on this idea of the four heads and those little figures.

George Martin: I'm not sure they ever stopped being a good rock-and-roll band. I think once they'd got their first success under their belts that seemed to spur them on to greater songwriting efforts. John and Paul, having found out that it was comparatively easy to make a hit with "Please Please Me" and then "From Me to You," said, "Great, we know how to do it." It then became a production line, and their ingenuity was actually spurred on by their success at that stage. They were always thinking of fresh ideas and new things, and each song that came out seemed to be a good one. I don't think they really started developing their best songwriting skills, in a really strange way, until *Revolver*. I think that was the beginning of the breakthrough, and certainly "Tomorrow Never Knows," on the end of *Revolver*, was the beginning of the so-called psychedelic bit, which was the forerunner of *Sgt. Pepper*.

Chapter Eight

Pop Art, *Pepper,* and Post-Touring

On June 10, 1966, The Beatles released the single "Paperback Writer/Rain." At the end of July some radio people in Birmingham, Alabama, discovered the interview from London's *Evening Standard,* which had been reprinted in *Datebook,* an American teen magazine. In the article John Lennon inadvertently stated that The Beatles were more popular than Jesus Christ.

John Lennon: Christianity will go. It will vanish and shrink. I needn't argue about that. I'm right and I'll be proved right. We are more popular than Jesus now. I don't know which will go first, rock and roll or Christianity. Jesus was all right, but his disciples were thick and ordinary.

Tommy Charles: The response so far has been sensational. Here in Birmingham we've had a 99 percent cooperative attitude, and as you may have heard, all across the country radio stations are jumping on the bandwagon. I think within another 10 days to two weeks you're going to see a tremendous increase in the number of stations that have banned The Beatles' records, and I think this is good. It came about because of a magazine article in *Datebook* magazine, which reprinted an interview in London with Maureen Cleave in which John Lennon was quoted as saying that Christianity was on its way out and that The Beatles were more popular than Jesus Christ. We felt it was an absurd and insane statement. We felt we had a public service to do and we banned The Beatles' records and we've also asked listeners to bring all of their Beatle paraphernalia and Beatlemania to the station. We have a big bonfire scheduled for August 19. I just talked to a reporter. He asked me about my religious affiliation and if I was a religious fanatic or something. I told him I wasn't, that I attended church sort of regularly, but that this had nothing to do with it. It was just that I was completely repulsed by the idea that a group like The Beatles, who are idolized by so many young people, could come out and make a statement like that. I think responsibility should go up with their success.

Radio stations that had never played The Beatles instituted a ban on their records. The Grand Dragon of the South Carolina Ku Klux Klan attached some Beatle records to a wooden cross and set it on fire. A Baptist minister in Cleveland said that he would revoke the membership of any member of his church who agreed with John Lennon's remarks or played Beatle records.

Brian Epstein: The quote that John Lennon made to a London columnist more than three months ago was quoted and represented entirely out of context. Lennon is deeply interested in religion and was at the time having serious talks with Maureen Cleave, who is both a friend of The Beatles and a representative of the London *Evening Standard*. What he said and meant was that he was astonished that in the past 50 years the church in England, and therefore Christ, had suffered a decline in interest. He did not mean to boast about The Beatles' fame. He meant to point out that The Beatles' effect appeared to him to be a more immediate one upon certain of the younger generation.

Ironically one of the radio stations in Texas that organized a public bonfire of Beatle records was knocked off the air shortly after making the announcement. A bolt of lightning hit the station's transmitter tower, knocking the news director unconscious and causing extensive damage to the station's transmission equipment.

Maureen Cleave: I was astonished that John Lennon's quotation was taken out of context from my article and misinterpreted in that way. I don't think for one moment that he intended to be flippant or irreverent, and he certainly wasn't comparing The Beatles to Jesus Christ. He was simply observing that, to many, The Beatles were better known. He was deploring, rather than approving this. Sectors of the American public were given the wrong impression, and it was totally absurd.

Murray Kaufman: Among the young people there were more people interested and concerned about what The Beatles were doing in their music and their events than in going to church and listening to the teachings of Jesus Christ. That appeared in an article, and when John Lennon said to his friend Maureen Cleave, "Yeah, it's really great to find that The Beatles are more popular than Jesus Christ," he wasn't saying The Beatles had taken the place of Jesus Christ but that [Christianity] had a big problem. Young people weren't able to relate to religion as it was being presented. It's really interesting to note that after that statement [Christianity] started doing things like having rock concerts in churches and trying new approaches to attract young people. I think the statement did provoke and inspire churchmen who believed that what John was saying was the truth. And they started to do something about it. If you look back on those times, and it wasn't too long ago, some of the things in civil rights and some of our habits and our values were archaic by today's standards. John's statement may have been an unfortunate use of words, and the press built it up more than it should have, but it started a discussion among theologians. If a theologian had said the same thing, the statement wouldn't have gotten more than a half sentence in the press, but because John Lennon said it, some good came out of it.

On August 5, 1966, The Beatles released the single "Eleanor Rigby/Yellow Submarine" as well as the album *Revolver.* The Beatles gave a press conference concerning the debate over what John Lennon had said about Christ and Christianity.

John Lennon: I was just talking with a reporter [Maureen Cleave] who also happened to be a friend of mine. It was sort of an in-depth series she was doing, so I wasn't really thinking in terms of PR or translating what I was saying. I wasn't saying The Beatles were better than Jesus or God or Christianity. I was using the name "Beatles" because I can use them easier. I was using it because I could talk about The Beatles as a separate thing and use them as an example, especially to a close friend. I could have said TV or cinema or anything else that's popular — motor cars are bigger than Jesus — but I said Beatles because that's the easiest one for me. I never thought of the repercussions. When I first heard the controversy in America, I thought it couldn't be true. It was just one of those things like "Bad eggs in Adelaide," and when I realized it was serious, I was worried stiff because I knew how it would go on and on and I couldn't control it. I couldn't answer for it when it got that big because it had nothing to do with me then. From what I'd read and observed of Christianity, it just seemed to me to be shrinking. I wasn't knocking it or saying it was bad. I was just saying it seemed to be shrinking and losing contact.

Paul McCartney: And we all deplored the fact that it is, you know.

John: Nothing seems to be replacing Christianity, so we're not saying anything about that. It's silly saying it's all fine and, yeah, we're all doing this and we're all not doing it. We were brought up Christians. I don't profess to be a practicing Christian. I think Christ was what he was, and anybody who says something great about him, I believe. I don't have un-Christian thoughts.

Paul: I don't think this means the Americans lack a sense of humor. Some Americans lack humor. Some Britons lack humor. Everyone, somewhere, lacks it. But there are just more people in the States, so you can pick on the minority.

John: We are still looking forward to our tour of America, even though we've been quoted as saying that we only wanted to play in California while we're here. I think somebody probably said which place do you like best in America and we probably said we were looking forward to spending some time in L.A. because we know a lot of people there.

George Harrison: We usually eat well when we're there [in California]. We eat different foods from hotel food, not that there's anything wrong with hotel food, but it's a break from hotel food because we've got a house there to use.

John: We could have hidden in England and said, "We're not going." It occurred to me when I heard all of the fuss that I couldn't remember saying it. I couldn't remember the article. I was panicking. I was thinking, I'm not going over there. But if I straighten it out, it will be worth it and good.

Reporter: To what do you describe your immense popularity?

John: You answer that one.

Ringo Starr: Ask Tony Barrow that one.

Paul: I don't know really. If you want an honest answer, none of us know at all.

Reporter: Do you hope to someday see these places you just fly into and out of?

George: We can go everywhere we want to go "when the bubble bursts." [Lots of laughter.]

Reporter: John, your music has changed immensely since you first started out. Is it because you've become more professional, or is it because you're trying to impress the public?

John: It's not trying or being professional. It's just a progression.

George: We're trying to impress ourselves in a way. That's why we try to do things better because we're never satisfied.

Reporter: Why is it that American journalists haven't treated this "Bigger Than Christ" story right?

John: I don't know. When it came out in England, a few people wrote into the papers saying, "So what that he said that. Who is he, anyway?" Or they would say, "He can have his own opinion." Then it just vanished. It was very small. But by the time it got over here and was put into a kids' magazine, it just lost its meaning or its context and immediately everyone started making their own versions of it.

Reporter: John, it appears that a great many ministers have agreed with you in the full context of what you said and that most of the concerns and oversimplification of what you said came from what we call the Bible Belt, which is notorious for its basic Christian attitudes.

Paul: Yeah, they seem to think that by his comments John's trying to get at them, but he isn't at all. It's just a straight comment on something, which may be right or may be wrong, but he's got to answer as he feels honestly. If they think that for him to say that is wrong, then they don't believe in free speech. I thought everyone here did!

Reporter: Mr. McCartney, could you tell us what the meaning is of the line in your latest song concerning "Father Mackenzie who writes sermons that nobody hears"?

Paul: It was a song about lonely people, that one you're talking about — "Eleanor Rigby." It's a song about one lonely person who just happens to be a priest who's darning his socks at night, and he's lonely. That's all there is to it.

Reporter: What about your further comments also in that same interview that America is a lousy country where anyone who's black is called a nigger?

Paul: If you say anything about, say, the way civil rights are treated over here, then there's bound to be criticism. There are extremists who think we're wrong in saying that colored people are the same as white people, but I honestly believe that. If anyone wants me to give the showbiz answer of "Oh, we're just good friends," I will. But I personally believe it's better to be honest about it.

Reporter: Doesn't the same thing exist in England?

Paul: Of course it exists. It exists everywhere. But it's about time people did something about it. It just needs to be said occasionally, that's all.

Tommy Charles: We accept his [John Lennon's] apology and the manner in which it is offered. We think it is the least we can do. An offhand remark like that isn't only dangerous, but it can be very impressionable on the young folks. We think The Beatles made a wise decision.

Tony Barrow: I'd been with The Beatles from the start, from 1963. We'd had other people, called press officers or PR aides of one sort or another, who had gone out with The Beatles on the road at various times while I stayed back at home base because we were launching a lot of other acts. But by 1965 I was back on the road with The Beatles again, not just supervising from London but personally setting up and running the press conferences on the road. So I was involved in the last two years of touring, which included what was to me the greatest experience. I won't call it a concert, but a peak experience of the entire Beatles' career. That was the Shea Stadium show of 1965. Not the one in 1966. The magic wasn't quite as thick upon the ground the second time.

Nineteen sixty-six was my second year back touring and, of course, The Beatles' last year of touring at all. In fact, 1966 was a horrendous year of one crisis after another. The first of these was Japan when threats were being made by a certain faction, an element among students in Tokyo who reckoned that the Budokan venue The Beatles were going to play at was a sacred place. Sacred to great sporting tournaments of one sort or another and therefore shouldn't be used for such frivolous purposes as rock concerts. They said that if The Beatles played at the Budokan, the boys would be murdered. I actually managed to determine what was happening from some of the kids down in the Tokyo Hilton foyer. These Japanese kids read the papers to me, which is the only reason I knew about the murder threats. The Beatles never really knew what was happening. They just saw a lot of armed guards everywhere. They never knew they were under threat of death in Japan.

We then flew straight from there to Manila in the Philippines and, of course, all hell broke loose. This was the second of three major crisis points of 1966 when it was claimed that The Beatles had snubbed the first lady [Imelda Marcos] and failed to turn up to see her at the presidential palace. Of course, one doesn't snub people like the Marcoses in a territory such as the Philippines. One lives to regret it. Immediately there was an anti-Beatles thing that grew up overnight.

Now I have to tell you that from time to time Brian Epstein and myself, and others involved with The Beatles, did quite lie our way out of certain formal functions on behalf of the boys because they hated these overformal white-tie affairs. I also have to tell you that on that particular occasion we weren't trying to white-lie ourselves out of it at all. For there hadn't been a proper invitation.

We hadn't been given the idea that there was a crowd of over 200 sons of the aristocracy of the Philippines lined up to meet The Beatles and that there was a formal luncheon the president and his wife would attend. None of that had got through to us at all. We were told about an informal drop-in or a call-in type invitation, and Imelda Marcos, President Marcos's wife, might be there, but we had no idea it was such a formal occasion.

Now, incidentally, there is one other thing about Manila that no one ever thinks about. On that day, July 4, The Beatles played to a larger number of people in live performance than they did at any other show, anywhere on earth, in their history. That little point has been forgotten. They gave two performances in a 45,000-seat stadium, and that outdid the Shea Stadium show by 35,000 or so.

The third and final phase of that horrendous year was the last tour of the United States, where we began with Beatle records being burned and John Lennon under the direct threat of assassination from religious zealots in the southern United States, the Bible Belt states. It was the misconstruing of his comment about Jesus Christ's diminishing popularity, which wasn't in any way boastful. It was just a comment he made. By the time it reached certain southern states, it was taken very badly by certain religious factions and there was the threat of death hanging over that whole tour.

I do recall that once we did get down to that area, the southern states, that a firecracker was let off during the concert in Memphis and everybody, all of us at the side of the stage, including the three Beatles on the stage, all looked immediately at John Lennon. We would not at that moment have been surprised to see that guy go down. Of course, that was 14 years too early for that. John had halfheartedly joked about the Memphis concert in an earlier press conference, and when we got there everything seemed to be controlled and calm, but underneath somehow, there was this nasty atmosphere. It wasn't a happy day at all. It was a very tense and pressured kind of day.

Reporter: John, may I ask you what is it, in your estimation, that can and does really inspire young people today?

John Lennon: I don't know, honestly. I just know that what we're doing inspires them to a degree, but it doesn't inspire them to do anything else than to enjoy themselves.

Reporter: What you do excites them and makes them enjoy themselves. What is inspiring them?

Paul McCartney: They get inspired by people who talk honestly to them and not by people who take the long way round and talk in riddles. I think if they believe us on some things it's because we can say it like they would think it, because we're exactly the same and we don't pretend to be anything better than we are.

Reporter: Is there a possibility that The Beatles someday will break up?

John: Well, all . . . everything is possible. There's no answer to that. We obviously aren't going to go around holding hands forever. We've got to split up or progress. I mean, it might happen. Yes, it is quite possible.

Reporter: With the *Revolver* album, are you trying to create trends?

Paul: No, I don't think we ever try to establish trends. We try to keep moving forward and do something different and if in the meantime it starts trends, that's okay, but we never try consciously to start them.

Reporter: You're certainly original.

Paul: Thank you.

Reporter: In regards to songwriting, have you ever attempted to or would you attempt to write anything on your own without Paul or without another writer?

John: Well, I've written many things without Paul before. For years we've worked together and separately.

Reporter: What about with, say, another writer?

John: Another writer I don't need.

Reporter: How can you sleep with that long hair?

Paul: Great! That's it! We can't sleep with this long hair.

John: People have only had short hair since the last world war. So they've been sleeping all those thousands of years with long hair.

Paul: It's not a problem. I tell you. It's just as much a problem as having short hair, which to you seems to be normal.

John: It's more a problem having short hair, having to keep it short.

Reporter: Would you ever have your own record company?

John: We would never start our own label. It's too much trouble, you know.

George Harrison: When we started to get famous and did our own songs more it was very exciting. Then we started doing these big tours and we had to play our records to promote them and sing our hits and stuff. By the time of our last tour, we were in a rut. We just played the same stuff to different people all over the place. It got boring. Nobody could hear us and we felt very little satisfaction. We always hated the hotels, the guards, the police escorts, the press, and many other things, but we always loved the fans and performing.

I don't know if you saw the Shea Stadium film [documenting The Beatles' 1965 appearance there], but when I look at the film, we tried to have a good time. But the show we did was for ourselves. And the fans were sort of miles away and they were making their own scene. There were so many police and kids flying around. It was really crazy. The audience was buzzing away and leaping up and down and doing all that, and we were just playing loud. But the sound was bad, and we joked to each other to keep ourselves amused. It was very impersonal. Worst of all, we became terrible musicians because we couldn't hear ourselves and we didn't really care anymore.

Then we got into a big political thing, with all that "Bigger Than Christ" and Manila and things and I just got sick of it. I think we were all nervous wrecks, being flown around everywhere, with press conferences everywhere we went. It was just too much, and that's why I can't see us going on the road again because it would be the same. Exactly the same, and possibly even wilder now, because a lot of people say, "Oh, it wouldn't be the same and we'd all be quiet." And they'd get petitions saying,

"Come back and tour and we promise we won't shout." But we'd have to play in those big baseball places again or a little club. And the only point in playing a little club would be for ourselves and the handful of people who would fit in there. So there's just no way. I don't want to repeat that fiasco of airplanes and everything.

Louise Harrison: One night, when we were in Chicago, we'd been sitting up on the 11th floor of the hotel talking and chatting before the concert and the police came to the fire escape to lead the guys down to take them through the basement into the building next door where the concert was being held. And I remember looking at George as he stepped out onto the fire escape. He turned and looked at me, and I always sort of got the impression that it was like the look that would be in the eye of a deer that was looking into the barrel of a gun. I can't exactly express what it was like, but that was what it brought to my mind.

Tony Barrow: The end of that tour [in 1966], the final concert at Candlestick Park in San Francisco, was poignant. I carried a cassette recorder around on all those last tour dates to pick up as many interviews as I could that took place in press conferences. I wanted to take them back home to let journalists and people here in London who hadn't been out on the tour listen to them. I also assembled all kinds of post-tour press kits and whatever. Paul [McCartney] said to me on the way in to San Francisco, "You've got your tape recorder, haven't you?" I said, "Sure, of course." He said, "Tape tonight, will ya? Record tonight." I knew what he meant because it was fairly common knowledge among the Beatles, and not beyond The Beatles, that this was to be the last concert tour. Therefore tonight was to be the last concert they would ever give.

There was nothing extraordinary about the performance at Candlestick, and it wasn't a capacity crowd. It was a tight 30- to 35-minute performance, and there were extra things in there, just bits of patter and dialogue in between the songs, particularly between John and Paul. They put in things that they had never said before. It was kind of "end of term" time in a way, and all of that I have on tape at Paul McCartney's request. I think it's probably the most unique Beatle recording in existence.

That same night, when we all got back on the chartered aircraft that was going to take us down the California coast to L.A., the very first thing that George Harrison said as he sank back into his chair on the plane was "Well, that's it. I'm not a Beatle anymore!" And that, as far as The Beatles themselves were concerned, was the end of the matter. They were all going to continue writing songs and they were all going to go to the recording studio, and all the labels and sleeves would say the word "Beatles." But it didn't matter. As far as they were concerned, "Beatles" meant live touring. And that was all over on August 29, 1966.

Brian confidently expected he could change their minds. One afternoon in his office that following autumn he actually got as far as showing me a list of U.K. tour dates he had in mind for the early part of the following year. He said, ambiguously, when he snatched the piece of paper back from me, screwed it up, and threw it in the waste bin, "All hell will break loose if they ever see that, or if they ever hear about that!" I never queried him on whether he meant The Beatles or the press. I know he wouldn't have gotten past Messieurs Harrison and Lennon, in that order.

Murray Kaufman: I think it was a matter of growing up. The day The Beatles first came to the United States, you have to realize, George was just turning 21. Paul was 21 and the oldest, Ringo and John, were 23. You do an awful lot of growing up in two or three years. And the terrible thing about being that kind of superstar is that no matter who you meet, I don't care whether it's a security person or Lord and Lady Harlick, they all want something. They either want you to pose for a picture, or to autograph something. The Beatles always used to hate going to affairs like the ambassadors' parties. They'd come back and say, "They are the rudest people." They couldn't wait to get away. I remember John was receiving an award for his book *In His Own Write* and he was very uptight. So he went to this luncheon and they were very upset because the only thing he said when he got up was "Thank you. You've got a lucky face." Then he sat down. So, when they finally refused to go on tour anymore, I wasn't at all surprised.

Paul McCartney: I remember being frightened many times. As we waited for an armored car to take us to our guarded hotel rooms, I would sit and say to myself, "I really don't want to go through this any longer. We have the money. Let's take off for Brighton!"

John Lennon: We'd had enough of performing forever. I couldn't imagine any reason that would have made us do any sort of tour again. We were all really tired. It did nothing for us anymore. That was really unfair to the fans, we knew, but we had to think of ourselves.

Ringo Starr: By the end, none of us enjoyed touring. You couldn't really. When we started, it was about making good music. That's why I wanted to be in The Beatles, because they were the best band around. Once you have to go out and play your biggest hits and you've got to manufacture it, it doesn't work. I think of it as the worst time and the best time of my life. The worst part was that 24 hours a day you had press and people fighting over you, as well as fans climbing up and down the drainpipes, trying to get into your rooms, knocking on your windows and doors. It was insane. If it had gone any further, I would have gone crazy.

Sean O'Mahony: We covered most of the tours. We photographed them, as well. It was always crazy. In fact, the tours to me were summed up by the security guards as they rushed The Beatles using various devices through the crowds, eventually getting them inside a dressing room until the doors would finally clang shut like a cell door. You realized, "My God, we're trapped for nine hours to do two concerts." Then, when you thought you were in for a bit of peace at last, the security guards would turn around with their books and demand signatures. To me that summed it up. There was little peace, no place for it on a tour. That's what really gets to all the big stars. This feeling that they're trapped and that they can never get away from the autographs, never get away from the interviews, never get away from being on show! That's what they hated.

After the last American tour ended, George Harrison and his wife, Patti, left for a two-month journey through India. George met Ravi Shankar there and took sitar lessons from him as well as thoroughly absorbing the entire Indian experience.

George Harrison: I went to India partly to learn the music and partly to see what the country was all about. I'd heard stories about men in caves up in the Himalayas who were very old and wise, and about people who could levitate. I had heard of people who had been buried underground for weeks on end — mystic stories that had permeated my curiosity for years. When I got there, I found all of this was happening all over the place, with people materializing everywhere. In the West everybody was vibrating on a material level, but in India they had this great feeling going on of something else that was spiritual. Once you get to the point where you really believe you're trying to do things for the truth, then nobody can touch you because you're harmonizing with a very great power. So the more you're into this spiritual thing, the more you understand you're not doing it!

There are always choices, and it happened like that with me just through action, reaction, action reaction, and I got into Indian music. The first time I listened to it, it was a Ravi Shankar album. When I played the music, it was technically and spiritually the most amazing music ever. And even though, intellectually, I didn't understand it, I felt within myself as though I knew it. I just knew it back to front, and it seemed so obvious and so logical. Through that I got involved with the sitar and Ravi Shankar, who was probably the person who influenced my life the most. Maybe he's not that aware of it. I really love Ravi Shankar, and he's been like a father figure and a spiritual guide, as well.

Later I realized that Indian music was like a stepping stone to the spiritual thing, because I also had a great desire to know about the yogic thing. I always had a feeling for that. I went to India and I liked it a lot and most of the people I knew in there were Hindus. It was just a natural sort of involvement with it. But it was because of that that I was led right round the cycle and got to understand the thing about Christ and Christianity and what Christ actually was.

So I have a great respect for Indian music, history, and philosophy. Maybe it has something to do with my past lives, but I feel a great connection with it. Also because in this age the West and East are getting closer, they can benefit from each other. We can help them with our material things and they can help us with the spiritual thing, and we all need both of them. You need the outer aspect of life as well as the inner because the outer is empty if you don't have the inner spiritual side to life. And vice versa.

On November 9, 1966, John Lennon went to an art exhibit at London's Indica Gallery and met Yoko Ono for the first time.

John Lennon: Yoko was having an art exhibition at a gallery in London where I used to go to see what was happening. Someone said there was an artist who was going to have an event and I said, "Well, what sort of event?" He said, "It's like a happening, only it's an event." I thought that was all right. Then he said something about black bags. "Everybody's going to get into bags." I was thinking, Oh, come on! I don't want to get into a bag. I want to be the one that doesn't do it, you know, a spoilsport. So I thought, Well, let's go and see. He invited me there the night before it opened. There were just a few people in the gallery, and I was wandering around trying not to look like John Lennon. Yoko didn't know me from Adam, anyway. And then we met. She had a painting on the ceiling. You went up this ladder, and with a spy glass you read a little word that said, "Yes!"

Yoko Ono: I was never into pop music, and when I met him I didn't know the name John Lennon. He came to a gallery and there was a painting of mine. To see it you had to go up a ladder and hold a magnifying glass to the ceiling to see it. And when you did that it said, "Yes." That was the first piece of mine that he saw. He told me later that he loved it because it was so positive and that at last there was someone who thought like he did. If it had said, "No," then he probably wouldn't have looked at the rest of the show. When we first got together, we were so happy and excited with each other that we just thought, This is so great! It was like Man meets Woman on common ground and East meets West and all the rest. We never thought everyone was going to hate us like they did, but John was a hero to a lot of people and they just didn't want to give him up.

Peter Blake: I met Yoko when she did the show at the Indica Gallery. I knew her as an artist separately from John before they met. She was staying with an artist with whom I once had a show. When she was putting that show on, she asked me, because I taught at the Royal College, if I knew any young students who could help build the exhibition. So I recommended three boys who actually made most of those pieces. They did all the woodwork and actually built them. I knew John separately, and then he went to the exhibition and met Yoko and then I knew them both. John loved exhibitions. He had two exhibitions at the Robert Fraser Gallery.

On November 24, 1966, with their touring career behind them, The Beatles began the next phase of their career. They started work on the song "Strawberry Fields Forever."

George Martin: "Strawberry Fields" came hard on the heels of "Tomorrow Never Knows." We went into the studio just before Christmas and recorded "Strawberry Fields," "When I'm 64," and "Penny

Lane" all around the same time. This was the beginning of the new album, *Sgt. Pepper.* But Brian [Epstein] came and said, "You know we've got to put a single out because it's time for one." I said, "Well, I really want to save these for the album." Brian said, "We're going to have something." So we released "Strawberry Fields" and "Penny Lane" back to back, and therefore *Sgt. Pepper* was bereft of those two. Now, if you listen to those songs in that context, you'll see they do actually fit into the style of *Sgt. Pepper.*

When John first brought me "Strawberry Fields," it was a very gentle song and he sang it beautifully. It was gorgeous. I loved the word imagery, I loved the harmonic changes, and I loved the tune. I thought it was terrific. Then, when we came to record it, it turned out much heavier. Obviously John felt the same way himself, because he came to me a few days afterward and said, "That really isn't quite what I had in mind. Could we do it again?" I said, "To tell you the truth I, too, was disappointed with the way it turned out. How do you want to do it differently?" He said, "I'd like you to score it for me, put some strings and brass on it, and do a different version."

I actually think he was kind of jealous of some of the stuff I'd been doing with Paul. So we did that. We went back into the studio and cut another version and I think I changed the key of that version because I wanted to get the bottom string of the cello. So I moved it up a notch when we recorded it. The second version had a tremendous rhythm track with everybody contributing to it. There must have been about seven or eight people doing things that evening. There was mayhem, but it was great fun.

Again John went away and thought about it. He came back to me and said, "You know, I do like what we've done, but there's some bits in the first one that I think are terrific. Could we keep some of the bits in the first one and some of the bits in the second and put them together?" I said, "The problem is they're in two different keys and they're also in different tempos." He said, "I'm sure you can fix it," and walked away and left me to it.

Well, of course this was a tremendous challenge. But luckily, by speeding one up and slowing the other down, I brought them into line from a key point of view. I actually changed the key and the pitch and it worked! So the final version of "Strawberry Fields" is, in fact, two recordings welded into one with a certain help from the Almighty! If you want to know where the two songs are actually joined, it's exactly one minute in from the beginning. "Strawberry Fields" was unique. I think it broke fresh ground, and without wanting to sound too pretentious, I think it was a new kind of art form.

Peter Halling: The Beatles were always very kind to the musicians. They were very nice chaps. It was all on the same level. Everybody was the same. There was no *Upstairs, Downstairs,* and it was all quite natural. We'd arrive for the session and you could see that The Beatles were very appreciative of the musicians turning up. Sometimes they used to try to set the atmosphere at number two studio. You'd find it rigged up with blue and green lights to try to get us in the mood, I suppose. I remember one distinct night we were called to a ten o'clock session to do just one track, "Strawberry Fields." There was food and drink and, of course, it all became very great fun. We finished at about one o'clock in the morning. Sometimes they wanted to boost up the bottom line, so they would have six to eight cellos doing a certain thing. Sometimes there would be four or five bass flutes to get this very weird sound. They'd try everything. Nowadays things have changed because you've got synthesizers that have taken our jobs.

David Mason: George Martin told me that Paul [McCartney] had seen the television performance where I was playing [Bach's] Second Brandenburg Concerto on a live broadcast from Guildford Cathedral. Paul had seen this and he saw this small trumpet, which is much smaller than the average one, and thought it sounded nice. He thought it could be a gimmick or something new. The Beatles were always looking for new ideas, and he asked George Martin to get me to come along and experiment. None of us knew what we were going to do, and I took along all these trumpets and mostly played that one, the smallest, and said, "Well, do you like this?" Paul said he did like it. Then I asked, "Well, would you like it with a mute in?" He said, "No, I don't want that." He had heard all the usual ones, and this was just something new.

"Penny Lane" was Paul's song. He did the whole thing, even directing me. George [Martin] only wrote it down. I think the reason was because they'd had another classical musician in the previous week and he had wanted an arranging fee, so they were going to make sure they didn't have to pay me an arranging fee. Paul sat at the piano, played his few chords, and sang a bit, then went, *"Dum da digga dum."* He said, "Can you do that?" Then I did it and he said, "No, up a bit. Yes, that's better. That sounds nice. Yes, we'll keep that bit in." Then George wrote it down. We took three hours actually writing it and deciding what they wanted on this record. I think we took 10 minutes to record it. In those days I don't think they had the ability to wipe a take they didn't want to keep. They had two master tapes and I only had two goes at it. Luckily it came off well on both of them. They seemed to be quite happy. But I don't think any of us, George Martin or any of The Beatles, ever realized it was going to be anything particularly outstanding. Otherwise I would have had a royalty payment written into the contract.

I remember that most of the sessions were in the middle of the night — midnight to three in the morning. It was the only time they could get together. As classical musicians, our whole life is oriented to symphonic work, and there is a very big difference between that and pop music. I've done sessions for film with all the big orchestras at Pinewood [Studios] and other studios for the major things, but that's all written out and straightforward film music. I hadn't really done the jazz/pop/commercial side of things until I did "Penny Lane." After that I was asked to go along to all sorts of funny little studios underground somewhere in the middle of the night. I'd turn up and there would be nobody there but a few long-haired musicians who'd say, "Oh, you've come to play the trumpet." I would say, "Where's the music?" They would reply, "We haven't got any music, man. No music." So I would say, "Well, what do you want me to play?" They would hum and haw for a bit and eventually it would come out — "Could you do something like you did for The Beatles?" They had thought that I had made it up on the spur of the moment.

On February 17, 1967, while The Beatles continued recording what would become the *Sgt. Pepper* album, they released the single "Strawberry Fields Forever/Penny Lane."

Murray Kaufman: The biggest perfectionist of them all was Paul McCartney. Brian Epstein told me a story about "Penny Lane." They were ready to go to press that night, or the following day, to start pressing the album. Paul got an idea in the middle of the night and called Brian up at three in the morning and said he just had to make a change on the record. As Brian told it, the change that Paul wanted wouldn't have made one iota of difference in the hit potential of the record, but Paul felt he didn't want that record out unless the change was made. And they allowed him to go in and do it. It was something to do with the instrumental part actually. But he's always been that way. Paul has always been the utter perfectionist.

Geoff Emerick: During the recording of *Sgt. Pepper*, The Beatles were always together. We used to start about four in the afternoon and finish about four in the morning. We did work the hours out and it was roughly 700 hours of recording time, which in those days was a lot. I think that was spread over a period of three or four months. Of course, that's nothing now.

George Martin: I don't know how much work goes into recording Wagner's *Ring*, but recording *Sgt. Pepper* was the most indulgent thing we'd ever done. We were only able to do it because we had been enormously successful and no one at EMI dared to question what we were doing. So, in fact, we went on our own, plowing our own lonely furrow, and it took us about five months altogether. There were times when I wondered whether we were being too self-indulgent and pretentious. But when I started putting it together I thought, No, this really is good and I'm quite sure we've done the right thing. I told myself that if people didn't like it, we'd do something different next time. If people did like it, we'd still do something different. The important thing was that we'd satisfied ourselves. If it had fallen flat on its face, we would have shrugged our shoulders and said, "Well, too bad. Let's have another go." The very first time anybody heard it [*Sgt. Pepper*] they were knocked out by it, and that encouraged me enormously. I thought it was good to have done it. I was quite pleased.

It was Paul who had the concept idea of having a fictional band because he'd happened to write this song, "Sgt. Pepper's Lonely Hearts Club Band," which was really just a little ditty. There was nothing very profound about it. The best thing about it was that the song gave him the idea of making an album with a band within the album. And we all then got enthused with the idea and starting working on it to that end. But it wasn't really until we came to put it together that it crystallized. It was almost as though it were growing by itself and had a life of its own. There was no "grand design." It really wasn't planned. The way the album fell together didn't have any inner meaning. People were looking for it all the time. They were playing it backward and turning it upside down and doing all sorts of things, looking for the clue, the cipher, to this enormous enigma. Well, the great joke was that there wasn't one. Of course, at the time, The Beatles were happily getting stoned occasionally whereas I never touched the stuff. I think if I had been smashed out of my mind all the time that we would have never made such a good album. On the other hand, I think that some of the psychedelic flavors that came through on the album were partly the result of their going into their little dream worlds, which I don't think did any harm.

Julian Lennon: I was at Heath House, a private nursery school in Weybridge, and I was about four years old. One day I painted a picture of my "girlfriend," Lucy O'Donnell. It wasn't very good, all blurry and watery. The top was all dark blue sky with some very rough-looking stars, green grass along the bottom, and Lucy with long golden hair. I showed it to Dad and he said, "What's that then?" I said, "That's Lucy in the sky, you know, with diamonds." He made the song up from that.

George Martin: I suppose it sounds a bit theatrical, but with "Being for the Benefit of Mr. Kite" I knew exactly what I wanted to do. I wanted to make a mush of noise but still with the characteristic of a steam organ-calliope kind of sound. And I didn't want any of the notes to be identifiable. So that was what I did. Geoff Emerick, the engineer, thought I was quite crazy when I got him to cut all the bits up from tapes into 15-inch sections and then fling the pieces into the air at the end and say, "Now put them back together again." He really thought I was mad, but then he saw the sense of it once we did it.

Geoff Emerick: What I remember most about "Being for the Benefit of Mr. Kite" was the brass-band section. Rather than getting a brass band to play a written piece, we just got an old brass-band outtake from something else and snipped it up into pieces. Then we threw them up in the air and rejoined them, hoping they would all make up some weird, different tune. Of course, it came back identical, which was a million-to-one chance. It was quite fun doing that. I remember that overdub because George [Martin] played "Being for the Benefit of Mr. Kite" on the harmonium. George was pumping away at the harmonium while Paul was doing keyboards, and all the percussion parts were done on the same track. Everything was done live. I think we spent about six hours doing that, and eventually George collapsed onto the floor out of sheer exhaustion.

Peter Blake: I didn't hear much of the recording. One night I went over to Paul's house. They'd just done "Lovely Rita," and he played it for me. We were also there when they recorded "Good Morning, Good Morning," and I also sat in on some of George Harrison's recording. We went in one night, and there was a big carpet in the middle of the floor with all the Indian musicians. George was always a real gentleman and very sweet. We hadn't really talked to him much before. The sad thing is that I was concentrating so hard on getting the cover [for *Sgt. Pepper's Lonely Hearts Club Band*] together that I didn't really appreciate it. I mean, I was doing my job and they were doing their job. For instance, I never got their autographs. And although I've got signatures and post-cards and things like that, I was very conscious of not asking them for their autographs because we were professionals working together and you don't do it. But I wish I had.

Geoff Emerick: They brought in the Indian musicians for "Within You, Without You." I can't remember if there was any guitar work or anything, but all the rhythmic Indian stuff was from the Asian musicians. I don't think anyone had ever done anything like that before. I mean, tablas had been around, but you could hear when someone was in front of you or just playing it in the background. There is a certain depth somewhere in that drum. Therefore, normally for classical work, they miked it miles away, but we tried to get inside the drum and get this bottom thing that you could really hear and really contain.

Peter Halling: Once some Indian musicians came to the studio to record the song "Within You, Without You," and I was told, "Look there's no music. Just play whatever you like!" I would just muck about and they would say, "Marvelous, marvelous!" The Beatles were lovely people and great fun to work with. They would make cuts and changes all the time, sort of cutting and pasting as they went along, much like a painting, which was totally different from all other session work that I did. That was how these sessions ran.

We were contracted for three hours, and sometimes the musicians would say, "Look, I can't stay any longer." But The Beatles would say, "Oh, don't worry, you'll be paid." And they would stay for another two or three hours. So you would pick up double money. Some of these musicians were very high-class musicians who tended to look down on this type of music, but I think the experience with The Beatles changed all that.

We were called up constantly, especially when they were doing a "long player." They would get stuck and they would be doing one track for two or three days. One title! It was unheard of. But they were experimenting with all sorts of sound ideas. Anything they would say to you would be intelligent. They would say they wanted to have this certain type of sound. They were most obliging, and when they wanted to know something, you didn't mind showing them what you could do on your instrument. They would say, "That's right, great, we want that." I would put a mute on or take a mute off or play ponticello or something from the catalog of sounds. If somebody said, "No, that's not right. That's not what I want," they would disappear into the booth. Then George Martin would say, "We'll take a break now." He would then scribble some stuff out. You'd come back afterward and they would give you a scrap of paper with five or six bars on it saying, "Insert goes in here."

That was the interesting part till they got what they wanted. When we were finished, they would say, "Thank you very much. Marvelous." And damn it, about a week later we'd be called back to do another thing because the whole piece had been destroyed and they would start again. Many times that happened. They would get a new string section in sometimes if they weren't happy. Sometimes you'd go to the studio and you'd do a first take and they would spend another three hours trying to better it. Eventually they ended up with the first take that was done in the first 10 minutes.

Geoff Emerick: The recording was really open to experimentation and I really wanted to get into the drum and get the depth from it. In those days the way you were taught was to mike things like drums from quite a distance because you'd destroy the mike if you got any closer. So we went completely against that ruling. As far as the great bass sound goes, it really came from Paul [McCartney]. First of all, there was never any DI [direct in] on the bass in those days. It was always a matter of miking the amplifier. That unique sound was all Paul's.

Paul McCartney: I listened to a lot of different bass players — mostly Motown records. They were great and the bass player, who I found out later was James Jamerson, was an influence. So smooth, melodic, and solid. I really liked Marvin Gaye records. And, of course, I've always liked Brian Wilson all the way through The Beach Boys. But *Pet Sounds* blew me away. It's still one of my favorite albums. When I first heard it, I thought, Wow, this is the greatest record of all time! Brian took the bass into very unusual places. The band would play in C, and Brian would stay in G. That kind of thing. It gave me great ideas. That musical invention of Brian Wilson was eye-opening, I mean, ear-opening.

George Martin: One of the best examples of a true collaboration between Paul and John was "A Day in the Life." It was ground-breaking in style. Typical of John, the lyrics were taken from things he'd read all over the place. He would pick up a newspaper cutting and say, "I'll use that." The person who "blew his mind out" in a car crash was a friend of his named Tara Brown. And there's a *Daily Mail* cutting where the mayor of Blackburn, Lancashire, was complaining about the state of the roads and that he'd counted 4,000 holes. John thought that was funny, and so little references like that appeared in the lyrics. Regardless of the origins of the lyrics, the way John sings that song still sends chills through me. The other essential part of the song came from Paul because his is the middle bit, the "Woke up, fell out of bed," and so on. It was from another song that he was working on, but when John came to him and said, "I need help here," Paul contributed this piece. It was also Paul's idea to leave 24 bars of the drum pattern, which we filled in later with an orchestral climax. So it really was one of their strongest collaborations, and I still think it's a marvelous track.

Peter Halling: What they wanted us to do on "A Day in the Life" wasn't unusual for classical musicians. I mean, glissando is nothing. We get glissando in classical music constantly. Stravinsky's *The Firebird,* for example. That's legitimate, lovely stuff. There was nothing funny in going up in semitones. No, that wasn't anything difficult or different. Modern music is full of effects. It was an effect, after all. If the guy is paying for it, and that's what he wants, he's gonna get it, isn't he? Sometimes The Beatles would amend it and say, "I don't like it." Then we would say, "Then try it this way." I've spent three hours experimenting with sounds with those boys. They would bring us into the studios to experiment with textures and new sounds, but now synthesizers do that. Now you can sit there and experiment yourself, but in those days they had to experiment with new sounds with us.

Alan Civil: I remember a little car, a mini car, in which all the windows had been blackened to hide the driver's identity. It kept going back and forth to some hotel where The Beatles had an arrangement with the restaurant, and various sorts of tureens would come along. You would see the most marvelous silver-plate serving dishes. They would open it up and the food was just sausages and beans, real sort of Boy Scout food. Everybody would play their lowest note, say, and go up and up and play higher and higher. And you'd say, "How the hell are they going to use this?" And there was Ringo dashing around with his movie camera. It seemed almost like a party, with booze, fags, and such. It was crazy. You couldn't believe it was a session. A lot of classical musicians didn't really condone this type of session. They thought it was rather beyond, well, beneath their dignity to mess around like that.

Geoff Emerick: Recording "A Day in the Life" in those days was really different. Today we work with 48 tracks on an album. Back then there was no way we could possibly keep two four-track [machines] together in sync. So there wasn't even eight tracks. It was all finished on the four-track. We very rarely bounced down. Maybe if we had to copy guitars and stuff we would do that. But all the finished masters are just four tracks. There are no eight tracks or anything. In fact, *Sgt. Pepper* wasn't even monitored in stereo. Stereo took a long time to establish itself in England. The best copy of *Sgt. Pepper* is the mono version, because we spent three weeks mixing that and the stereo we mixed in only two and a half days. Nobody realizes that all the actual effort went into the mono mix because we never monitored in stereo. It was all from one speaker. That's how we all heard it.

On June 1, 1967, The Beatles officially released the album *Sgt. Pepper's Lonely Hearts Club Band.*

Peter Blake: The Beatles were well into the music for *Sgt. Pepper* and they were friends with Robert Fraser, who was a seminal figure in that whole art scene. He was a gallery owner and I was with his gallery. They actually had a cover prepared by Simon Mariaka of The Fool [graphic artists]. Knowing their work, it was probably a psychedelic, Jimi Hendrix kind of cover. Robert said, "Look, in 10 years' time this is going to be just another psychedelic cover. Why don't we ask a fine artist, you know, a real artist to do a cover?" They had tended to do that already. They'd used Bob Freeman. They'd used Klaus Voorman. So Robert talked to me and asked if I'd be interested. Of course, I was very interested. We had a meeting with Robert, myself, all The Beatles, and Brian Epstein and we talked about what was possible.

By that time The Beatles had invented the concept of a band within a band, and the concept of a concert with an overture and then into a concert and then a reprise at the end. There was this Sgt. Pepper and a sort of German marching band. They also had the idea of the uniforms. I wouldn't be surprised if they had designed them themselves, because they were all quite individual.

So we talked about the idea of a concert in a bandstand, in a park, and then it slowly evolved that maybe there could be a crowd around the park. I said, "If we're having a crowd, how about working with a collage technique and make a giant collage? By making cutout figures, we could have a magic crowd of really anybody you want. I mean, anyone in the whole world, dead or alive or mythical or whatever you want, we could do."

So this evolved as an idea and we asked each Beatle to make a list of the people he would like in this magic crowd. Robert and I also made lists. That was typical and amusing because Paul's list was a long list and quite complete. John's was a very long, good list, and George gave us a list of about six different gurus. Ringo just said, "Whatever the others have is fine by me. I won't put anyone in." I don't think he actually gave us a list at all. From [all these lists] we made a working list of people and put all the photographs and references together. Then we had life-size blowups made and cut out. A lot of the credit for it must go to Jann Haworth, who I was married to at the time. She did most of the actual physical work.

When we had all the cutouts done, we built it against one wall of the studio. It had to actually be constructed, taking into consideration the camera angles. It had to be a great deal wider at the back than it was at the front to make it appear straight. We then decided that The Beatles would stand with the crowd behind them, with some kind of municipal flower arrangement in front. We did the flowers and got that all arranged. The Beatles were recording that day and really couldn't come in. So all these flowers, which we had to keep alive, had to be held for two more days. All the hyacinths, which were about ready to bloom, had to be slowed down. Eventually The Beatles came around and we got the shot.

When the photograph was done, EMI kind of panicked. They suddenly thought, Well, you know, we could be sued or we could be in trouble. So they wrote to everybody to get permission to use their photographs, and somewhere there must be a big file of letters they wrote. One of the stories is that they wrote to Mae West, who wrote back and said, "What would I be doing in a lonely hearts club band, boys? You know what I mean? You can't do this to me." So then The Beatles all wrote back a personal letter saying, "You know we love you, Mae, and we'd love to have you in the picture. She wrote back and said okay.

I had put Leo Gorcey and Huntz Hall, the Bowery Boys, on my list. Leo Gorcey wrote back and said, "Yeah, you can put me on, but I'd like a fee." But EMI wouldn't pay it, which I think they should have done. So Gorcey just came out and there's a gap now. There's a gap and then Huntz Hall.

John had put Hitler and Jesus on his list. It was generally agreed that it was just too controversial to put them in. But they're there. They're actually behind the four Beatles. They're in the group, but at the last moment it was decided it was too much. So The Beatles are standing in front of them and you can't see them. That was John's sense of humor. There had been the "Christ" controversy by then, so I think it was John just being naughty again.

It was probably The Beatles' idea to have the lyrics printed, so it was designed by the graphic designer. We also wanted to do an inside sheet. What we were trying to work out for that — and again everyone contributed ideas — was a packet. A sort of transparent packet with lots of presents, like a badge and sergeant stripes and all kinds of things. But it just wasn't practical. We already had a double-fold album, which was one of the first double-fold albums, if not the first. But having got that through EMI, they weren't going to accept the bulky package, as well. It was a packaging problem, you know. We had to abandon that since time was running out. So all those ideas were squeezed together on this sheet of cutouts, which was my idea. The point was that you cut them out and stuffed them into your clothes.

Murray Kaufman: When Brian Epstein came on my show and heard WOR-FM for the first time, he flipped out because it was something new as radio. He'd never heard radio like that. He brought me over an advance copy of *Sgt. Pepper*, which no one in the world had heard, and let me hear it. Listening to "A Day in the

Life" was a trip in itself. It was unreal. My favorite song, and the one that made me realize they had the pulse of the country, was a song that never was a hit in itself. Still, it said to me that The Beatles were completely in tune with life. That song was "She's Leaving Home." The lines in that song about parents giving their daughter everything money can buy really knocked me out.

What we'd heard growing in *Rubber Soul* and *Revolver* had blossomed into full maturity. They were beginning to learn their instruments. They were becoming better musicians. It's like a ballplayer all of a sudden getting experience and people saying, "Gee, you know, this kid's going to make the team." It was also the time that Lennon and McCartney weren't writing together very much anymore. Lennon would write songs that he would do lead on, as would McCartney, even though both of their names appeared on the credits. "A Day in the Life" happened to be two different songs. John had written a song and Paul had written a song and it just so happened by putting them together it came out to be a hell of a song, but they never wrote it in concert. That's when the dichotomy really started, just around the *Sgt. Pepper* time. Also, George Harrison started to become a little upset that he wasn't getting enough of his music in there.

Red Robinson: When The Beatles initially got under way with their records, Top 40 radio was Top 40 radio. It's the things they did subsequent to what I call the bubble-gum years with "She Loves You," "I Want to Hold Your Hand," and the moptops. The next stage was with *Revolver* and *Sgt. Pepper*. Happening in tandem with all of this were the things going on with the antiwar movement in the States and with Haight-Ashbury. It was as if these two separate philosophies melded, and The Beatles were at the forefront because they were experimenting with different sounds and different ways of doing things with George Martin. So that was the second renaissance of rock and roll, and out of it came varieties of things. Interestingly Paul McCartney told me in an interview that his whole inspiration for *Sgt. Pepper* was *Pet Sounds* from the Beach Boys. He thought "Good Vibrations" was the [best thing] he'd ever heard. I tend to agree with him on that point. So they went on with new sounds. It changed radio after that. The subculture was now where it was all coming from — and this new thing called FM radio where they could talk forever and play 10-minute cuts. It was albums like *Sgt. Pepper* and what came after it that gave FM its start.

Roger McGuinn: After *Sgt. Pepper* they didn't need to perform. I think that what happened was they got so sophisticated that they really couldn't reproduce their albums on stage anymore, you know, without hiring a full orchestra. And some of the effects were difficult to get. Nowadays, with all the electronics, the state of the art is a lot more together than it was then.

James Taylor: The *Sgt. Pepper* album had a huge impact on me. I clearly remember bringing it home and saying, "Oh, wow, look at this!" I checked out the cover, read all the lyrics through, and listened to it over and over. I liked "She's Leaving Home" and I loved "With a Little Help from My Friends." Wow! Unbelievably great coming after *Revolver* and *Rubber Soul.* Those were such amazingly great albums. Later I was signed to Apple and was actually there, but I never sat down and talked much with either John Lennon or Paul McCartney about their records. They were pretty well occupied in those days.

George Martin: I think the strain of fame and touring had taken its toll. The Beatles were going through a period when they secretly wanted not to be famous and they wanted to be ordinary people again. This could be a psychological reason why the record *Sgt. Pepper* existed in the first place because the boys were referring to some other entity, something quite separate from them. It was as if other people were doing the record and not themselves. When we got into recording songs like "Strawberry Fields" and "Sgt. Pepper," I think we were actually creating what amounted to tone poems. I mean, it sounds a bit pretentious to say you're doing that, but I did really feel I was. In the same way that Ravel would use the resources of a symphony orchestra to create marvelous paintings in sound, so we had different resources.

We didn't have a symphony orchestra. We could have, I suppose, but I don't suppose we would have done it half as well as Ravel did. But we had other means. We had electronic means and we had various tricks in the studio. We had the ability to do almost anything. I mean, not just in terms of money but in terms of risk. If we felt at that time it was right to break a milk bottle over a cast-iron desk, record that sound, and multiply it, then we would have done it. We had no restrictions on our imagination. We did all sorts of things. We rarely stuck to the same sound. So we would always have different drum sounds and we'd have a different bass sound. We were always trying different things, and that's why you'd get a varying quality. Some people would say, "I think the drums on that track are better than the drums on this." Well, it's just a question of taste. We were trying different things. It seemed to have a life of its own, to be honest. I mean, I was talking to Paul recently. *Sgt. Pepper* is still a watershed for him, as well as for me.

Chapter Nine

Revolution,
Evolution,
and
Apple Corps

On June 19, 1967, Paul told *Life* magazine that he had taken the hallucinatory drug LSD.

Paul McCartney: I don't regret that I've spoken up. It happened because some newspaperman came up to me and said, "Hey, did you take LSD?" So I thought that I could be cagey or maybe a little evasive or I could tell the truth and give an honest answer. I said yes. And then it was blown up [out of proportion] as usual. I mean, I just spoke the truth, and it's sometimes painful. I know I've done wrong, Mom!

Billy Graham: I am praying for Paul [McCartney] that he finds what he is looking for. He has reached the top of his profession and now he is searching for the true purpose of life. I wish him well.

On June 25, 1967, The Beatles performed "All You Need Is Love" for a worldwide television audience. It was released as a single on July 7.

George Martin: We were asked to represent England in a live global broadcast called *Our World,* the estimated viewing audience of which was something in the order of 350 million people. In those days, remember, television, particularly in Britain, wasn't a really big thing. Not every home had one. So to think that we'd be seen by 350 million people was really quite staggering. The boys had to come up with a song, and I think Paul was working on "Hello, Goodbye," which wasn't accepted, and John had written "All You Need Is Love," which seemed to fit with the overall concept of the program. Now, since it was a live broadcast, I said, "We must do some preparation for this. We can't just go on in front of 350 million people without some work." So we laid down a track on the four-track machine that The Beatles would play live to during the broadcast.

I must also mention that the week just before the broadcast was an absolutely horrendous one for me. I was moving house that week. My wife was pregnant with our first daughter and, two days before the broadcast, my father died. It really was a horrendous week, and added to that there were cameras and crews running through the control room pointing at me and Geoff Emerick as we prepared for this live show in front of the whole world. Then, about 45 seconds before the red light went on in front of 350 million people, the phone rang in my control room. It was the producer of the show in the van outside saying, "George, I've lost all contact with the studio. We're about to go on, so you'll have to relay instructions if I get into any problems." Well, at that point all I could do was laugh. I said, "If you're going to make a fool of yourself, this is the way to do it — in front of 350 million people." And, in a curious way, that calmed my nerves. Of course, the boys performed beautifully and it was a very successful television show and a very successful recording, too. I'll never forget it.

Geoff Emerick: Everyone was partying when we were setting up the orchestra. Mick Jagger, Marianne Faithfull, and many others were there. The orchestra members were shocked. They didn't know what was going on. First of all, they were asked to wear evening dress, which was unheard of for a recording session, and then there were various funny party novelties floating around. There were all sorts of funny hats and the like. It was really weird.

David Mason: That was the occasion with Mick Jagger and The Rolling Stones. They came along with all their friends. They had all this confetti and balloons, and all this noise going on. We were getting quite annoyed. I played bits out of the Second Brandenburg Concerto and my colleague was playing the flugelhorn for something else. The saxophone player played "In the Mood." They just kept repeating it back and it really got out of hand. I believe there was a big party afterward, but we didn't stay. Obviously we weren't invited.

On August 24, 1967, The Beatles met the Maharishi Mahesh Yogi at one of his lectures at London's Hilton Hotel. They followed him to Bangor, Wales, by train the next day.

Maharishi Mahesh Yogi: I teach a simple system of transcendental meditation that gives people the insight into life to begin enjoying all peace and happiness. Because this has been the message of all the sages in the past, they call me saint.

Reporter: You seem to have caught the imagination of the pop stars in this country.

Maharishi: What is this "pop stars"?

Reporter: People who sing with guitars. Have you anything to say about that?

Maharishi: You mean The Beatles? I found them to be very intelligent and sensitive individuals.

Murray Kaufman: The Beatles met the Maharishi [Mahesh Yogi] and initially fell under his spell. Eventually John [Lennon] put it the best way when he wrote the song "God." He said, "I don't believe in Beatles and all the other things." And he says there is no guru. There isn't anyone. You believe in yourself and you believe in what you believe in. But George definitely is a believer. He went to India supposedly for two weeks and he stayed three months. He is a believer in their philosophy.

On August 27, 1967, Brian Epstein was found dead of an apparent accidental drug overdose at his home in London. The news of his death broke up The Beatles' gathering with the Maharishi in Wales.

John Lennon: We don't know what to say. We loved him and he was one of us. So you can't —

George Harrison: You can't pay tribute in words.

Reporter: Did the Maharishi give any words of comfort?

John Lennon: Yes, his meditation gives us confidence enough to withstand something like this. Even in the short amount of time we've had.

Clive Epstein: Even in the last year of Brian's life they were beginning to go their separate ways. I mean, The Beatles stopped touring in August 1966, and a lot of Brian's functions had always been connected with their live performances, their films, and their touring. I should think that in the last nine months of his life he had felt to some extent that he wasn't required to provide the management as he had earlier. And what would have happened had Brian lived? I can't say. The only thing I do know is after he died obviously The Beatles wanted to develop in their separate and individual ways.

George Harrison: I can't imagine where we would be if Brian hadn't died because it's impossible to imagine. But because he died we suddenly had to find out and be responsible for ourselves, which we were, anyway. The business side of things was abstract then because we always imagined, "Well, Brian does that and every-thing is fine." Even when it wasn't fine. But with nobody being there, it was directly up to us to work out what we had to do with ourselves.

Alistair Taylor: When Brian died, Clive [Brian's brother] asked me to stay on as general manager and obviously I said yes. It was a very sick scene at NEMS, however, because Clive had no direct connection with the company. He was a director of NEMS, but he didn't bother at all with the day-to-day running of it. And we had all the infighting of people like Victor Lewis and Robert Stig-wood, who were trying to grab what they could. I was very unhappy and the boys spotted this. John Lennon said, "Okay, come on over to Apple and be our general manager." I'd helped to set up Apple in the first place. Before Brian died we were setting up the company that became Apple. So I moved out of NEMS and took over as GM of Apple until 1969 when Allen Klein appeared on the scene.

In the beginning it was stimulating. It was fun, but it was also difficult. They were all happy memories. The memories of diffi-culties and problems are there, but here we were working for four of the most fascinating people the world's ever known. It was the biggest phenomenon that has ever happened, and if anybody didn't find that stimulating and fun, they needed their head [examined]. It was great. It was difficult, though, and I made myself quite ill through it. I got glandular fever because I kept canceling holidays. I never took holidays and was working almost 24 hours a day, sometimes for seven days. Literally going in with the milk, as we say in England. Showering, putting on a fresh suit, and going back to the office.

It was exhausting, but it was fantastic. I wouldn't have missed it. I wouldn't go back to it now for all the tea in China, but the times I did have were nothing but happy, exciting memories. Nevertheless, I made one big mistake. I should have walked out of the business the day Brian died, because it was never quite the same. Brian and I had this very strange relationship. There were people a lot closer, in many ways, to him. It was a very strange kind of respect we had for each other, and we had an understanding. Let's not mess about. Brian was a homosexual. I am not, but I loved that man like I loved my father.

Sometime after Brian died there were rumors that he'd been murdered. That was absolute rubbish. Philip Norman, who as a journalist I greatly respect, may have had a lot to do with those rumors. He had a year off when the *Sunday Times* were on strike and he said, "How do I fill in a year and make some money?" He wrote the book *Shout!* In the back of the book there was a credit to a guy called John Fielding. John Fielding was a top member of the Insight Team on the *Sunday Times*. It's probably the finest investigative journalist team in the world, and I did hours and hours of interviews with John Fielding about Apple. He spoke to lots of other people, as well. Philip Norman had access to all this John Fielding material from the Insight Team. The Insight Team was going to do an exposé on The Beatles and on Apple. And their solicitors put the knockers on it. They said, "No way, no way," and it was shelved until Philip Norman got all that information. But where he gets this idea about Brian being done away with and others he said had been murdered — it's great fiction.

Billy J. Kramer: I thought that Brian was a very sensitive person. Deep down he was also a very generous person. All I know is that Brian was very good to me, regardless of the fact that he was a homosexual. As far as I'm concerned, it takes all sorts to make this world go round. For a long time I was not even aware that Brian was gay. He never came across that way. To me he was very thoughtful. He used to send my family birthday and Christmas cards. These things are never mentioned. He took care of me when my mother died, for instance, and he always dropped in to see my dad and took him out for meals and drinks.

Dezo Hoffman: Brian was a lucky boy. He came from an entirely different background from the boys and he was a terribly frustrated actor. He wanted to be an actor, but he never made it. I could tell you stories, but I don't want to go into it things like that because the poor boy is not with us anymore. On top of that, he got lots of credit that he didn't deserve because the boys really did everything for themselves. They didn't need professional managers or press officials. They needed to keep away the people. They needed more police. They needed Brian because they couldn't sell themselves, so they needed a man to front them. But let's just say he didn't know how much to charge for a gig and sometimes they worked for nothing. They already had a number-one single and they still worked for 100 pounds a week!

George Harrison: Yeah, it's like it's karma. My karma. It's like saying, "Oh, Brian Epstein did die and we did go to America and we did get Apple." It's like everywhere you go you've got a number of choices. You can say there's a crossroads and you can go left or you can go right, but if you just follow yourself, your natural instinct, you don't have to decide really which one you want to go down. You naturally go down one of them, and it's like that all the time.

On September 11, 1967, The Beatles boarded a bus and began filming *Magical Mystery Tour.*

Spencer Davis: Nineteen sixty-seven was an incredibly busy year for the Spencer Davis Group. The parents of one of our road managers owned a pub in Cornwall. When we had a break, we would all go down there and stay. So off I took the Mrs. and the two offspring, jumped in the mini, and raced down there to grab a couple of days' rest. Anyway, I was watching the news and an item came on that said The Beatles were on a bus on the way to the West Country. They were going over a narrow bridge and the bus didn't quite make it, so they got stuck. I made a few discreet inquires and found out they were going to the Atlantic Hotel, which was in Devon. I called the hotel and got Mal Evans [The Beatles' personal assistant]. I said, "What's going on?" He said, "We're having a magical mystery tour, and Paul and the boys would like you to bring the family and come on over." So I went over and they were busy filming away, and if you look on the back of the *Magical Mystery Tour* album cover, you can see John in the back and I'm with him and Paul. My wife is sitting with George Harrison, with Lisa, my youngest daughter, on her lap. So we ended up on the cover, and I got some wonderful outtakes of those photos where my other daughter, Sara, is misbehaving herself and Paul McCartney is giving her a real dirty look.

On December 7, 1967, The Beatles opened the Apple Boutique at 94 Baker Street in London. On December 8, the EP *Magical Mystery Tour* was released. One song, "I Am the Walrus," written by John Lennon, created a stir due to its strange lyrics and sounds.

John Lennon: I got the idea for the song "I Am the Walrus," which developed very subconsciously as I kept hearing police sirens in the middle of the night at my Weybridge home and their sound fascinated me. It was so hypnotic, you know, *dee doo dee doo dee dooo* fading in and getting loud and then fading away again. In the studio we began with electric piano and Ringo's drums. Paul put down his bass line separately and then all the session musicians came in to put their parts on and we did a lot of mixing and such. And finally the voices were added.

Iain Taylor: The idea of taking a word and playing with it is very much a Liverpool tradition, and I think it comes from the Irish and Welsh oral culture. You use words in creative ways. There was a lot of that in Liverpool and a lot of Liverpool comedians used it. In John Lennon's "I Am the Walrus" there are Liverpool folk rhymes imbedded throughout it. Nobody, to my knowledge, has ever been able to discern it. One of the lines that appears in the song was taken from one of those schoolboy doggerels to try to make your friends sick: "Yellow matter custard, green snot pie, dripping from a dead dog's eye, spread it on a butty nice and thick, then wash it down with a cold cup of sick." John fragmented and built it into that particular song, which is a dreamy, surrealistic kind of pastiche.

On December 26, 1967, the BBC broadcast the film *Magical Mystery Tour.* Unfortunately, though it was shot in color, it aired in black-and-white.

Victor Spinetti: *Magical Mystery Tour* was ahead of its time. It should be taught in colleges and universities. The Beatles wrote it and directed it themselves. The critics hated it, but all The Beatles were saying was "If you look to the left, that's fine, but if you look to the right, you'll see the sunset and the trees and the waterfalls." The message was to celebrate the fact that you were alive. They were saying that we were all born to go on a journey, so look, learn, laugh, sing, and love. That's what the movie is about. It says that we aren't magical, but that *everybody* is magical.

In February and March, 1968, George Harrison and John Lennon enjoyed time with the Maharishi in India. While The Beatles were away, EMI released the single "Lady Madonna/The Inner Light." Paul only spent a month in India and Ringo only 10 days, even though he took a large consignment of baked beans. On their return to London's Heathrow Airport, Paul and Jane Asher were confronted by reporters.

Reporter: What is transcendental meditation?
Paul McCartney: You sit down, you relax, and then you repeat a sound

to yourself. It sounds daft, but it's just a system of relaxation. That's all it is. There's nothing more to it. We meditated for about five hours a day in all. That was two hours in the morning and maybe three hours in the evening. And then the rest of the time we slept, ate, sunbathed, and had fun.

Reporter: One Indian MP accused this place of being an espionage center and you, in fact, of being a spy for the West. Well, what happened?

Paul: Don't tell anyone. It's true. We're spies, yes. The four of us have been spies. Actually I'm a reporter and I joined The Beatles for that very reason, but the story's out next week in a paper that will be nameless.

Reporter: Jane, did you go for a holiday, or did you go to meditate, as well?

Jane Asher: Oh, to meditate, yes.

Reporter: And what effect has it had on you? This presumably is your first big meditation?

Jane: Mmm. It . . . I think it calms you down. It's hard to tell because it was so different, life out there, but it would be easy to tell now that I'm back and we're doing ordinary things.

Two and a half weeks later, John Lennon and George Harrison returned to London from India.

Reporter: John, do you think the Maharishi is on the level?

John Lennon: I don't know what level he's on.

George Harrison: He's on the level.

John: But we had a nice holiday in India and came back rested to play businessman.

Donovan Leitch: From my point of view we were all speaking about peace and love. When we met the Maharishi, we thought, Here's the man who's going to tell us something. McCartney said the same thing and I think Lennon said the same thing — "We're going to go over and he's going to tell us how to really lay this peace on the earth because we know this man is advanced." It's true to say all yogis are very advanced. They've studied. If we dropped acid, we couldn't go to one fraction of the depth that you could go with meditation. We understood this and that there was a great philosophy in yoga and that the Christian faith in the West wasn't supplying it. We were looking for this guy to tell us something. Maybe he was a god or an angel. But he was a man, and that was great. The main thing with the Maharishi for me was that he laughed. He said he was going to turn on the business world. We realized that we were also turning the Maharishi on. It was two ways. The press were outside. The Beatles, one Beach Boy, me, and Paul Horn, we were on the inside. The Maharishi taught us how to meditate.

Funny story. In the Maharishi's bungalow there were four Beatles, a Donovan, a Beach Boy, Mia Farrow, and embarrassed silence. John Lennon, the wit of the 1960s, goes up to the Maharishi, pats him on the head, and says, "There's a good guru. You know, behave yourself." And that was the dialogue. We weren't going there to learn something so much as share something with this man. And the message that was beamed out across the world was peace and love and meditation. Very essential. So my experience was very positive. I wrote some marvelous songs there. So did The Beatles. They got the *White Album* and all that.

On May 4, 1968, Paul McCartney saw Mary Hopkin on a talent-spotting television show.

Paul McCartney: I phoned Mary Hopkin and she came down and I listened to her sing in the recording studio. She was sensational, so I decided to record her. I had heard "Those Were the Days" about two years earlier when I was out at a nightclub feasting on steak and lettuce. These two people came on and they sang this song. I think I was there about two nights that weekend. I heard the song twice, and it was one of those things I couldn't get out of my head. So I started playing it on my guitar. I always thought, you know, that it would be a hit song. But no one ever did it. I tried to get The Moody Blues to do it. They nearly did it, but it never worked out for them. It's better that they didn't actually because Graham Edge was saying to me the other day that if they had done it, they wouldn't have been into this thing they're into now. They would have had a mammoth hit and been pop stars all over again. So I recorded Mary Hopkin and she had the hit with it.

Mary Hopkin: I was on a television show called *Opportunity Knocks* when I was 18. It was sort of a national talent contest. After the first appearance, I was contacted by Peter Brown of Apple Records. At the time I had never heard of Apple. The only thing I'd heard of was the Apple shop in London. After the call, I didn't think much of it, but Peter rang back again and I found out that it was Paul McCartney who wanted me to come to London. I was totally shocked. Anyway, I went up to London and Paul asked if I was interested in signing with Apple. He showed me "Those Were the Days," which was a song he'd had around for a few years. He had played it to various people, but hadn't found anyone to record it. So he thought I was suitable. About two months later we recorded and released it, and it all happened from there.

On May 30, 1968, The Beatles began recording what would become *The Beatles* album, popularly known as the *White Album*. On July 17, the animated feature film *Yellow Submarine* was premiered in London.

Paul McCartney: The only thing that's a pity about *Yellow Submarine* is that we couldn't be part of its production because we were very busy with other things and therefore the producers couldn't use our voices on it. We did try to do it later, but it's impossible to record the voices after the drawings are completed. It's especially difficult with cartoons. So that's the only disappointing part from our perspective, but it's still a great film. We really can't take any credit for the making of *Yellow Submarine* because we didn't make it! It's a film, a cartoon, about us, so it's like saying the seven dwarfs made *Snow White* by Walt Disney, but Walt Disney made it really.

Tom Halley: King Features came along with the script for *Yellow Submarine,* and that came after two TV series of The Beatles that were produced at TV Cartoons in London. George Dunning's input here, I think, was responsible for the look of *Yellow Submarine* because he's quite a genius. The creative look of it, I'm sure, is inspired as much by the music as by the individuals, those of us who developed the characters and laid out the particular situations. I think *Yellow Submarine* is unique. I think there have been pretenders and copiers who have failed miserably because they don't understand the philosophy of the design, the graphic qualities, and certainly they wouldn't have that superb sense of color. I think *Yellow Submarine* will always be unique for its time. And the genius of it is that The Beatles' music was both a catalyst for what happened but also linked the whole film together.

    The design is almost two-dimensional. When I was animating some of the Meanies stuff, it had a more three-dimensional feeling to it and the Meanies were fun to animate. They were real Meanies. The Beatles were somewhat different. They had to be very accurate, certainly, with some of the faces. It was quite difficult to get the look of Paul. George was much easier. He had good, strong cheekbones. You could get hold of him. And John, with the glasses and that, was reasonably easy. Ringo wasn't too difficult to get. But the film was made in a year and, all things considered, it was successful. It reflects points of truth about people and society. That's one part of it. Also people identify with The Beatles' music. An audience looking at the film will immediately [understand] the Blue Meanies, you know, the heavy landlords, the heavy politicians, the lawmakers, and all that sort of thing. People seem to cheer when they're defeated.

Reporter: Did you write a lot of music while you were in India?
Paul McCartney: We're recording all that now. We've just gone into the

studios and we're recording the material that we wrote in India. I think it will take a couple of months to complete all the recordings.

Reporter: Are you concerned about being seen now as businessmen because of Apple?

Paul: It doesn't bother me how people see us. It really matters to all of us what we really are. It matters to me personally what I am, and I don't feel at all like a businessman. I also don't feel like a performer anymore because I haven't performed for so long. I feel more like a recording artist these days.

Reporter: Are you being deluged with new artists at Apple?

Paul: Well, we are trying now to avoid doing too much of that because it means that every bum on the road who asks for a shilling gets it. But there are some people who want to do something special where they need a bit of money. Obviously if we're running a company that involves money, you can't just give all the time.

On August 22, 1968, while The Beatles worked on the *White Album,* Cynthia Lennon filed for divorce from John Lennon. On August 26 EMI released the single "Hey Jude/Revolution."

George Martin: There were a lot of influences at that time. The Beatles were getting further and further apart, anyway. They were writing and recording their own songs. I was recording not a band of four, but three fellows who had three accompanists each time. George would do his own thing and the others would join in, a little more reluctantly than they used to. And Paul would do his own thing and sometimes John wouldn't turn up. I remember on "Ob-La-Di, Ob-La-Da," for example, Paul came along with this kind of ska thing and John actually wasn't in the studio. We got the thing more or less together, but we were having a bit of difficulty with it. Then John came in, slightly stoned, and said, "What's this rubbish you're doing?" He went over to the barrelhouse piano and said, "Right then. Here we go. One, two, three, four, *da da da da da dum dum dum.*" It was a corny introduction, but it worked. We said, "Great, okay," and enjoyed it from then on. But that was the kind of incident that would happen when they weren't working terribly close together. In the *White Album* this became more and more obvious. Paul's "Blackbird" was almost entirely his and the others hardly turned up on it.

George Harrison: I wrote "While My Guitar Gently Weeps" at my mother's house in the north of England. I had my guitar and I wanted to write a song. I do this often, actually. If I haven't particularly got an idea for a song, then I believe it's a bit like the *I Ching,* where everything at that moment is relative to that situation. So "While My Guitar Gently Weeps" was typical of that. I opened a book that was around, and the first thing I looked at became the song. It was something about "gently weeps." Then from that the whole thought started going and I wrote the song. Eric Clapton played guitar on it. Lots of people don't realize that. Some people wrote letters to me saying, "You've got a really good blues feel with that guitar." We didn't publicize it, but we didn't, like, keep it a secret. Eric's a good friend of mine, and I really dig him as a guitarist and as a guy.

Chris Thomas: George Martin said, "I'm going on holiday. You take over The Beatles for a little while." So, of course, I was very nervous. But I didn't really think I was there to produce The Beatles, because I didn't really have any experience at producing. George just said, "Go down there and make yourself available." The Beatles had done 10 songs in the previous three months, and we did 10 songs in those next three weeks. So, when George came back, he was quite pleased that things were moving along. I was surprised at just how good The Beatles were playing in the studio. Considering the fact that they weren't doing any gigs, you'd imagine they'd be a bit rusty and that everything was just sort of pieced together but, no, they were great! The Beatles were a very, very good band. And they were a very funny band, as well. I had some really funny times with them.

Every night they used to have a meeting. They were running

Apple, so they'd arrive from home and go straight to the studio. Then, at one point in the day, they had to discuss business matters as well as everything else. They recorded as a band. I hadn't worked with them before, so I couldn't really tell, but I got the impression that everybody else was like the backing man. They'd all play together on the backing track. It was the four of them playing live definitely. Paul wouldn't play bass necessarily. He'd probably play the instrument he wrote the song on. He might play piano or guitar again and put the bass on later. So it was a band in that way, except they didn't play together on "Blackbird," for example.

We were doing George's song "Piggies," and I was wandering around the studio looking for any weird instruments hanging around from a classical session. Sometimes you'd find old things and you'd use them on the record. You might get an idea for it. I saw the harpsichord, which was actually set up in number one, the big classical studio. I said, "Why don't we use the harpsichord?" So we went into number one and started playing around on it and George actually played me "Something" that night. I said, "That's great! We should be working on that." He said, "Do you really think it's good?" I said, "Yeah." Then he said, "Well, maybe I'll give it to Jackie Lomax." I really wanted us to do "Something" that night but, of course, it was left for about a year or so till the next album. We did "Piggies" instead.

I said to Paul one Monday, after things had been going quite well, "*The Girl Can't Help It* is on TV Wednesday night and I've never seen it." He said, "Really? Oh, great. Maybe we should go and see it. We can all go around to my place and watch it." He came that Wednesday for the song, which was actually "Birthday." Everybody rolled up at about 5:00 p.m. I think we got the backing track down by about half past eight, when it was time to whiz around to watch the film. We watched the film, came back, did the vocal on "Birthday," and finished it off. We did the whole thing in 12 hours, plus watching the telly.

I remember doing the backing track for "Happiness Is a

Warm Gun," which took a long time. I remember they did over 100 takes of it, all the way through to two or three in the morning. Then they came back the next day and went all the way through again. But that wasn't unusual for them. I think George Martin had found an advertisement in a magazine that said "Happiness is a warm gun," because we were talking about it at the time. When the *White Album* was started, it was just when Robert Kennedy was shot. George Martin mentioned the ad to John, and shortly after the song came along.

With "Revolution 9," The Beatles said, "We're about to do a sort of collage or montage of a few things." They went up to the library at EMI and found loads of old tapes. They just nicked anything, like Cliff Bennett and the Rebel Rousers, Oxford and Cambridge music tests for A levels. Loads of things. They took everything down there and made copies of the bits they wanted. Sometimes they played them backward. Sometimes they chopped a little bit out. They literally did anything they liked with the bits of tape. Then they assembled some really good-sounding loops. One of the ones they "bunged" on was this Oxford music exam. A guy was playing the piano and said, "Number 9," then he played another bit. Obviously you had to identify the bits that you knew. That's where "Number 9" came from, and there's no significance in it.

John Lennon: "Revolution 9" was to me like a sound picture, more an abstract sound picture, a montage of feelings in sound. It was really an unconscious vision of what happens, or what I think happens, when it happens. It was just like sketching a revolution in sound. I had about 30 or 40 tape loops going like we did with "Tomorrow Never Knows," and we fed them on to one track of the tape machine. That ominous voice repeating "Number 9, Number 9" was one of these loops. It was some kind of an EMI test tape that I found in the library. I would cut up classical music tapes, all sorts of things from upstairs. We would make copies of the masters and chop them up into these loops and things. The others started losing interest in doing it, so that's why I'm cred-ited with it. There are many symbolic messages going on in it, but it just happened. You know, cosmic meandering.

Chris Thomas: The Beatles had been trying to do "Helter Skelter" before actually. They were doing it much slower and it didn't quite work out. When we were sequencing the album right at the end, Paul decided that it had to be mixed again. I was listening to running orders with John while Paul was in there remixing the song with Ken Scott as engineer. Ken came in and said, "Paul's gone to sleep. You've got to come and help me." And when we did the mix, we faded out and just faded it back up again and sort of left it. Then we said, "Yeah, it's all right. That goes on." That's all it was. There was no hidden meaning.

On November 22, 1968, The Beatles released the *White Album*.

George Martin: I must say, by the way, about the *White Album,* that I struggled very hard to make that a single album because I thought there was an awful lot of excess material in there. It should have been pruned down. I lost my battle and I didn't realize until afterward why I lost it. It was because the contract, which I didn't know about, when they re-signed with EMI, gave them an expiry time that was dependent on months and years of time but also dependent on the number of titles. By recording and issuing as many titles as they did, they cleared the way for a new contract in which they could have higher fees. I didn't know that at the time.

George Harrison: I think, in a way, it was a mistake doing four sides [for the *White Album*] because, first of all, it's too big for people to really get into, both for reviewers and also the public. People who've bought the album have their own favorites, but there's a couple of things we could have done without on the album. Maybe we could have made it a compact 14 songs. "Revolution 9" was all right, but it wasn't particularly like Beatle music. Then again it has good points because "Revolution 9" worked very well in the context of all those different songs. That was the great thing about it. But if people spend enough time listening to it, there were all different types of music and songs and there was nothing really shocking about it. I don't think there was anything particularly poor about it. But it was a bit heavy. I find it heavy to listen to myself. I listen mainly to side 1, which I like very much, with "Glass Onion" and . . . "Happiness Is a Warm Gun."

Paul McCartney: There may be some sort of correlation between the speed of making the record and how good it is. I think there is some sort of secret in not having too long to think. I mean, we humans rely a lot on thinking, whereas animals don't. They just kind of go to it. And I think when we humans get spontaneous and don't think about it, like a boxer who doesn't look at too many tapes or an actor who doesn't look at his rushes all the time, I think it applies also to recording. Now you can sit around waiting for them to fix a computer that's gone down and waste five hours. We could have made an album in five hours! Just give me a tape recorder, man. Turn that mike on and I'll make the album. It only plays for 40 minutes, so it should only take 40 minutes to make. But, in truth, I think that's a little bit easy to say because, I mean, there are also some real good albums that have taken a long time. *Sgt. Pepper* took a long time compared to albums of its time. The *White Album* took a long time, comparatively speaking. And I've done a few albums that have taken a long time, but I do like to record quicker rather than longer. But there's no hard and fast rules.

Peter Blake: The cover art for the *White Album* used the same link — Robert Fraser. Also with Fraser's gallery was Richard Hamilton. So Robert set it up for Richard to do the *White Album* cover, and he, very consciously, made it a contrast to *Sgt. Pepper,* which was very fussy. In a way, though, he used the same concept. I mean, the giveaway inside and the big poster.

On January 2, 1969, The Beatles began filming *Let It Be* at Twickenham Film Studios in London.

Glyn Johns: The *Let It Be* project was originally to be a television show. The idea was that The Beatles would meet at Twickenham Film Studios and rehearse the material for the show. They would actually shoot them rehearsing the songs and I was there to record them. The songs were all new, and there was to be a live album of the show released. A documentary film was to be made of the making of the show, and that ended up being the movie called *Let It Be* that was shown in the cinema. It was an abortion of a film if I ever saw one. Anyway, that's neither here nor there. There was a very lengthy rehearsal period during which George Martin had very little reason to be there. He'd phone in and say hello every now and then. I was left entirely to my own devices and, in fact, was used by the band as the producer in George's absence. I found it quite embarrassing, because as far as I was concerned, George Martin was their producer. He was extremely charming about the whole thing and seemed to understand, so there was no friction between us whatsoever.

We eventually realized the TV show wasn't going to happen. Basically The Beatles changed their minds about the TV show. So we got two-thirds of a documentary film made with no finish to it. Meanwhile The Beatles were in the process of building a recording studio at their new offices on Savile Row, and it was decided we would move over there. It had never been used and was literally just a room in which the carpet was laid the day before we went in.

We borrowed some equipment from EMI — their spare remote equipment — stuck it in the control room, and moved there from the Twickenham sound stage. The idea was that The Beatles would continue to rehearse, which was exactly what they did. The rehearsals in Savile Row were the first time I actually had any equipment. All the vocals were live, and I recorded most of what went on. I was incredibly impressed with what happened during those rehearsals. Apart from anything else, there was a lot of rather negative publicity about the band at that time. However, they were in extremely good spirits and extremely amusing. I don't think they were aware of it themselves.

Anyway, I sat in my control room and was blown away by what was going on, particularly after their paranoia about their ability to actually play live was displayed to me on several occasions. One night I took a couple of reels of the eight-tracks away with me to Olympic Studios and mixed two days of rehearsals with a lot of chat and humor and so on. I thought it would make the most incredible Beatles album ever, because it was so real. If you cast your mind back to 1969, they were totally untouchable. They were on pedestals 90 feet high and they were superhuman. So here they were being perfectly ordinary, very amusing, and quite capable of just sitting down and playing normally. So I put it together and gave a copy to each Beatle the following day and said, "This is just an idea, so take this away and listen to it and see what you think." And it was very rough indeed. I had just put bits and pieces together. The next morning they all came back and said, "No, it's a terrible idea. Forget about it." Each of them individually. So I thought no more about it. We finished the sessions and I went off to America to work with Steve Miller or somebody.

Then I returned to England. Several weeks went by and I got a call from Paul, asking me to meet him and John at EMI, which I duly did. I walked into the room and they said, "Remember that idea that you had?" I said yes. There was a big pile of tapes in the corner of the room, so they said, "Well, there are the tapes. Put them in your car. Take them away and do the album as you want to do it." So I said, "What are you saying? That you want me to make the album entirely on my own, without you lot even being there?" They said yes. That's quite extraordinary when you think about it.

Now, I have to tell you, I don't know that they did that because of their confidence in me. I think possibly it was because they were pretty disinterested in the project. Anyway, I took the tapes away, very excited, as you can imagine. I was thrilled about it. I made the album and I'm extremely proud of it. Always have been. Everybody thought the album was wonderful. I presented it to them in the same manner that I'd done the first idea, and it went down very well. I asked each member of the band if I could have a production credit on the record, since clearly I had produced it, and they all agreed to that. As far as we were concerned, it was going to be released immediately. It wasn't, because Allen Klein wanted to hold the album until the film had been finished, and the film took something like a year to straighten out.

By this time we had actually started work on *Abbey Road*. Then The Beatles broke up, Allen Klein got involved, and it was all extremely unsavory. McCartney and Lennon fell out. Everybody went their separate ways, including me, of course.

Paul McCartney: We started off coming to Apple with great theories like, when you come into business, you don't need to be the big businessman. You don't need to answer telephones every minute. You don't need to do it all like that. But, in fact, you do a bit. You need to at least have someone there to answer the phones. We were disillusioned about that for a bit. We thought, Christ, does it have to happen like this? Then we realized there are certain areas where we're not needed. Like the machine of business doesn't need us. There's no need for us there. But where that machine goes does need us. And that's what we've always been good at. That's what The Beatles have always been.

We never knew how to press a record, but we could make the record for you to press. At first we even thought, We'll manufacture all our records and radios and everything. We'll do this, we'll do that, we'll do the lot, ya know. We'll take over the world. And we thought that's the way it would all go. But the thing is, once you become a big corporate giant, you've got to take the responsibilities of being a big corporate giant. And you tie your own hands as you do it because then you become owned by your shareholders, and so on. It goes round and round and round. That's just one way that we don't want to go. So we're giving it all back to the big men. You know, all the people who want to own it all, can have it. We're doing it from another angle now. It is, in fact, a much better angle, which is finding the people who can make great records and films. So we have to put someone in here who we hope will know a good young filmmaker when he sees one. Now a lot of people don't, or their idea of the talented young filmmaker is different.

So, anyway, the way we're doing it now is we're just playing it completely by ear and we're learning all the lessons as we go along. And it is getting a lot better. I think if you'd seen Apple a few months ago, it was just total chaos. It's chaos now, but before it was just total. It's now a bit more together. People are beginning to see what it is we're trying to do and there's nothing really that can go wrong. I mean, all that can happen is that we lose all our money, which I don't mind one bit. It would become a relief in a way for me. Or else the building gets blown up or something, which again will be quite a relief. I don't mind. I really don't mind because the thing is we've passed the point where we have to worry about, "Oh, you know, what am I doing tomorrow? Is my job safe?" We used to think like that, but that's no longer the point. It's nothing to do with it anymore. I don't mind what happens tomorrow 'cause I know that whatever it is, it'll be all right. If Apple happens, it'll happen. If it doesn't happen, then that's hard lines. And nobody at Apple will worry. The worry will be from the people that hoped something would happen for once.

Essentially we're not businessmen. We probably will, just because of our experience, be able to get it together. But if we don't, there's the next line of people who will learn from our mistakes. They'll do it. I mean, it's not as though this thing isn't going to be done. Look at all the kids in the universities at the moment. They're not thick. They'll know what to do, and if they get greedy when they get control, they'll learn. We were greedy. I mean, we wanted fame, to be rich, to be liked by everyone and so on. I wanted the lot. I don't deny that. Every kid of 18 wants the lot. You just want every little piece. You want a great car, a great bird, you want to be dressed immaculately, you want whatever it is that you want, and you set out to get it. But the point is, once you've got it, you can't get any more. There's no further you can go. It hit us at about age 24. We realized there's still a lot of life to go after that, so you've really got to rethink what's important.

Alistair Taylor: The very basic idea of forming Apple was [to make] business fun. It would still be a business. Profits had to be made, but not excessive profits, not rip-offs, in other words. Why be greedy? Why sit in gray suits behind a desk being angry with people and arguing and bartering all the time? Why not sit around and tell the truth and make money at the same time? I get laughed at even by my own wife about that because I believe it could have worked. It was a beautiful philosophy. I still maintain if The Beatles had handled it right, it could have worked. It could have been phenomenal. It could have been a revolution in business. But in the end I got very uptight about it because The Beatles blamed everybody but themselves. They said people were ripping them off, people were doing this, but you know they were the ones who were doing it. You can't imagine what it was like. Paul [McCartney] would come in and say something and then John [Lennon] would come in an hour later and completely change it. Then we went through a period when we weren't allowed to do anything until someone had thrown the *I Ching*. Well, you know, it was all our faults.

Philip Norman: MPL [McCartney Productions Ltd.] is what Paul wanted Apple to have been. I think probably with the added ingredient of genuine philanthropy, he did want to encourage people to write and paint and that sort of thing. Unfortunately that genuine desire was plugged into the great, seething, floppy, woolly-minded mass of the hippie subculture, which was not where it should have gone. I think he still has a strong feeling for the arts and that he's rather missed out on education or felt a belated desire to receive education and wanted writers and painters and filmmakers to have the encouragement and the backing that The Beatles in their early years couldn't get. I think that did come from Paul. It was Paul, as much as John, who drew up that famous newspaper ad, the one-man band, that their office manager, Alistair Taylor, had posed for. Paul composed the caption — "This Man Has Talent, Send Your Tapes to Apple, Wigmore Street." Although Paul, evidently, always wanted to be a tycoon, he was more affected by the sort of free and easy philanthropic influences of the 1960s. Now I'm sure MPL doesn't want any young filmmakers to receive encouragement, or perhaps even any justice. But, yes, I think he wanted Apple to have that side. It was Paul who used the phrase "Western communism," which was communism in its purist form.

Alistair Taylor: One of the ideas I had at Apple was that since we did a lot of entertaining — taking people out for lunch and whatnot — we should have a small kitchen where we cooked and had our meals if we were entertaining anybody instead of going out and spending 30 pounds at a restaurant. We had this beautiful house in Savile Row, so why not take advantage of it? Everybody in the journals and books reported that we had two Cordon Bleu chefs. What we actually had were two young girls who trained at the Cordon Bleu school of cookery. That's very different from two Cordon Bleu chefs. Everybody still took guests out for lunch, and most of the extravagances were [due to] Peter Brown and Neil Aspinall sitting down and having superb four-course lunches with classic wines in the dining room at Apple. This was all self-destruction, which Peter Brown mentions in his book [*The Love You Make: An Insider's Story of the Beatles*].

All the invoices used to come through me, and I was getting these horrendous drink bills. I've forgotten the exact quantity. It was bigger than Brown put in his book. So I called the boys in and said, "Look, this is a farce." I meant to be fair. We all had our own drinks covered, and possibly my weekly thing would be something like one full bottle of spirits and some mixes. Neil was the same, Peter Brown was the same, to be fair, and then suddenly you'd get Derek Taylor with two crates of brandy, two crates of

Coke, eight bottles of Scotch week after week. But the answer I always got [from the boys] was "Oh, don't be a drag, Alistair. Forget it. Relax and enjoy it."

Then suddenly they started listening to [Allen] Klein. You know, the whole idea of getting Klein in really came from me — great to admit that! I said at one of these meetings, "We need a 'Beeching.'" Now I meant a Beeching type. Lord Beeching was a very fine businessman in England who straightened out the railways. I could see what was happening, and I looked around and there was myself who was a glorified accountant with some managing experience but not in that league. There was Neil Aspinall, who had never finished his accountant's training and who was a road manager. There was Peter Brown who, like me, had been a shop assistant in Liverpool selling records. Here were three people, the three people supposedly running Apple, which is a multimillion-pound company!

What the hell qualifications did we have? I didn't want to run the company. Neil was good at things, and Peter Brown was very good at lots of things. I'm not going to knock them on their abilities. But as good as we three were in our fields, add it all together and we still weren't capable of running a company like Apple. The money was coming in so fast, but there were no controls. When I tried to control Derek Taylor, I just got laughed out of court. That's when I said we needed a "Beeching," and the next thing I read was that John and Yoko had gone to see Lord Beeching. They had taken it literally. It evolved from that and, of course, we ended up with Allen Klein. So [the man] whose head is on the chopping block first is the guy who thought the idea up. Klein fired me.

Paul McCartney: The idea of Apple is that even if you are a clerk in an Apple office or in anything to do with Apple, we really do try to turn you on. There is a definite effort to turn people on in this building. The people who don't want it, who don't like it, will go back to being hired clerks because they'd rather do that. But if you want to come here in order to be a sort of turned-on clerk, that's great. I think occasionally too much of it goes on and you don't actually get much work done because everyone's so busy turning each other on. But it is nicer. I mean, it's really a different atmosphere in this place from any building I've ever been in. It's great, you know. I get sort of amazed every time I come in here.

We were going to call ourselves Apple, and John just came in the next day and said, "Shall we call ourselves Apple Corps?" Everyone snickered. Then we said, "Yeah." So we rang up the man and said can you register us as Apple Corps? That's all it is. We do things like that. We really do silly things. It's like the magazine *Private Eye*. It's all got sort of smutty, but it's got jokes and stuff. And it's a very sort of schoolboy humor, like lavatory-wall humor. [People think we have] a very far-out sense of humor, but it's not far-out at all. We're very far-in. We're very ordinary. I like a good joke and a bottle of brown ale, you know. I really do.

George Harrison: We got very involved with this business thing, which we were always actually involved in. Maybe people think it's a drag, the Beatles doing that business thing, but we were always involved in it. We just didn't notice it because Brian Epstein did it. When he died, we suddenly realized that there were a lot of people who we had contracts with and involvements with and, you know, it was just ridiculous. We had to try to solve that problem and sort it all out. It was just as much part of our past as, say, playing our first Ed Sullivan show. We were fairly responsible, but the business side of it was abstract then because we always imagined that Brian took care of it and that everything was fine, even when it wasn't fine. But with nobody being there it was directly up to us to work out what we had to do with ourselves. And, consequently, we came to find out, to our horror, all this past thing that we were involved with — contracts and business and tax, and all those things. With Apple now I'm quite happy, but it's like a rumor. You know, if you say to one person such and such a thing and he says it to somebody else, by the time it comes back to you it has nothing to do with what you originally said. And that's the main problem with Apple, or I'm sure with any business. You say to somebody, "Okay now. There's the thing. Go do that." And it comes back just slightly different and takes a lot of time to sort out. Really, what Apple was trying to be was just a service for The Beatles. As somebody, I think Derek Taylor, put it, "It's just for our whims."

Derek Taylor: Apple is an organization that has developed without anyone really planning it this way. It's a service that exists to implement the whims of The Beatles, which fortunately do, normally, turn out to be commercial. However, if they didn't, we'd still have to do it, and that's okay, because that's the gig. The gig is not Apple. The gig is working for The Beatles.

Alistair Taylor: So much was done purely on a whim. Then the novelty would wear off. We had Magic Alex, or Mad Alex, as I called him. The whole idea was that John [Lennon] was going to buy an island and have Alex design this house, which was going to be a glass bubble suspended in midair. In the end I took John out to the island and I let the dust settle. Nobody knew it belonged to John for months and months. I took him out to see it and he got these great plans. Then it slowly faded. I left Apple and the next thing I read in the papers was that he gave the island to a group of hippies. So he got the island and I don't think he ever saw it again.

Victor Spinetti: I was staying at John Lennon's house one weekend when the police broke in and started searching for drugs. They tore the rooms apart, woke Julian up, ripped his mattress apart, tore everything up in the house, then asked for John's autograph and left.

On January 30, 1969, The Beatles played an unannounced noontime concert on the roof of their offices at Savile Row in the heart of London.

Glyn Johns: That [the rooftop concert] was my idea actually. Yes. They said that they had this desire to play to the whole of London. It was

in the middle of winter, and we were sitting up in the dining room
at Savile Row having lunch. We were all there, including [*Let It Be*
director] Michael Lindsay-Hogg. We were talking about the
building, and Ringo said there was a wonderful roof on it that The
Beatles were thinking of making into a roof garden. I said, "Oh,
that's fantastic." Then I looked over at Michael and said, "I have an
idea. We should go up and look at this roof." So we all went upstairs
and looked at it and thought, What a great idea it would be to play
on the roof — play to the whole of the West End [of London].

On March 12, 1969, Paul McCartney married Linda Eastman at a ceremony
in London. On March 20, John Lennon married Yoko Ono at the Rock of
Gibraltar, a place that John said was "quiet, friendly, and British."

Peter Brown: The love relationship between John [Lennon] and Yoko
[Ono] was very sincere, so naturally they wanted to get married
in a very special way. John called while I was on a trip to Holland.
He said, "Stay there. We'll come over and get married in Holland."
I said, "Don't do it, John." When Paul [McCartney] got married a
week earlier, the supposedly secret ceremony became a media
circus. John was determined not to go through that, so he said,
"Peter, find me a spot where we can get married as quickly as
possible without any problems." I looked everywhere and finally
discovered that Gibraltar was in the unique position of being part
of the British system and remote enough so that it didn't have a
press corps.

In March 1969 Dick James sold his ownership of Northern Songs to
Britain's ATV.

Stephen James: We felt Northern Songs was such a vibrant company
that the best way all the people involved could appreciate their
interest was for us to go public and be quoted on the London
Stock Exchange, which we did in 1965. In later years, in about
1968 or 1969, there were problems in the Beatle camp with Brian

[Epstein] having died and different factions coming in and pulling John Lennon in one direction and Paul McCartney in the other. My father and I could see that The Beatles weren't going to be able to remain together. There was just too much pressure on them. Being the only publishing company to be publicly quoted in the City [London's financial district], we felt that the institutions and the main investors in the City that didn't really understand the music business wouldn't understand how a company like Northern Songs could continually increase its profits and carry on if The Beatles broke up. Since we could see the writing on the wall, we felt it was in everyone's interest — although it was argued by certain other people that it wasn't in their interest — to sell the company to Lew Grade's company, ATV.

On March 26, 1969, John Lennon and Yoko Ono began their "bed-ins" for peace at the Amsterdam Hilton Hotel.

John Lennon: Can you think of a better way to spend seven days? It's the best idea we've had yet. We're doing a commercial for peace on the front pages of newspapers around the world instead of a commercial for war. We're holding a bed-in for peace and we're selling peace. Everybody has got to be aware that they can have peace if they want it and as soon as they want. We plan to do this bed-in for seven days, and I think this is the fourth day. I'm not sure, you know. There's so much going on in this bedroom. I don't know what day it is. Actually we snuck out yesterday morning to the American embassy to apply for a visa, but it was a great secret. Yoko and I are filming all the time. We're making a film of this event. It'll be an amazing film when you see the goings-on in the bedroom. We got a radio station in here, we got people chanting "Hare Krishna," we got visitors coming in one after the other in strange outfits. It's really fantastic. You'll dig it.

On April 11, 1969, the single "Get Back" was released. The label credited "The Beatles and Billy Preston."

John Lennon: We've often used other musicians on millions of records, you know. We just named Billy on the cover of *Let It Be* because Billy was playing a pretty funky piano solo. That's all. He used to play with Ray Charles's band, and he came over and signed up with Apple. George is producing an LP with him. He's a groovy cat. He comes in and sits in on the session and then lays it on you, so we thought we'd give him a credit. I can't understand people's problem with it. It [the album cover] says, "With Billy Preston." It doesn't say, "Billy Preston instead of The Beatles." I don't understand how these myths get going.

On May 8, 1969, John Lennon, George Harrison, and Ringo Starr signed a deal with Allen Klein, making him manager of much of their business affairs. Paul McCarney refused to sign.

Philip Norman: There comes a point where it's simply impossible to assess the virtue of someone like Allen Klein. He came in and sorted out the mess [of Apple Corps]. The mess was abominable, but he did come in and sort it out. Though to do Ron Cass, who was the head of the Apple record label, justice, he and Peter Asher had sold millions of records by the time Allen Klein came in. That was an area Allen Klein had no knowledge of at all. But he certainly did renegotiate their contracts. He was clever. He knew exactly how to appeal to The Beatles in the basic way of saying, "You should have had all this money and you haven't got it. I can get it for you." In everything he got them, he would take a percentage. On another level, he was very, very clever. When Paul McCartney wanted the Eastmans, father and son, to take over business affairs for the band, and Lennon and the others wanted Klein, Klein managed to engineer a meeting between the Eastmans and himself. Eastman started shouting at Klein, who was the underdog. The Beatles, of course, sided with the underdog. Well, I'm sure Klein gave Lee Eastman ample reason to shout at him, but nonetheless it was a great coup. The Beatles thought Klein was the one who was taking all the abuse, so they went with Klein.

Alistair Taylor: I never met Allen Klein. It's the only time in my life I've been fired from a job and never met the person who did it. I never met him, and I'm very proud of that. If you're going to get fired, it's great to be fired by someone you've never met. And it wasn't just me. There was a numbered list of 16 people, and I was number one on the list. He just removed anyone who was remotely close to The Beatles. They gave him carte blanche. I spent a day trying to phone the boys purely to find out. I wanted to be sure they knew that I was on that list because I couldn't believe four very close friends could do this to me. Having said that, I've been in business a long time and I appreciate that if you give someone carte blanche you can't start saying, "Ah, yes, but don't touch Alistair Taylor and don't touch so and so." I just thought it would have been nice if one of them had had the guts to say, "Look, Al, I'm sorry. That's the way it is." I'd have accepted that, but with a couple of them — I'm not going to name them — I actually got through to the houses. I had all the private numbers obviously, and I could hear them talking in the background while I was told they weren't there. That hurt. After 10 years of slipping them money under the table for drinks, [everything] was forgotten.

Peter Brown, in his book, funny enough, is very kind to me. In fact, I'm about the only person he's got anything decent to say about, which doesn't alter my opinion of it. Somebody said to Paul, "What is it like to sack someone like Alistair Taylor?" They quoted my name, and he said, "Oh, well, it's just got to be done." I feel they just chickened out. I thought Paul and I were very close. Obviously we weren't! It hurt. I just didn't work for them, for God's sake. I mean, I've been on holidays with them. They confided in me. I could write a book that would make Peter Brown's look like Enid Blyton, and yet they did come to rely on other people doing everything, including jobs like that. A very strange quartet!

Derek Taylor: Apple is not such a grim memory as some other things. I find having done a book [*As Time Goes By: Living in the Sixties*] and revising the book, some periods were almost unbearable.

November 1964 appears to be a grim time. It was the time that we were all trying to find a name for the *Beatles for Sale* album. Eventually, as usual, The Beatles came up with the name. They normally did. But that album reminds me of dreary times, and I find that Apple, although it was again very hard work, was fun. A lot of it was hilarious, and for three years we just behaved in an extraordinary fashion in the middle of the straight world. We thought we had certain answers that we didn't appear to have, but we certainly had a good time.

Was Apple a success? No, it was a flop. Actually, a lot of people had a great deal of fun. John and Yoko ran a sensationally extensive peace operation from there [Apple]. It was very widespread what they were doing. Steven Spielberg told me that The Beatles were responsible, in part, for ending the Vietnam War. I only quote Steven Spielberg because he's now claimed as one of our geniuses, and I personally think he is a genius. We believed in what we were doing. We believed in helping people. The fact is you can't really help that many people, particularly when you're on [Johnny] Carson's show and you say you can help everybody.

I think Apple flopped because we were disorganized. I was certainly taking on too much as usual. George was doing his Billy Preston, Doris Troy, and Hare Krishna. But George wasn't really committed to Apple the madhouse. He wanted a more peaceful life. He was seeking more tranquillity than some others we could name. Paul, who had started off with a bang, became disenchanted very quickly because it wasn't his Apple. He wanted a more orderly Apple. He wanted the sort of Apple that MPL [McCartney Productions Ltd.] has become — extremely efficient and a graceful kind of office building in the middle of London, where things get done properly and bills get paid promptly. In fact, Paul McCartney's office has got the reputation of paying its bills more promptly than any other organization in the record business. Paul wanted Apple to be a reflection of his own approach, which has always been pretty methodical. Paul was well taught by his father, and his father would not have approved of Apple. My father came. He thought that Apple was a wonderful place. He was 80 when he arrived there. He thought it was the most fabulous place. He caught sight of Allen Klein and said, "Oh, look out for that man."

Philip Norman: I spent about five to six weeks at Apple. Everyone who went to Apple could have whatever they wanted. Most people asked for money or food or drugs, and I asked for access to the band. It was an incredible time. John was with Yoko doing his media saturation for peace. Harrison was upstairs having photos taken with a Buddha and banks of flowers. Ringo was somewhere else trying to sell his house, and Allen Klein was busy having long meetings trying to rationalize the business. As a result of that, McCartney didn't come around that much.

You could see why Apple fell apart even then. There were all these incoherent, greedy people walking in and thinking just because they were wearing caftans and bells that that made everything all right. That was the terrible lesson of Apple, because it was supposed to be for a utopian kind of youth. But the youth kept on being what they have always been — a younger version of older people who have the same mixture of good and bad qualities.

On May 26, 1969, John Lennon and Yoko Ono made a surprise visit to Montreal, Canada, and began a bed-in at the Queen Elizabeth Hotel.

Paul White: When John and Yoko arrived in Canada, I got a call from him. He said, "I need $5,000." Our lawyers said, "Why should we give them $5,000?" I said, "I think it's because they've probably earned it." John had just arrived and he didn't have any money, so we had to send one of our people down, literally, with a cashier's check, because he didn't know what he was going to do.

On May 30, 1969, The Beatles released "The Ballad of John and Yoko/Old Brown Shoe." While John Lennon and Yoko Ono continued their bed-in in Montreal, many celebrities and hangers-on visited them. Timothy and

Rosemary Leary, Tommy Smothers, Murray the K, and members of the Canadian Radna Krishna Temple were some of the people who dropped by. On June 1 Lennon and Ono decided to make a recording.

André Perry: At the time we were doing a lot of work for Capitol Records in Canada, and in the middle of the night I got a call to get my buns down to room 1742 of the Queen Elizabeth Hotel to make a recording with John and Yoko. So I woke up some people from RCA, rushed over, got the four-track machine, and tuned it up. We did the recording for "Give Peace a Chance" late in the evening and the flip side of it with Yoko. We did it with just the three of us — John, Yoko, and myself — in the hotel room. We spent the whole night doing it until about five o'clock in the morning, and that was quite a moment in my life to have that intimacy together.

The main problem we had was that the room was so small. The ceiling was only seven feet high. It was a very strange suite in the hotel. It had Gyproc walls, resonating walls. People banged on them, causing what we call in recording, standing waves, which you really do pick up on the microphones. We decided to do two tracks of it, which were the main voice and guitars, and after that we overdubbed some of the singing in the background under more controlled conditions. The action in that room was tremendous. There were about 60 people in the room, and as you can well imagine, I had people under tables. I had them everywhere. I had a small table to put the console and the four-track on, and there were people all over the place. The Hare Krishna people were under the table.

John's generosity, as far as I'm concerned, was phenomenal. When the record was released, I received a phone call from the Capitol people in Toronto. They were stunned and said, "André, we just got the label copy from England, and you won't believe what it says. It says 'recorded by Le Studio, André Perry,' with the address, the telephone number, and the province." I was totally, absolutely, amazed. So that was, I think, John's way of saying thank you. He was a very warm kind of person in that way and very generous. Of course, it really helped me to get things going.

What touched me the most was all that time we spent together, the four or five hours recording what was to become the B side, and the whole way John went about it. After the recording, I went and mixed it in the studio. When I came back the next day to play it to him, I was amazed. It was like he had a way of inspiring confidence immediately and developing confidence in other people. He had a way of sensing very rapidly in people's eyes, or the way you behaved, what you were all about. Contrary to a lot of artists who might have been somewhat heavy about their way of proceeding, he left it up to me, which I found very surprising, especially from someone like him. I met him after that in New York at Elton John's launching, and he remembered absolutely everything. I was very surprised, considering the amount of people he must have encountered.

On July 4, 1969, the single "Give Peace a Chance" was released by the Plastic Ono Band.

John Lennon: It was just a gradual development over the years. Last year was "All You Need Is Love." This year it's "Give Peace a Chance." Remember love. The only hope for any of us is peace. Violence begets violence. If you want to get peace, you can get it as soon as you like if we all pull together. You're all geniuses and you're all beautiful. You don't need anybody to tell you who you are or what you are. You are what you are. Get out there and get peace. Think peace, live peace, and breathe peace and you'll get it as soon as you like. Okay?

The Beatles are four middle-aged teenagers who've got to make a democratic decision on whether they go on tour or not. Right now we're not agreed on it, so I don't know. But John and Yoko are certainly ready to perform. Meanwhile Paul's driving through Europe last time I heard. Ringo is in the Bahamas, sort of half filming and half on holiday, and I don't know what George is doing. He's probably working.

Alistair Taylor: Yoko and I were quite good friends. I've read a great deal about all the tension. I was there and certainly there was some tension, because John and Yoko were doing something the boys had never done before. I mean, the women simply did not appear. And Yoko just didn't appear. She would be sitting at John's feet! I must confess I was never aware of great tensions between the wives. It didn't go down particularly well, but there was no what I would call real "agro" at all.

On August 8, 1969, with sessions coming to an end for the *Abbey Road* album, The Beatles were photographed crossing the street outside Abbey Road Studios. The four members of the group recorded for the last time on August 20. On September 13, the Plastic Ono Band played and were recorded at the Rock and Roll Revival in Toronto.

Klaus Voorman: What happened was that somebody said to John, "How about you coming to Toronto? There's a big rock-and-roll festival going on." John said, "Yeah, sure." He thought he was going to watch the bands, to watch Chuck Berry. He just wanted to see these bands play. After a while they called back and said, "John, are you coming?" John said, "Yeah, I'm coming." They said, "What's the lineup?" John said, "What lineup?" They said, "You're coming to play, aren't you?" John didn't know that they wanted him to play. So he suddenly, somehow, got conned into putting a band together. Yoko said, "Come on, John, you can do it." So he just called us. We had Alan White, who I couldn't understand because he talked with a strong Newcastle accent. It was very difficult. I knew Eric Clapton. We all met and rehearsed on the plane. I wasn't really nervous because it didn't matter whether we were good or bad. John was nervous, but I wasn't.

Little Richard: I remember at the show [the Rock and Roll Revival] that people were throwing bottles at Yoko Ono. They were throwing everything at her. Finally she had to run off the stage. They would have beat her to death up there. Oh, boy, it was very bad. It was the first time I saw a Japanese person get a whipping like that!

On September 26, 1969, The Beatles released the album *Abbey Road.*

George Martin: The *Let It Be* songs were great. Obviously I didn't like what was done to them afterward. That was an unfortunate and a very unhappy time. The unhappiest time of all. I mean, after *Let It Be,* I really thought that was the end of the road for all of us. I didn't really want to work with them anymore because they were becoming unpleasant people — to themselves as well as to other people. And I really thought we'd finished. So I was quite surprised when Paul rang up and said, "Look, you know, this is silly what happened to *Let It Be.* Let's try to make a record like we used to. Would you come and produce it like you used to?" I said, "Well, I'll produce it like I used to if you let me. I can't do it otherwise. I can't do it without your cooperation." So Paul rounded up John, George, and Ringo and we started work on *Abbey Road.* It really was very happy, very pleasant, and it went frightfully well.

There was still obviously a schism. John got disenchanted with record production. He didn't really approve of what I was doing. He didn't like "messing about," as he called it. He didn't like the pretentiousness, if you like, of record production. And I could see his point. He wanted good old-fashioned, plain, solid rock, and to hell with it. "Let's blast the living daylights out," he'd say. Or if it was a soft ballad, "Let's do it just the way it comes." He wanted authenticity and that kind of thing. And he objected very much to what we did on *Abbey Road* on the second side, on the long side, which was almost entirely Paul and I working together with contributions from the others. So we compromised. One side was very much what John wanted — a collection of different songs — and the second side of *Abbey Road* was what Paul and I wanted.

Geoff Emerick: The *Abbey Road* sessions were very good, very fast. I think the whole album was completed in four to five weeks. *Sgt. Pepper* was done on a four-track. Some of the tracks would have maybe a guitar, a vocal, or a piano overdub all on that one track, and while it was fresh in your mind you had to mix it. Otherwise, once you'd finished the track, you'd forget all the switches, or how you were going to pan and reequalize the track, or change from vocal to guitar to piano and so on.

We'd probably lay down drums, one guitar and piano, or two guitars and piano. The drums we couldn't keep separate. They're normally on with the bass. So with bass and drums on one track, one track was left for the lead voice and one track for overdubs. If anything else was wanted, we could maybe bounce once on a few of the tracks. We would go four to two and back to four. But it was very complicated. On the mixing board there were only eight inputs and four outputs. I always remember the transition from doing *Sgt. Pepper* and going on to do the *Abbey Road* album, where EMI had changed from the valve-[tube] desk to the transistorized desk. In no way could we get the same bass drum or bass sound, so I don't know whether we did progress or not.

George Harrison: I wrote "Something" while we were still recording the *White Album,* but I never finished it off. I could never think of words for it. Also, there was a James Taylor song called "Something in the Way She Moves," which is the first line of [my song]. So I thought I should try to change the words, but they were the words that came when I wrote it. In the end I left it as that and just called it "Something." Actually I think Joe Cocker has recorded this song, but when I wrote it I imagined someone like Ray Charles doing it. That's the feel I imagined. But I'm not Ray Charles. I'm much more limited in what I can do, so it came out like this. It's probably the nicest melody I've written.

"Maxwell's Silver Hammer" is just something of Paul's that we'd been trying to record. We'd spent a hell of a lot of time on it. It's one of those instant whistle-along tunes that some people hate and some people really love. It's more like a "Honey Pie," fun sort of song. But it's pretty sick, as well, because the guy keeps killing everybody. It's one of the tunes on which we used the Moog synthesizer. I think it's pretty effective.

"Oh Darling," to me, is another Paul song that is typical of the 1950 to 1960 period. The chord structure and everything is really nice. But this is really just Paul singing. We do a few "oo's" in the background, just very quietly, but it's mainly Paul shouting.

Paul McCartney: I thought of "Oh Darling" as sort of a black song in format. There wasn't a lot of melody. There wasn't a chordal magnificence. It was fairly straightforward. I always figured I had to really put a good performance in. So I did. I just tried every which way. I tried a hand mike, a stand mike, a boom mike, this mike, that mike, and in the end I just thought, Oh, to hell with it! By then I had toughened up my voice, got a little bit of an edge that I had wanted to make it a little funkier.

George Harrison: "Octopus's Garden" is Ringo's song. It's the second song Ringo wrote, and it's lovely. You know, Ringo gets bored playing the drums. At home he plays a bit of piano, but he only knows about three chords. He knows the same on guitar. If you're deep in your consciousness, it's very peaceful. So Ringo's writing cosmic songs without noticing.

The last song on the first side [of *Abbey Road*] is "I Want You (She's So Heavy)." It gets sort of very heavy. It's John playing lead guitar and singing. It's good because it's basically a bit of blues. The riff that he sings and plays is a very basic blues thing. But again it's a very original John type song. The middle bit's great. John has an amazing thing with his timing. He always comes across with different timing things. For example, "All You Need Is Love" — "Nothing you can do that can't be done, da da da, da dl da dl da dl," which skips beats out and changes from three-part, three-quarter, four/four/four, you know, all in and out of each other. But when you question him as to what it is, he doesn't know. He just does it naturally. The bridge section of the song is a bit like that. It's got a really good chord sequence.

"Here Comes the Sun" is the other song I wrote on *Abbey Road*. It was written on a nice sunny day [in the] early summer in Eric Clapton's garden. We'd really been through hell with business, and it was all very heavy. On that day I just felt as though I was sagging off from school. I just didn't go in one day, and it was the release of being in the sun on a really nice day. Then the song just came. It's a bit like "If I Needed Someone," with the basic riff going through it. That's how I see it, anyway. Quite a simple tune.

"Because" is one of the most beautiful tunes. It's three-part harmony. John, Paul, and I all sing it together. John wrote it, and the backing is a bit like Beethoven with three-part harmony right through. People might think it's a Paul McCartney song rather than a Lennon song because of the sweetness of it. Paul usually writes the sweeter tunes and John writes the sort of "rave up" things or the freakier things. I think this is my favorite song on the album because it's so simple. The lyrics are so simple. The harmony was pretty difficult to sing. We had to really learn it. I think that's one of the tunes that impresses most people, you know. Straight people dig it and the music people dig it, but hip people dig it, too.

Yoko Ono: I was playing [Beethoven's] Moonlight Sonata one day. The piano has been my security blanket all my life, and whenever I'm nervous or something, I tend to go to the piano. So I was playing Moonlight Sonata and John said, "Oh, it's beautiful, beautiful. Could we just hear the chorus and could we, well, play it from this end, and sort of backward?" It worked. It wasn't quite the reverse, but that was the inspiration for "Because."

George Martin: "Because" wasn't one of the typical songs John [Lennon] was bringing in at the time. I thought it was strange because it was just a very simple and beautiful song. I was very surprised when he allowed it to be done in that way. Again the three of them were terribly good at harmonizing, anyway, and when we actually did the vocal backings, there was George, John, and Paul singing as a trio. I would give them lines to sing, then go out and record them and double-track them. In fact, I triple-tracked the three of them, and it was just like working with a very experienced, very good professional group. They took direction admirably. It's amazing, really, when you think of their arrogance. They knuckled down beautifully.

George Harrison: The big medley of Paul and John [on *Abbey Road* has] all the songs shoved together. It's really hard to describe. "You Never Give Me Your Money" has two verses of one tune, then the bridge is like a different song altogether. It goes out of that into this quite melodic bit. Then "Sun King" is John's thing, which is funny, too. I think John called that one "Lost Paranoia." John wrote "Mean Mr. Mustard" and "Polythene Pam." "She Came in Through the Bathroom Window" is a very good song of Paul's with good lyrics. It's really hard to explain what they're about. Anyway, on "Golden Slumbers" all these link up. "Golden Slumbers" is another very melodic tune of Paul's. "Carry That Weight" is almost part of "Golden Slumbers." In fact, "Carry That Weight" keeps coming in and out at different times. And "The End" is just the end. It's a little sequence that ends it all. You really have to hear all that. With *Sgt. Pepper,* and even the *White Album,* I got an overall image of my own of the album. With *Abbey Road* I was at a loss. People have said it's a bit more like *Revolver.* It still feels very abstract to me. I can't see it as a whole. You get an image of an album and it all gels and fits together, but I can't do that with this one. It's a bit like it's somebody else's record. It doesn't feel as though it's us, even though we spent hours doing it. But I think it's a very good album.

Geoff Emerick: On the track "Golden Slumbers" we used two studios. The guitar solo at the end of it was played by George [Harrison] and it was done live with the orchestra. That wasn't an overdub. When arrangements like that happened, normally they were in Paul's head. Paul can't write music, so the only way he could interpret it to the orchestra was through George Martin. He wrote the notes down and then the orchestra played them, and if something was wrong, then Paul would discuss it with George. Paul would say, "I want it to go so-and-so," and George would translate that to the orchestra.

Alan Parsons: I worked on the recording of *Abbey Road* as a tape operator, assistant engineer, or what have you. I noticed that during
the sessions you wouldn't often find all four Beatles there at once.
It would be Paul McCartney with George Martin, or George
Harrison with George Martin. They would each come in to do
their individual parts and their individual songs. I think I was
enormously impressed at that time by the way they didn't use
normal, conventional musical instruments to make the record.
They used all sorts of strange ideas and processes with instruments. Remember, they were one of the first pop bands, if not the
first, to brilliantly use the Moog synthesizer, and earlier they were
the first to use the Mellotron. The Moog was used on *Abbey Road*
quite a bit. It was actually George Harrison's. I was surprised
when I saw Ringo blowing through a straw into a glass of water
to get the underwater effect for "Octopus's Garden." Then, on
"Maxwell's Silver Hammer," he banged an anvil for the hammering
sound on the track.

George Martin: As we got up to the last stage, which was *Abbey Road*,
The Beatles were developing even beyond what they had done
before. Of course, after *Abbey Road* they each went off in their
separate directions. Even in *Abbey Road* they were still frag-
menting. *Abbey Road* was a collection of individual songs. There
were John's songs, and Paul's songs, and George's songs. There
wasn't a great deal of collaboration in the songwriting itself. So I
tended to deal with one person at a time, and the others would
come in as backup. It was that kind of situation, rather than
dealing with a group.

    Paul asked me if I would do *Abbey Road* after the awful busi-
ness of *Let It Be*. It was a conscious attempt, really, to get back to
Sgt. Pepper. I asked Paul to think in classical terms, to think in
terms of writing a symphony, if you like, because what the boys
were doing was writing the equivalent of a symphony in today's
standards. I said, "Think in those terms and think of form, and
try to think of a song you can introduce as a particular theme and

then bring it back in a different key, maybe as a counterpoint to another song." Paul accepted all this and worked on one side of *Abbey Road*, which is one long piece.

The guys saw the sense of it. They would bring me little bits. John would bring in a little ditty and say, "Have you got room for this anywhere? Can we slide this in somewhere?" They collaborated very well like that. Basically, though, John didn't like the idea of the continuous movement. He said, "No, it's not rock and roll. Let's have good ol' rock-and-roll songs. Each with a beginning and an end, and that's it." In fact, *Abbey Road* was a compromise between one and the other. There was a tussle, an artistic tussle, and it was very difficult to hold them together in that way. There wasn't a cohesive feeling between them to do the same kind of music. They had to express themselves individually. They had to get away. And, really, when you think about it, it was amazing that they stayed together for so long. It was almost a decade, you know. And, heaven knows, they deserved to have that freedom.

On October 6, 1969, The Beatles released the single "Something/Come Together." Also, in October, Detroit DJ Russ Gibb said that he had received information that Paul McCartney had died some years earlier and that it had been covered up through the use of a look-alike. He reported that several clues had been included on subsequent Beatle albums.

George Martin: All of a sudden things began to add up. I started to get letters and cards from people outlining how obvious it was that Paul was actually dead. They said that they understood all our clues on the covers over the past few years and, you know, I started believing it myself. They would say, "Look on the back of *Sgt. Pepper*. He is the only one of the four with his back to the camera, and on *Magical Mystery Tour* he is shown wearing a black carnation and he's not wearing shoes on the *Abbey Road* cover." Little things like that. People read more and more into the things that Paul had done differently than the others. Well, if he was dead, he darn well had a very good impersonator. One afternoon

Paul was at my home playing the piano and having some tea. We laughed about all that was happening, but really it wasn't that funny after a while. Rather sinister, actually, when people start to find your telephone number and call you at three o'clock in the morning, asking you if Paul is really dead!

Peter Blake: We went to visit Paul at his house. We talked about the rumors and he said, "You know, I'm not Paul McCartney. You met Paul when you were working on *Sgt. Pepper* and he didn't have a scar on his mouth. Look, I've got a scar. I'm a stand-in." And, just for a moment, I wasn't sure. Then he told me the story that he'd fallen off his bicycle. He still has that scar and he still has a slightly crooked lip because of it. But I was prepared to believe it and I knew Paul very well by then. But if this person says, "I'm not actually Paul," you believe it. And, of course, it was him. He was kidding.

There were all these myths about The Beatles and Paul being dead at that point. I mean, one of the myths is that on the cover of *Sgt. Pepper,* around the flower bed, there are marijuana plants. And it certainly looks as though there are, but I didn't know they were, and if they were, it was somebody else's joke. There are real plants around the edge with spiky leaves. If they're marijuana plants, I would be surprised. But that's one of the myths. I think it was completely accidental. I think the myth built up on an accident. Another is about a design in the middle of the flower bed. There are some white-shaped hyacinths. Now there was a young boy with the firm of flower people who said, "Can I make a guitar in flowers in that scene?" It was a very corny, nice idea. So I said, "Sure go ahead." He made us a white guitar. Well, if you really look very hard you can read "Paul?" As if to say, "Is Paul dead?" So that was another totally accidental thing. It wasn't meant to be, but it is there.

There are four shapes with a fifth shape at the end that could be a question mark. Someone spotted it and said it was deliberate. And you can then read it and make yourself believe that's what it says. Another myth was that there's a hand above Paul's head and that this is a sign of death, therefore Paul is dead. In fact, it's a very corny English singer called Issy Bonn. He had a big song called "My Yiddishe Mama." In the photograph he was waving to his fans. And it was pure chance that it was over Paul's head. On the other photographs we took it's somewhere quite different.

Philip Norman: I think there's no doubt that in almost every way Paul McCartney is an extremely likable person. But a likable person, however likable, becomes just that bit less likable if he really wants to be liked. I think that's the great flaw in his character. He's always really wanted to be liked. And I know absolutely lovely people who have this defect. They just want to be liked. And however nice they are, they get less nice if they have that great desire to come out well with everything and to be on everybody's good side. I start to be suspicious of them. It just rubs me up the wrong way, however nice somebody is. John Lennon was a human being. No better and no worse than any other human being. He managed, under intolerable pressure, to stay normal, reasonable, and very pleasant to his fellow creatures. And I think that's an amazing achievement and says a lot about the Liverpool character as well as his own character. Lennon never tried to be liked and was, as a result, always that much more likable.

Chapter Ten

And in
the End

On November 25, 1969, John Lennon returned his M.B.E. to Queen Elizabeth, protesting Britain's involvement in the Nigeria/Biafra dispute. On December 17, Lennon and Ono appeared at the Ontario Science Centre in Toronto, Canada, for a Peace Conference press conference.

Reporter: Why do you think you can succeed?

John Lennon: A lot of people have failed. It's like saying, "Why bother keeping on with Christianity because Jesus got killed or something?" We don't think people have tried advertising peace before. If we can start there . . . Look, pretend peace is new. Then, because we've never had it, let's start advertising. Sell, sell, sell, and whatever gimmickry or irrelevancies are going on during the advert, it's the drink or the car that they buy at the end of it. Whether there's chicks or a white horse and snow and all that, the product sells, and we believe in selling.

Reporter: The last time you were in Montreal you mentioned you had acorns available. Do you still have any, and what has happened with these peace acorns?

John: King Hussein planted his, if you'd like to know. He's the only one, we believe. We will keep sending them until everyone has planted one. We sent them to all the world's leaders' addresses we could find and we've had about 20 replies so far. I don't know who. I can't remember.

Reporter: Is there any one thing that started this peace campaign?

John: It sort of built over a number of years, but something that struck it off was when we got a letter from a guy called Peter Watkins, who made a film called *The War Game*. It was a long letter stating what's happening and how the media is controlled and how it's all run. Everybody knows that bit, but he sort of said it in black-and-white for hours and hours and it ended up with "What are you going to do about it?" He said people in your position, and our position, because he's a filmmaker, have a responsibility to use the media for world peace. We sat on the letter for three weeks and thought, Well, we're doing our best. All you need is love. Finally we came up with the bed event, and that's what really sparked it off. It was like getting your call-up papers for peace.

Reporter: Is it true you were planning to go to Biafra?

John: Yeah, at the time Yoko was pregnant and we decided not to go. She had a miscarriage. We thought and thought about it and we were scared of going somewhere where [war] was happening because we didn't want to be dead saints. I'm scared to go into Vietnam and Biafra until I'm convinced I can do better there than out of it. I'll stay out of it. I will go to Russia, but I'll think twice about China because I don't want to be a martyr.

Reporter: Do you think your campaign is naive?

John: If anybody thinks our campaign is naive, that's their opinion. That's okay. Let them do something else. If we like the idea, we'll join in with them. Otherwise we do it the way we're [doing it]. We're artists, not politicians, not newspapermen, not anything. We do it in a way that suits us best, and this is the way we work. Publicity is our game because The Beatles were that. That's the trade I've learned. This is my trade, and I'm using it to the best of my ability.

Reporter: Have you tried to pitch your colleagues, The Beatles, into doing this?

John: Well, no, because this is the first time there's been a peace-oriented idea, or festival for peace. I'll try to hustle them out, and maybe I'll get one or two or something like that. I got George [Harrison] and some other people the other night for UNICEF, but I can't speak for The Beatles 'cause I'm only me. But if I can get them, if I could get Elvis, I'll try. I'll try to get them all.

Reporter: John, I remember you saying you thought we'd have peace by the year 2000. Do you still think that?

John: Well, I don't want to think that. I say by 1970, you know, and then I believe in that positive-thinking bit. So let's say 1970, and when we get there, we'll say, "Oh, we're wrong. Let's say 1971." I mean, we'll get it as soon as people realize they have the power. It doesn't belong to Mr. Trudeau, Mr. Wilson, or Mr. Nixon. We are the power. The people are the power, and if people don't know what to do, then let's advertise to tell them they have an option.

Reporter: What about the future of The Beatles? Do you expect to remain a foursome?

John: I've no idea. If we're comfortable enjoying being The Beatles, we'll do it. When we don't, we won't. That's always been the case. The last four years, every time we've made a record, it's been a decision of whether to carry it on from there. Now the point is, in the old days, Paul and I would knock off an LP and write most of the songs on it. Nowadays there's three of us writing equally good songs wanting that much space. The problem now is, do you make a double album every time, which takes six months of your life, or do you make one album, spend three or four months making one album, and get two tracks each? That's the problem. It's just a physical problem, and whether we'll do it or not, I've no idea.

Reporter: John, you've said you're a pacifist. Are there any circumstances in which you personally could support a war?

John: No!

Reporter: I'm wondering what your attitude would have been, for example, during the last war?

John: I can only say, don't talk to me about 1939. Talk to me about 1930.

Yoko Ono: It was all our responsibility. The Germans say, "Oh, it was Hitler." The world says it was the Germans, et cetera, et cetera. It was all our responsibility then. I know from people who were there. I was only a child being bombed and all that, but I just don't believe it was all our responsibility before it happened. I don't believe in killing whatsoever.

Reporter: How seriously do you consider that your pursuit for peace, your manner of clothing, your hair, would alienate more people rather than ever convince them to come over to your side?

John: Many people ask why I don't get a butch haircut and a suit. Politicians do that. Now how many of the public are gullible when it comes to politicians with a nice picture of the family, the dog, and a whore on the side and church on Sunday? I could do that, but I don't think people would believe it. That's the politicians' way. The youth certainly don't believe it anymore. There's an old

Chinese saying that says, "The castle falls from within." I like to leave one door open. If you close all the doors, the energy will attack from all sides and you stand the chance of losing, but if you leave the door open, they'll concentrate there. Our door is hair, some type of irrelevancy to distract so that the attack doesn't hit us. It hits the irrelevancy. We try to be natural. If I feel like cutting [my hair], I'll cut it.

Reporter: Are you focusing this peace movement on the youth of today as opposed to adults?

John: Yes, we are aiming at youth. Our hope is with them because they will be the establishment.

Yoko: The old people will come around, too. Say if there's a Hitler in this world now, we are hoping we can stop him from doing something because everybody, all the youth, is watching and it's very difficult for a Hitler to operate.

Rabbi Abraham Feinberg: You have more power on the youth in the world than all the bishops, rabbis, and priests put together. That's true. Do you ever have a sense of fright over the power that you have?

John: It's an abstract power. If we have something specific sometimes and we want to use the power, say, we wanted to plug a certain product that wasn't peace, I would contact the press and try to get it over, but it probably wouldn't work. So I haven't got any power I can get hold of and do something with.

Rabbi Feinberg: Well, you're using it now for peace, and I think the whole world should be grateful to you and Yoko for doing it.

John: Well, thank you for that.

Reporter: Do you believe in God?

John: Yes, I believe that God is a powerhouse, like where you keep electricity, like a supreme power. But he's neither good nor bad, left or right, black or white. He just is, and we tap that source of power and make of it what we will, like electricity. You can kill people in a chair, or you can light the room with it. I think God is that.

Yoko: We talked about having belief in youth, and that being said, what can we do? This question was always coming up even when we had this bed-in in Montreal. Look what's happening now. Maybe it was twisted around a little by reporters, but the Woodstock Festival, the Isle of Wight Festival, there were thousands and thousands of people there with no violence. Maybe a few mishaps, but no violence, and that's fantastic, very historical. We were at the Isle of Wight and it was beautiful to be able to get together and be quiet and show the violent people and make them ashamed to be violent.

Reporter: Could you give us your personal definition of peace?

John: Peace . . . just no violence and everybody groovin', if you don't mind the word. If people want to be violent, let them kill each other, if it has to be that.

Reporter: Do you think the peace movement could be used as a substitute for the problems that youth in society today are having with drugs?

John: I think the drug problem is a hang-up and a drag. Everybody needs something because of the pressure of society, so it could have been alcohol or something. So the problem isn't what they're on. It's whatever made them go on whatever they're on. The only times we took drugs were when we ran out of hope, and the only way we got out of it was with hope. If we can sustain that hope, then we don't need alcohol or drugs or anything. But if we lose hope, what is there to do?

Reporter: Would you have had that hope without the success of The Beatles?

John: The Beatles had nothing to do with the hope. The Beatles made it, they stopped touring, and they had all the money they wanted, all the fame they wanted, and they found out they had nothing. Then we started our various trips with LSD and the Maharishi and all the rest of the things we did. And the old gag about money and power and fame wasn't the answer. We didn't have any hope because we were famous. You see all those other people, Marilyn Monroe and so on, who had everything The Beatles had. That's no answer. We have the same problems. John and Yoko have the same problems and fears and aspirations as any other couple on Earth do. Regardless of the position we're in or the money we have, we have the same paranoia as everybody else, the same petty thoughts. We have no super answer that came through The Beatles or through power. The Beatles, in that respect, are irrelevant to what I'm talking about.

On December 23, 1969, John Lennon and Yoko Ono met with Canadian Prime Minister Pierre Elliott Trudeau to discuss their peace campaign and plans to call 1970 "Year One for Peace."

John Lennon: We felt we had made a communication direct with the establishment, and it was surprising to find they were straight. Of course, it is snobbery to assume that the whole establishment is one big thing, like it is the same to assume that all Jews are this, or all blacks are that, but we're all guilty of that. I feel that way quite a lot of the time. These people are trying and they are driving a very big machine. There are lots of copilots and they've got to be very careful how they do it. But it certainly gives hope that there are straights who are trying to communicate with us and all the youth. They want to know, but they aren't sure how to approach us, and so we must stretch out our hand the same way as they're trying to stretch theirs.

Reporter: Do you feel confident the new year is going to be a very positive year for peace?

John: Yeah, we think this decade was the beginning of the end and that it was a positive decade, not a depressing one, as people are trying to put around. It was the decade of all the music and the generation becoming aware, the freedom and all the jazz and the moratoriums, the Woodstocks and the Isle of Wight and everything. And this is just the beginning. What we've got to do now is keep hope alive, because without it, well, we'll sink.

Reporter: Why are you here?

John: The main reason is to set up this peace festival, a three-day event at Mosport Park [near Toronto] in July, and to see the people who are arranging it again, and then go to Montreal and make some peace promos for radio.

Reporter: An effective crusade for peace looks like it's going to be a multimillion-dollar project. Are there sources for that kind of money?

John: There's a lot of money around, but can it be gotten? Well, we'll see. I think we can say that we can take this festival round the world and drop a load of money in each country. Leave it in the country in which it's earned and leave a few people we trust to see that it's used for peace and that nothing bad happens to it. We can be on the phone and it won't rely on us so much.

Reporter: What about live appearances?

John: I've done more live appearances in the last year than I've done in the last five. Last year I appeared about five times.

Reporter: What about The Beatles?

John: As soon as they're ready. We had half The Beatles at the Lyceum Ballroom. That was George [Harrison] and me plus Delaney and Bonnie and a 17-piece band we had up there. It was a great experience. It should be like that. If we were doing that and all the Beatles wanted to come, it would be great. There would be no great thing about it. No "Oh, The Beatles are coming back onstage!" like they expect Buddha or Mohammed to come on and perform. That's the fear The Beatles have, including me, about performing. So much is expected of us. George has been on tour with Bonnie and Delaney and I've been drifting around playing. Playing isn't the hang-up. It's going on as The Beatles that's the problem for us.

Reporter: Are you more involved with the peace movement than music now?

John: I'm trying to use both actually. My songs are all about peace. We make music and films mainly, and they're about peace. It's like The Beatles singing "All You Need Is Love" and I'm singing "All You Need Is Peace."

Yoko Ono: And this "Instant Karma" that he just wrote is really like the second step from "Give Peace a Chance," which was a simple message. But "Instant Karma" shows that getting peace is not just going to charity balls and such but a deeper level to change your mind.

Reporter: Do you still get excited about performing?

John: You never lose the excitement or the fear or the nerves before a performance. I'm still excited about releasing new material. There's some more Beatle records coming out, and I'm still excited by the whole scene. When I haven't got an idea for a song in my head, then I'll say, "I'm not really interested," but as soon as I've got a song that I like and a record I like, I'm back on.

Reporter: What about The Beatles these days?

John: We've just finished two albums in the space of five months, so we're pretty together musicwise and our lives are getting pretty together, as well. Our houses, our wives, and things. It's all fab for The Beatles for the moment.

Reporter: Have you gotten rid of some of your own violence?

John: We were pretty violent at the start together. We were pretty violent with each other and then we worked that out in a fit of throwing cups of coffee everywhere all over Ringo's curtains at his house when we were staying there.

Reporter: Do you ever get depressed by the opposition toward your peace campaign?

John: Now and then we get depressed, but in the end you really have to just laugh at them. There's nothing else to do because they're like bears in a cage. They've been in captivity so long they don't know they're in a cage. So you just feel sorry for them.

Yoko: Being upset by them is almost like being upset by a tombstone. They are really dead and we don't get upset by a tombstone. We just have to realize that 80 percent of the whole world are tombstones and 80 percent of our mind is a tombstone because history is a big thing. There is nothing to get angry about really.

Sean Lennon (at age 7): Peace is a very good thing, and salmon is very good when it's smoked.

On March 6, 1970, The Beatles released the single "Let It Be/You Know My Name (Look Up the Number)." Three weeks later Ringo Starr released the album *Sentimental Journey*. On April 17 Paul McCartney released his first solo album, *McCartney,* then on May 8, the album *Let It Be* was released.

Glyn Johns: After The Beatles finished recording *Abbey Road,* the band split up and it became very acrimonious between them. Months later I heard that John Lennon had called Phil Spector in. He'd evidently had a complete change of heart about the album that I had put together. Mind you, he was going through a very strange period in his life. I actually think he was stark raving mad. He'd decided to give it to Spector, who I think did the most abortionate job I've ever heard in my life. He totally and utterly wrecked the album. I really think that he crucified what was a bloody good record. Apparently, I'm told, Paul [McCartney] agreed with my opinion of the Spector version. The other thing is that I never actually got paid. I got paid engineering money — and don't misunderstand me I got paid handsomely for the engineering job that I'd done — but I was never paid for the production work.

George Martin: "The Long and Winding Road" was another McCartney track that was a very, very good song. Unfortunately, when it was released, it had been scored for orchestra by Phil Spector. Orchestrating is always difficult, particularly when you're working with someone like The Beatles. I'd always tried very hard to maintain a kind of classical style that was very clean, whereas I felt the version that was released was very much laden down by the choirs and the scoring. I think Paul felt the same thing, too. He said that it wasn't as good as it could have been. People, nevertheless, loved it and have accepted it, but in my opinion it could have been better.

On May 13, 1970, the film *Let It Be* was premiered in London.

Glyn Johns: In my opinion Allen Klein was a disaster area altogether. He wrecked that film [*Let It Be*]. It could have been an extremely good film, and it was directly as a result of his involvement with it that it wasn't, in my opinion. There clearly was a lot of humor, and the feeling that was on the original record existed on film. It could have been magnificent. I mean, they actually filmed an enormous amount of footage, and that was probably the problem. That they actually had so much. And it wasn't directed well. There was no continuity on a lot of it, and all the rest. There were hours and hours and hours — weeks and weeks of film — with no continuity, no direction, and God knows what else, so a lot of it obviously was unusable. However, I did see the very first rough cut of the film, which was extremely good. But Allen Klein saw it evidently and said he only wanted to see the four Beatles. He didn't want to see anybody else in it. Which is a bit difficult in a documentary when everybody and their mother was wandering around.

On November 30, 1970, George Harrison released his album *All Things Must Pass*. On December 11 John Lennon released the album *John Lennon/Plastic Ono Band*. Seeking to dissolve the partnership of "The Beatles and company," Paul McCartney filed a lawsuit in a London high court on December 31.

Paul McCartney: When The Beatles broke up, it was very difficult. I mean, I haven't been divorced, but from all the stories you hear about divorce, I think it was very similar. In other words, a loving relationship turned sour for one reason or another. With us it was mainly the business things. And probably a clash of egos. Yes, these things do happen. This is real life we got here, not some dream. So it was very difficult, after The Beatles, to come to terms with anything. You just felt like you'd lost the best job in the world, the best mates in the world, and it was really difficult. For a while there I think all of us felt pretty insecure and we just went off on different tangents.

John went to New York and got very avant-garde and did albums like *Summer in New York City* and got very anticommercial. Then, after a few years, he got fed up with that. When he did come back, he wanted to actually sell records. Unfortunately, as we all know, it was tragically cut short when he was, I think, getting more secure in his own life. Certainly from the conversations I had with him, he was feeling a lot better about everything.

And what's happened with me is a little different. The Beatle songs, near the breakup of The Beatles, were songs from a marriage that had just finished, and we wanted to put them behind us. At this point now they're not like that. They're just good songs. I had to look at never singing those songs again because of some pain that once happened to me, or that I was going to forget that and just get on with it and think, Well, they're good songs. I wrote them. I mean, most of the stuff we do in the show — I'm not being big-headed — but it's mainly my stuff. It's like "Strawberry Fields" would have been more of John's vibe. So it's my work and it would be really stupid to never exhibit that work ever again. And I'd say the best thing happened, once we'd made that decision, was I suddenly realized I'd never, ever, sung "Sgt. Pepper" live. Because we recorded it in one night. That was it. Put it down on disc. We walked away from it. The Beatles weren't touring, so I never did it again. "Hey Jude" I've never done live till this tour.

So I mean some of these real nice songs are suddenly there again, and they're really fresh to me now. I remember John once loved these little biscuits called Jaffa Cakes. He totally OD'ed on them. So much so that he could never look at another one in his life. Then what happens is that after three years you look back and you say, "Ooh, oh, I love them," but you've got to give it that time. So I think we all had to take a period where we proved we could do it on our own, and I certainly had to do that for my own mental state. When I got very successful records like "Mull of Kintyre," it felt really good. That was good for my confidence because I outsold anything The Beatles had ever done, so I had proof in my own mind that I could do it on my own. That wasn't particularly what I was setting out to prove, but at the back of my mind I had to answer the question — is there life after The Beatles?

Alistair Taylor: The big memory I have of George Harrison is the man of philosophy. I sat hour after hour in his garden ramblin' on about life and about plants. I always found him very gentle and very grateful for whatever you did for him. Ringo Starr is your guy next door. He's the guy you went to school with, a very nice, ordinary bloke who didn't like to bother anybody. John Lennon was probably the most difficult. John and I were great mates in many ways. He was always getting me to do things for him, but I never felt I got through to John at all. I mean, he's down in history and there's no question that he was the big rebel and everything, but I was never particularly aware of that. He was a guy you just never quite reached. Paul McCartney? Well, Paul was the most complex. Paul could be the most charming, delightful company. I used to love being with him, then he would turn around and be unpleasant to you. It was unbelievable, and he would do it in front of other people.

I have one memory of singer Mary Hopkin. Mary was actually living with my wife and me in our house. She had our guest room because she was only about 16 or 17, and every time she came down to London her mother used to come with her because they had to stay in a hotel. Obviously they weren't going to let Mary stay on her own. I said, "Look, this is crazy. All this money. Mary, move in with us. Live with us." So we were very close. One day Paul said, "Oh, bring Mary to the studio. We're rehearsing a number." So I did. I was just hanging around, and in front of Mary he turned around and looked up. I'd been there for 10 minutes. He said, "What are you waiting for?" I said, "I brought Mary up." He said, "You're not needed. Just go back to the office." That would have been all right, but in front of Mary and other people in the studio, I felt about half an inch tall. It was awful, but then the next minute he would be delight itself.

Yoko Ono: Until I met John [Lennon] I didn't really know what The Beatles were about. I suppose I had heard about them as a social phenomenon like most people in those days did, like Elvis Presley, who was another social phenomenon I wasn't involved in but sort of knew about. After I got involved with John, I knew what he had done and it was a beautiful thing. And John being Sean's father sort of makes me part of it. I feel a family pride for what they did. It's beautiful, as opposed to — and not to knock them or anything — certain groups who made their careers out of saying negative things. But what The Beatles were about was just simple love and, you know, "I Want to Hold Your Hand" and "All You Need Is Love."

That's the gist of it. And it's a beautiful thing. No wonder it was popular. It just changed the whole world, in a sense. I feel it every time I talk about it. The working class was something to be ashamed of before that, especially in Britain. Now even the shop-keepers know that if a young guy comes in who's speaking English with an accent, you're not supposed to be impolite to them just because they're young and they're not from an aristo-cratic family. So it changed everybody's consciousness. And you can make it when you're young. That's fine. Being young and being rich doesn't mean you were born to a good family. It just means you made it. Anything goes. Before The Beatles, if a young guy, or woman, came and started talking about something, people wouldn't listen. But now [people say], "Maybe this is one of those successful guys. Let's listen." It was a social revolution, you know. And, in that sense, I really admire what The Beatles did. When I did *Double Fantasy* with John, I had to realize yet again, almost like a new discovery, just how much he knew about rock and roll. He was like a living dictionary about all the little licks and this and that. It was amazing.

Allan Williams: Oh, yeah, people say to me all the time, "Allan, do you realize you could have been a millionaire?" And I say, "Well, I am a millionaire. I'm a millionaire of memories, and just being a cog in the wheel of the most historical, famous group the world has ever known, that's my reward." A millionaire couldn't have bought or had the fun that we had in the 1960s, and we're still here.

George Martin: The Beatles were always anti-establishment, even when I first met them. It was always them against the world. Anybody who was an authority figure was someone they were contemp-tuous of. It was part of their makeup. And, very fortunately for me, I didn't come into that category because they knew I was a maverick at EMI, so they sided with me.

Klaus Voorman: No, The Beatles didn't remain the same. I wouldn't say so. Basically Paul has stayed the same, but I mean he went through many changes. He's the one who stayed the way he always was, more or less. George was a real simple, little boy, a real son, a little kid, and very sensitive. He has definitely changed a lot from those first days when I met them. Ringo was always like a little dog. I loved him. You always wanted to cuddle him. I met him briefly when I did the *Anthology* cover in London and he was okay. He was nice.

Paul McCartney: I saw John [Lennon] before we came on this tour [Wings over America], and I checked out whether it was just me that felt sort of lukewarm on doing a show together. He said no, that he felt about the same as me. I'm pretty sure the other two, who I haven't seen recently, feel about the same way. An offer was made recently by someone outside the four of us. This fellow said, "How about it?" for this massive amount of money. So it gets all the papers asking, and everyone wants to know, and everyone gets involved in it. But really the truth is that none of us is interested in doing it. And it's not me holding it up, it's not John holding it up, and it's not George. From time to time, I think, people have a bit of a field day. I've seen in the papers in England that they say, "Well, Paul will do it. John will do it. Ringo will do it, but George won't do it!" And they keep doing this every two weeks and then it's "George'll do it, so and so'll do it," and so on. But it's really a lot of talk. The real truth is that we did what we did, we came full cycle, and we ended the group. It ended amid a lot of bad feeling. But that's sort of gone down and everyone understands, vaguely, anyway, why it all had to happen. So everyone feels kind of good about it now but really isn't very interested in doing it again. It's just the way it is.

Peter Halling: As a classical musician, you wonder what The Beatles' music is at times. Then you say, "It's music of the people, isn't it?" Folk music, yes. I think that classical music became too complicated and people couldn't take part in it any longer. They would listen to it, but the man in the street wants to take part in it. So The Beatles' music is a throwback to "folk music." They're very simple chords, things like that, and that's how it's evolved. Some of those Beatle songs are classics now and will be classics forever. They'll live on right through.

Gene Pitney: I got a letter the other day from a girl who is 18 and lives in Chicago. She said something that really caught me and I had to go back and read it again. She said she wished she had had a chance to live in the 1960s, that she really felt she missed something after seeing what she sees now and what happened then. And I started to think to myself, What was it like? I performed all the way through it. I wasn't an outsider looking in, but there was a feeling of optimism. There was something about whatever the problems were in the world, or personally, you could make them work out. There was an answer to it. To me that all fell apart at the very end of the 1960s and diminished into something that nobody ever believed in anymore. To me the 1970s went their way and I doubt we'll get that feeling again. In fact, I doubt we'll have that again ever. Everything was a positive. If it was a movement in music, it was a positive movement, the flower power thing. Even the psychedelic things were on the upside. They were all meant to be positive statements, and The Beatles were one of the most important aspects of the 1960s. They were the catalysts.

Richard Lester: For three years I was in the center of the universe, from *A Hard Day's Night* to *Help!* to *How I Won the War*, and I knew at the time that it would be the pinnacle of whatever I did. I said in the late 1960s that 30 years from now, if I'm knocked down by a bus, the *Evening Standard* poster will be, "Beatles Director in Dead Drama." You can't avoid that and I'm perfectly happy because at least I've had the opportunity to have had that experience. So life is downhill, okay, but at least you've been up and seen the view. The fact that a part of you lives on, apart from your own children, is a rare privilege and I'm perfectly happy. I'm thrilled to have made a film like *A Hard Day's Night* that will always be a good antique mirror. One that will say, "This is as accurate as I could produce what it felt like to be around that experience at the time."

Philip Norman: I think it's a story that gets more interesting every day. A story of a moment in contemporary history that, I think, is the last time we can remember believing that life got better every day rather than worse. And that's inextricably bound up with what The Beatles did and what they played and how they were. We know that the world was not much better than it is today, but it looked better and we felt it was better. I think it's deeply significant that 15- and 16-year-olds now turn to The Beatles. Deeply significant.

George Harrison: I've got a few Beatle boots and some ski boots from when we made the film *Help!* I've got some of those suits, the Pierre Cardin original suits, the collarless ones. I've got the jacket I wore at Shea Stadium and I've got my Sgt. Pepper suit and a lot of crazy psychedelic things that just look ridiculous now — hysterical things, fancy dress.

Astrid Kirchherr: It was a completely different time and we had different dreams. We had to fight for our visions to come true and that made it all so exciting. If we wanted a pair of pants, like tight bell bottoms, we couldn't buy them. We had to make them ourselves. Creativity just blossomed then and that was so wonderful. We used to sit around just like all young kids do and say, "Oh, what would you do if you had a million?" One day George [Harrison] said, "You just wait until we're the same as The Shadows!" And John [Lennon] burst out and said, "What do you mean, The Shadows? I want to be as big as Elvis!" It was like all kids' dreams. And when The Beatles did make it, I was and I still am very proud of them. When I see or hear that Paul [McCartney] has been knighted and that he wrote a symphony, my heart just opens up with pride and joy to know I was so lucky to get to know these wonderful people who deserved all this fame and fortune. When I think about all the songs they have written, and all the joy they gave to millions of people in the world, I know, for me, they're the biggest thing going in this century.

Horst Fascher: I think Paul McCartney is the warmest guy I've ever met. He's got a heart, a very soft heart. When my daughter was 11 months old, we found out she had to have a heart operation and I couldn't afford it. I couldn't find anybody to help me pay for this difficult operation. When Paul found out about it, he flew in the best surgeon possible to perform the operation and he paid for it all. Although my daughter died 13 days after the operation, I still think he is wonderful. I would do anything for him. Anything he asked, I would do it for him.

Tony Barrow: It was a magnificent time. Looking back, I think they were experiences one couldn't have got any other way because The Beatles hadn't happened before and will never happen again, however many claims there are about "Here comes another musical messiah." The Beatles will never be duplicated. They can't be. At the time, of course, we were all rather like people with our noses pressed right up against enormous Cinemascope screens. We couldn't see the whole picture for ourselves. It's only long afterward that we've all been able to go back and sit in the stalls and rerun the whole Beatlemania movie and understand the whole thing for ourselves. And realize for the first time, because we were so close to it, the huge social significance of The Beatles. The Beatles really influenced an entire generation of children. They influenced that generation as to how they should grow from children into adults, what their mode of behavior should be, what their attitudes should be, what their fashions should be, and what their toleration for adult domination should be. The whole thing changed. The seat of power changed, if you like. The balance of power fell from an average age of 40 to 25 overnight. That's what The Beatles did. Maybe not overnight, but through the course of time there was a generation of children who grew up with a whole new attitude and outlook that was brought about by The Beatles and all who followed them. The Beatles were the start of the revolution.

Derek Taylor: Tony Barrow was a typical NEMS believer. Another good Brian Epstein choice, like Dezo Hoffman. The whole damn lot of them were sold on the idea of The Beatles, I think, being saviors. I don't think that's too strong a word for it. We saw them in that sense. There is an evangelical phrase, "Do you take Jesus Christ as your personal savior?" I remember hearing that phrase, "your personal savior," 40 years ago, and I think that's what really happened. Not only in the psychedelic, sort of dangerous period, but in the very primitive Liverpool, "Please Please Me" days. People saw them as being some sort of answer to the miseries of the world or in our own little lives. They were the four-headed Santa Claus. It was a very cheering sight. No matter what happened to John [Lennon], that personal horror is separate from the aliveness of the black-and-white Beatles of that period — still capable of making people feel good again. So it's true. They are ageless and timeless.

Victor Spinetti: I was at a hotel in Salzburg [Austria] while we were filming *Help!* and I had the flu. We were all staying in the same hotel and I was lying in bed. Each of The Beatles visited me separately, and the way they visited me when I had the flu is what they are really like.

There was a knock on the door. Paul McCartney opened it, looked around, and asked, "Is it catching?" I said, "Yeah," and he closed the door. George Harrison walked in and said, "I've come to plump your pillows because whenever you're ill people come to plump your pillows." And he came in and plumped my pillows and tidied the sheets and did what he could to make me feel comfortable.

John Lennon walked in and said [in a very German accent], "You are in zeee state of Austria. You are going to be experimented on by zee doctors and your skin will be made into lampshades.

Heil Hitler!" Then he walked out. Ringo walked in, didn't say anything, sat on the side of the bed, picked up the room service menu, looked at it, and said, "Once upon a time there were three bears, Mommy bear, Daddy bear, and Baby bear . . ."

And that was the essential difference between the four of them. John, the surrealist. Paul, the one who thinks if it's catching he might not be able to do the shot tomorrow. George, the caring one. Ringo, the fantasist.

Murray Kaufman: I think the greatest impact The Beatles had on our lives was their attitude. Their music and attitude said it all for us. They kept pace with instant ice tea and birth control pills. From the time they put the press on, telling it like it was and not giving us the usual, expected, static answers, they endeared themselves to us. You have to realize that in the United States we never had self-contained groups. The most an act would have would be maybe their own guitar player or their own drummer, or their own piano player. But never self-contained groups. So The Beatles affected the guitar industry, which should set them up for life. They affected that. They affected dress. They affected the clothing industry. But most of all they affected attitude. When Frank Sinatra, Elvis Presley, and Benny Goodman came along, they were the superstars and they created eras. But from the beginning to the end of their reigns, they were the same, and to this day when you hear them, you know it. With every album The Beatles gave us a 180-degree change. A completely different change, a different sound, a different attitude. They kept changing with us. They kept pace with us. The Beatles inspired a lot of the political and social revolution that took place, because from a subliminal standpoint The Beatles represented change. The feeling that people had was that social change couldn't happen that fast. That changed because we saw The Beatles change right in front of our eyes.

When Brian Epstein died, that marked the beginning of the end. When Allen Klein came in, that was certainly the bell of disaster. I think that Apple was a disaster. They tried to become business people when they tried to do it themselves. I love Neil Aspinall, who was their roadie along with Mal Evans, but they weren't qualified to run businesses. They opened up boutiques and they opened up all these crazy things. Brian was the cohesive force that kept The Beatles together. He adapted himself and the running of the business to the lifestyle that they then demanded. They didn't always do the correct thing, but who does?

We only know them, selfishly, by what they represented in our lives. But they are indeed four lads from Liverpool with limited education and background who did remarkably well, who advanced our business and inspired a fusion of all music. You have to realize that after The Beatles, Peter, Paul and Mary actually sang, "I dig rock and roll music." I mean, they were the folk purists of the land. Bob Dylan became electrified and amplified. Black musicians were inspired by certain things that The Beatles did. The influence that they had was the greatest contribution they made. We can't actually sit down and make a list of these things. We can make a list of how many records they sold or how many albums they sold or what kind of appearances they made or how many people appeared, but attitude is a funny thing. It's a word that encompasses many things and effects a great deal of change. The Beatles had much more of an effect upon us than we realize.

George Harrison: They say, "Knock and the door will be opened, or seek and you will find." In those days we went through so much experience. It was almost like going through 20 years of experience crammed into three or four years. Some of those experiences were pretty heavy. They made me feel like I wanted to know what the point was of all this. We made our money and fame, but for me that wasn't it. It was good fun for a while, but it certainly wasn't the answer to what life is about. So I needed to know what it was all about and I got involved with Ravi Shankar and with Indian music. I went to India, I did a bit of yoga, and then I got into meditation. Through all that experience, somewhere down the line, the answers came to me of what the point of life is, and what we are doing in these bodies. And now I don't really have so many questions.

George Martin: There isn't an answer to the question "Why them?" Except that they were great. John Lennon used to say to me, "Elvis Presley is the greatest." I would always dispute that. And I still dispute it. I think Elvis Presley was great, but he didn't hold a candle to John or Paul or The Beatles generally. In my book The Beatles were the greatest performers and writers ever. And I think that's why we're still talking about them. I'm very, very lucky to have been part of that story.

At the time when we began they had no one else to look to and I was their boss. I knew about records, and it was a very good relationship. We got on famously. Gradually the emphasis changed because they learned very quickly indeed about recording, and in the end they knew more than I did. They always had enormous confidence that the world was theirs for the taking. Gradually the influence swerved. They were curious about everything. They were never satisfied with sticking to one style, one format, one sound. They started teaching me things. But we always remained extremely good friends and worked extremely well together. It was a good team.

I think I was part of a five-piece group. You know, in that I wasn't the one who performed, but I was part of them. We were all working toward the same end. I can't really say I was any more of an influence on them than Ringo [Starr] was, for example, or George [Harrison] was. We would all put our little two cents' worth in. My particular specialty in the beginning was introductions, endings, and solos. The rest of the song was theirs. Later on it became a question of orchestration and my injecting instruments that they couldn't cope with themselves. It was the knowledge of that and what one could do with it, and also recording techniques. The addition of things that they hadn't thought of — all the backward guitar stuff and that kind of thing.

For me their genius was in the songwriting. They wrote over

300 songs, and most of them are brilliant. Whether we will ever see another group like The Beatles is impossible to say, but I should think it very unlikely. There have been incredibly talented people since The Beatles and there will continue to be plenty of talented musicians and performers. It all comes down to the song, however. That's the fundamental part. Once you have that you can have anything.

Index*

Abbey Road, 271, 286–93, 307

Abbey Road Studios, 101, 104, 106, 113, 139, 168, 189, 209, 286

Ad Lib Club, 157, 183

Adler, Larry, 6

Aintree Institute, 53, 59, 73

Alice in Wonderland, 195

All Things Must Pass On, 308

"All You Need Is Love," 251, 285, 289, 305, 311

"All You Need Is Peace," 305

Altham, Keith, 127

American Top 40, 141

Anthology, 312

Apple, 247, 254, 255, 261, 263, 265, 271–77, 280–83, 317

Apple Boutique, 257

Arden, Don, 92, **93**

Ardmore and Beechwood, 95

As Time Goes By: Living in the Sixties (Taylor), 281

Asher, Jane, 133, **259**

Asher, Peter, 160, 280

Ashton, William. *See* Kramer, Billy J.

Aspinall, Neil, 133, 274, 275, 318

ATV, 278, 279

Baird, Julia, 3, 5, 10, 15, 39, 64, 67, 102, 109

"Ballad of John and Yoko/Old Brown Shoe, The," 283

Bambi Kino, 50

Barrow, Tony, 87, 107, 116, 131, 221, **222, 227, 315,** 316

Bassey, Shirley, 130

BBC, 99, 205, 258

"Be Bop a Lula," 14

Beach Boys, The, 155, 162, 241, 247, 260

Beat Brothers, 75

Beat Generation of America, 24

"Beatle Bath Water," 178

Beatlemania, 53, 55, 104, 126, 145–46, 149, 179, 217, 315

"Beatlemania," 168

"Beatles #2," 196

Beatles Book Monthly, 103

Beatles for Sale, 182, 282

"Beatles Movie, The," 164

"Because," 290

bed-ins, 279, 283

Beecham, Sir Thomas, 211

Beeching, Lord, 275

Beetles, 29

"Being for the Benefit of Mr. Kite," 238

Bennett, Barbara, 168

Bernstein, Sid, 139, 147, 151, 197

Berry, Chuck, 15, 46, 51, 55, 93, 116, 122, 136, 167, 193, 286

"Besame Mucho," 118

Best, Mona, 18, 22, 35, 53, 62, **100**

Best, Pete, 19, 30, 35, **36, 40, 43, 48, 49, 52, 54,** 59, **60, 62, 69, 70, 71, 91,** 99, **101, 102**

* Boldface indicates interviews.

321

Bill Black Combo, The, 179
Bill Haley and the Comets, 54
Birth of the Beatles, The, 198
"Birthday," 265
Black, Cilla, 64
"Blackbird," 264, 265
Blackboard Jungle, 13
Blackjacks, 35, 36
Blake, Peter, 119, 232, 239, 243, 268, 294
Blue Angel, 53
Blue Meanies, 262
BOAC, 169
Bonis, Bob, 170, 199
Bonn, Issy, 295
Bowery Boys, 245
Boyer, Charles, 20
Braddock, Bessie, 77
Brambell, Wilfrid, 170
British Invasion, 179
Brown, Ken, 19, 20, **23,** 52
Brown, Peter, 261, 274, 275
Brown, Tara, 241
Buckingham Palace, 203
Buddha, 305
Budokan, 223
Burgess, John, 135
Butcher Block photograph, 205

Cabaret Artists' Social Club, 30
Calder, Tony, 107
Caldwell, George, 151
Can't Buy Me Love, 133, 199
Canadian House of Commons, 191
Candlestick Park, 227
Capitol Records, 90, 130, 132, 135, 136, 141, 151, 155, 162, 206, 284
Cardin, Pierre, 314
Carnegie Hall, 138, 140, 147
Carroll, Lewis, 195

"Carry That Weight," 291
Carson, Johnny, 282
Casanova Club, 62
Casbah Club, 18–21, 22, 36, 52, 54, 59, 85, 102
Cass, Ron, 280
Cass and the Cassanovas, 74
cast of characters, xi–xv
Cavern Club, 61–65, 72, 73, 74, 81–84, 87, 88, 89, 115, 117
Cellarful of Noise, A (Epstein), 77
CFPL, 138
"Chains," 118
Chancellor, John, 149
Channel, Bruce, 108
Charles, Ray, 15, 94, 288
Charles, Tommy, 222
Chaseman, Joel, 146
Chelson, Joe, 120
Chris Barber Jazz Band, 7
Christ controversy, 217–24
Cinemascope, 315
Civil, Alan, 211, 242
Clapton, Eric, 264, 286, 289
Clark, Dave, 181
Clark, Dick, 198
Cleave, Maureen, 217, **218,** 219
Cliff Bennet and the Rebel Rousers, 266
Cliff Richard and the Shadows, 166
Coasters, The, 115, 156
Cochran, Eddie, 14, 20, 29
Cocker, Joe, 288
Cockroaches, The, 182
Cole, Nat King, 48, 155
Coleman, Ray, 181
Coleman, Syd, 95
Collingham, Anne, 131
Collins, Phil, 166
Columbia Records, 134

Condon, Les, 212
Condon, Richard, 197
"Coney Island Baby," 145
Cordon Bleu, 274
Cox, Maureen, 183
"Crazy Beatles, The," 41
Crazy Elephant, 120
Crickets, The, 29

Daily Express, 124, 128, 129, 168, 169
"Daily Howl," 11
Daily Mail, 129, 241
Daily Mirror, 129
Daily Telegram, 168
Dakotas, The, 115
Darin, Bobbie, 84
Dark Horse, 26
Datebook, 217
Davis, Billy, 119
Davis, Spencer, 257
"Day in the Life, A," 241, 242, 245, 246
Dean, James, 178
Dean, Terry, 90
Decca Records, 7, 75, 87–89, 107, 108, 116, 117, 123
Dee, Joey, 138
Del Renas, The, 53
Delaney, Paddy, 63, 81
Deltones, The, 53
Demmler, Otto, 132, 133
Derry and the Seniors, 37
Dexter, Dave, 134, 141, **155**
Dick Barton Show, The, 5
Dick James Music, 99, 131
Dion, 120
Disney, Walt, 262
"Do You Want to Know a Secret," 116

Dodd, Ken, 77
Donegan, Lonnie, 7
Donovan, 260
Double Fantasy, 311
Dunning, George, 262
Dupuis, Herbert, 191
Durband, Alan "Dusty," 25, 26
Dylan, Bob, 157, 318

Eastman, Linda, 278
Ed Sullivan Show, The, 140, 141, 161
Eddy, Duane, 30
Edge, Graham, 261
"Eight Arms to Hold You," 196
"Eleanor Rigby," 208, 210, 219, 222
Elvis Presley Fan Club of England, 199
Emerick, Geoff, 208, 210, **212, 236, 238, 239, 240, 242, 252, 287, 291**
EMI, 75, 90, 94, 95, 98, 106, 107, 116, 134, 135, 136, 137, 139, 141, 202, 203, 205, 236, 244, 245, 258, 263, 266, 267, 269, 270, 288, 311
Empire Stadium, 179, 180
"End, The," 291
Epstein, Brian, 73, **74, 75,** 76, 77, **81,** 82–84, **85, 86,** 87–90, 94–96, 98, 102, 104, 114–16, 121, 125, 128, **138,** 140, 141, 145, 152, **158,** 162, 169, 178, 180, 196, 197, 202, **218,** 223, 233, 253, 256, 317
Epstein, Clive, 86, 129, 253, 254
Eubanks, Bob, 191
Evans, Mel, 199, 257, 318
Evening Standard, 217, 218, 313
Everly Brothers, 94, 146, 198, 199
Excellents, The, 145

Faithfull, Marianne, 252
"Falling in Love Again," 118
Farrow, Mia, 260
Fascher, Horst, 39, 41, 92, 315
Fats Domino, 30, 44, 66, 93, 94, 199
Feinberg, Abraham, 302
Fielding, John, 255
Finnegans Wake, 195
Firebird, The, 242
Flamingos, The, 59
Flannery, Joe, 101, 108
Fool, The, 243
"For No One," 211
Four Seasons, The, 145
Four Vests, The, 136
Fourmosts, The, 77, 90
Foy, Jim, 95
Fraser, Robert, 243, 268
Freeman, Bob, 119, 243
'Frisco's Cow Palace, 203
"From Me to You," 114, 117, 121, 124, 131, 137, 213
Fury, Billy, 31, 90, 119

Garry, Len, 10, 13, 15, 25
Gaye, Marvin, 241
General Hospital, 198
Gentle, Johnny, 31, 36
George V, 161, 163
Gerry and the Pacemakers, 28, 29, 37, 114, 124
"Get Back," 279
Gibb, Russ, 293
Ginsberg, Allen, 24
Girl Can't Help It, The, 265
"Give Peace a Chance," 284, 285, 305
"Glass Onion," 268
"God," 253
"Golden Slumbers," 291
Goldwater, Barry, 172

"Good Morning, Good Morning," 239
"Good Vibrations," 247
Goodman, Benny, 317
Goon Show, The, 5
Gorcey, Leo, 245
Gorshin, Frank, 151
"Got to Get You into My Life," 212
Grade, Lew, 279
Graham, Billy, 251
Grand Dragon, The, 218
Gretty, Jim, **28,** 61, **64, 77,** 81
Guildford Cathedral, 234

Haight-Ashbury, 246
Haley, Bill, 11, 13
Hall, Huntz, 245
Halley, Tom, 262
Halling, Peter, 234, 239, 242, 312
Hamburg, 33–55, 66–71, 91–95
Hamburg Art College, 69, 70
Hamilton, Richard, 268
"Happiness Is a Warm Gun," 265, 266, 268
Hard Day's Night, A, 160–69, 161, 163, 164, 173, 175, 187, 188, 195, 196, 313, 314
Harris, Jet, 119
Harrison, George, 16, 23, 31, 41, 49, 51, 67, 81, 126, 145, 157, 206, 226, 230, 254, 256, 264, 267, 276, 288, 289, 291, 314, 318
Harrison, Louise, 17, 135, 150, 152, 227
Harrison, Peter, 36
"Harry Lime Theme, The," 31
Harry, Bill, 23, 27, 54, 59, 68, 73, 76, 81, 82, 87
Haslams, Mike, 90
Hawkins, Ronnie, 179

Haworth, Jann, 244
Heath House, 238
Helliwell, Bud, 145
"Hello, Goodbye," 251
"Hello Little Girl," 83
Help!, 165, 187–95, 196, 314, 316
"Helter Skelter," 267
Hendrix, Jimi, 243
"Here Comes the Sun," 289
Hessey's Music Store, 28, 64, 65
"Hey Baby," 108
"Hey Jude," 309
"Hey Jude/Revolution," 263
HMV, 95, 134
Hoffman, Dezo, 121, **156, 256,** 316
Holly, Buddy, 5, 15, 29, 198
"Honey Don't," 167
Hopkin, Mary, 260, **261,** 310
Horn, Paul, 260
"How Do You Do It," 98, 99, 104, 105, 113, 114
How I Won the War, 164
Howes, Arthur, 159
Howey Casey and the Seniors, 74
Hughes, Liz, 62, 72
Huntley-Brinkley news hour, 155
"Hurricane Smith," 202

"I Am the Walrus," 257, 258
I Ching, 264, 273
"I Feel Fine/She's a Woman," 182
"I Saw Her Standing There," 118
"I Wanna Be Your Man," 127, 132
"I Want to Hold Your Hand," 117, 128, 130, 133, 134, 141, 146, 149, 155, 159, 246, 311
"I Want You (She's So Heavy)," 289
"I'll Be There," 84
"I'll Cry Instead," 163

"If I Needed Someone," 290
In His Own Write (Lennon), 169, 229
"In My Life," 199
"In the Mood," 252
Indica Gallery, 232
Indra, 39, 45, 53
Insight Team, The, 255
"Instant Karma," 305
interviewees, xi–xv
interviews with press. *See* press interviews
Iron Door, 62
Isle of Wight Festival, 301, 304
Isley Brothers, 138
It's Trad, Dad!, 162

Jabberwocky, 195
Jacaranda Club, 28, 59
JAEP Music, 125
Jagger, Mick, 122, 157, 252
Jamerson, James, 241
James, Dick, 98, **278**
James, Ian, 13, 14
James, Stephen, 98, 113, 125, 130, 205, 278
Japanese crisis, 223
Jay and the Americans, 152
"Jingle Rock Island Line," 7
Joe Brown and the Brothers, 166
John, Elton, 285
John Lennon/Plastic Ono Band, 308
Johnny and the Moondogs, 23
Johns, Glyn, 269, 277, 307
Jollet, Lee, 90
Jones, Brian, 122
Jones, Peter, 104, 127
Jones, Philip, 114
Jones, Raymond, 74, 82
Joyce, James, 195
Justis, Bill, 16

Kaempfert, Bert, 68, 70, 71, 73, 77, 87
Kaiserkeller, 35, 40, 45, 49, 50, 51, 53, 92
Kaufman, Murray (Murray the K), 145, 146, **149, 152, 155, 157, 190,** 191, **197, 218, 228, 236, 245, 253,** 284, **317**
Keaton, Buster, 163
Kelly, Brian, 53
Kelly, Freda, 124
Kerouac, Jack, 24
King Features, 262
King Size Taylor and the Dominoes, 74
Kirchherr, Astrid, 45, 46, **47, 48, 67, 69,** 70, **91, 314**
Klein, Allen, 254, 271, 275, 280, 281, 283, 307, 308, 317
Klemperer, Otto, 211
Ku Klux Klan, 218
Koschmeider, Bruno, 49, 50
Kramer, Billy J., 114, 115, 159, **256**

"Lady Madonna/The Inner Light," 258
Leach, Sam, 7, 62
Le Coq D'Or Tavern, 179
Le Studio, 284
Leary, Rosemary, 284
Leary, Timothy, 283
Leitch, Donovan, 207, 259
Lennon, Cynthia, 22, 45, 59, **102,** 103, **124,** 150, **156,** 263
Lennon, John
   bed-ins, 279, 283
   broken wrist, 60
   childhood, 3–7
   Christ controversy, 217–24
   divorce from Cynthia Lennon, 263

In His Own Write, 169, 229
interviews, **8, 14, 29, 170, 173, 174, 194, 200, 206, 217, 229, 231, 266, 279, 280, 285, 299–306**
   marriage to Cynthia Lennon, 102–4
   marriage to Yoko Ono, 278
   returned M.B.E., 299
   salmon fishing, 8, 9
   Spaniard in the Works, A, 194
Lennon, Julian, 238
Lennon, Sean, 310
Leonard, Barry, 168
Les Stewart Quartet, 20, 21
Lester, Richard, 161, 162, 163, 164, 165, 188, 196, **197, 313**
Let It Be (album), 280, 287, 292, 306
Let It Be (film), 197, 269, 278, 307
"Let It Be/You Know My Name (Look Up the Number)," 306
Lewis, Jerry Lee, 62, 93, 94
Lewis, Victor, 254
Light Programme, 99
Lindsay-Hogg, Michael, 278
Linton, Paul, 132
Linton Records, 132
Litherland Town Hall, 53–55, 59, 116
Little Richard, 15, 30, 44, 46, 51, 54, 55, **93,** 94, 116, 193, 199, **286**
Liverpool Art College, 23
Liverpool Echo, 87, 88
Lomax, Jackie, 265
London, Laurie, 135
London Pavilion Cinema, 169
"Long and Winding Road, The," 307
"Long Tall Sally," 21, 54
"Lost Paranoia," 291
"Love Me Do," 15, 93, 104–9, 113, 116, 134, 137, 176

Love You Make: An Insider's Story of the Beatles, The (Brown), 274

"Lovely Rita," 239

LSD, 251

Lyceum Ballroom, 305

Magical Mystery Tour (album), 257, 293

Magical Mystery Tour (film), 256–58

Maharishi Mahesh Yogi, 190, 252, **253,** 258, 259, 260, 303

Manila affair, 223, 224

Marcos, Imelda, 223, 224

Mariaka, Simon, 243

Marsden, Gerry, 28, 77

Martin, George, 90, 95, **96, 97, 98, 99,** 100, **104, 105, 107, 113, 114,** 116, **117, 118, 125, 130, 132, 133,** 135, 138, 145, **182, 192, 193,** 194, **199, 201, 207,** 208, **209, 210,** 211, **212, 213, 232,** 234, **236,** 238, 240, **241, 247, 251, 263,** 264, **267, 287, 290, 292, 293, 307, 311, 319**

Maslow, Abraham, 59

Mason, David, 234, 252

"Maxwell's Silver Hammer," 288, 292

McCartney, 306

McCartney, Michael, 37

McCartney, Paul

  death rumour, 293–95

  interviews, **4, 12, 14, 15, 16, 31, 40, 65, 67, 70, 71, 104, 118, 119, 124, 129, 139, 170, 171–73, 176, 177, 190, 191, 200, 209, 229, 241, 251, 259, 260, 261, 263, 268, 271, 275, 289, 308, 312**

  lawsuit to dissolve Beatles, 308

  LSD, 251

  marriage to Linda Eastman, 278

McFall, Ray, 61, 62, 74

McGuinn, Roger, 189, 247

"Mean Mr. Mustard," 291

Medley, Bill, 177

Meehan, Tony, 119

Members of the British Empire, 191, 203, 299

Memphis concert, 224

Merman, Ethel, 159

Mersey Beat, 73, 74, 76, 77, 82

"Mersey Beatle, The," 74

Mersey Sound, 124

"Michelle," 200

Miller, Glenn, 125

Miller, Steve, 270

Mitchell, Guy, 11

"Money," 90, 116, 117

Monroe, Marilyn, 303

Moody Blues, The, 261

"Moon Glow," 42

Moon, Keith, 10

Moore, Tommy, 36

Mosport Park, 304

Motown, 157, 166, 200, 241

MPL (McCartney Productions Ltd.), 273, 274, 282

Murray, Mitch, 98

Murray the K. *See* Kaufman, Murray

Musique Concrète, 209

"My Bonnie," 71, 72, 74, 81, 84, 90

"My Bonnie Lies over the Ocean," 67

"My Yiddishe Mama," 295

Nelson, Jay, 179

NEMS (North End Music Stores), 65, 73, 75, 76, 77, 82, 83, 84, 85, 107, 108, 169, 254, 316

New School for Social Research, 139

New York Post, 150

Newell, Norman, 135

Newman, Edwin, 149
Nixon, Richard, 300
NME (New Musical Express), 114, 123
Norman, Philip, 43, 108, 255, **273, 280,** 283, **295**
North End Music Stores. *See* NEMS
Northern Songs, 125, 278, 279
"Norwegian Wood," 201
"Number 9," 266

"Ob-La-Di, Ob-La-Da," 263
"Octopus's Garden," 289, 292
O'Donnell, Lucy, 238
"Oh Darling," 288, 289
Oh! What a Lovely War, 160, 187
Oldham, Andrew "Loog," 107, 117, 123, 127, 128, 171
Olympia, 161, 163
Olympic Studios, 270
O'Mahony, Sean, 103, 229
Ono, Yoko, 8, 231, **232,** 278, 279, 283, 284, 286, 290, **301, 302,** 304, **305, 310**
Ontario Science Centre, 299
Opportunity Knocks, 261
Orbison, Roy, 113, 121, **123,** 124
Ormsby-Gore, Lady, 152
Ormsby-Gore, Sir David, 152, **153**
Orton, Joe, 197
O'Shay, Tessy, 151
Our World, 251
Owen, Alun, 161, 163, 165

"P.S. I Love You," 107, 109, 116
Palace Hotel, 201
Palladium, 77, 129, 159
Palmer, Tony, 134
Paolozzi, Eduardo, 69, 92
"Paperback Writer/Rain," 217

Paramor, Norrie, 90
Parlophone Records, 95, 107, 134, 155
Parnes, Larry, 29, 31, 36
Parsons, Alan, 292
Pendleton, Harold, 7
"Penny Lane," 232, 233, 235, 236
Perkins, Carl, 167
Perry, André, 284
Pet Sounds, 241, 246
Peter, Paul and Mary, 318
"Piggies," 265
Pinewood Studios, 235
Pink Floyd, 203
Pitney, Gene, 159, 313
Plastic Ono Band, 285, 286
Platters, The, 48
Playboy Club, 150
Plaza Hotel, 149, 150, 151, 156
Please Please Me, 117
"Please Please Me," 108, 109, 113, 114, 116, 131, 134, 135, 136, 137, 213, 316
Polydor Records, 68, 69, 71, 75, 87
"Polythene Pam," 291
Poole, Brian, 88, 89
Popjoy, William, 8, 9
Precht, Bob, 198
Presley, Elvis, 11, 15, 86, 90, 93, 95, 109, 136, 146, 147, 161, 179, 180, 199, 300, 310, 314, 317, 319
press interviews
    Beatles, 181, 182, 225, 226
    Christ controversy, 219–22
    death of Brian Epstein, 253
    Kennedy Airport (New York), 147–49
    Lennon, John, 173, 174
    London, 157, 158

Mahareshi Mahesh Yogi, 253
McCartney, Paul, 171–73, 176,
    177, 190, 263
Medley, Bill, 177
Members of British Empire, 191,
    203–5
Ormsby-Gore, David, 153
peace conference, 299–306
return from India, 258–59
Starr, Ringo, 174–76, 183
Taylor, Derek, 178
Washington, D.C. (Feb/64),
    153–55
Preston, Billy, 279, 280, 282
Prince of Wales Theatre, 129
Private Eye, 276
"Professions, The," 38
Pye Records, 90

Quarry Men, The, 9–27
Queen Elizabeth Hotel, 284
Quickleys, Tommy, 89

Radio India, 18
Radio Luxembourg, 107, 109
Radio One, 99
"Raunchy," 16
Ray, Johnny, 11
RCA Victor, 155, 284
Reader's Digest, 131
Record-Mirror, 121, 128
Record Retailer, The, 114
Rennie, Roland, 135
reporters. *See* press interviews
"Revolution 9," 266, 267, 268
Revolver, 207–13, 219, 225, 246, 247,
    291
Rice, Tim, 114
Richard, Cliff, 44, 104, 136, 137,
    146

Richards, Keith, 122, **127, 170**
Richards, Ron, 96, 105
"Right String Baby, Wrong Yo-Yo,"
    167
Righteous Brothers, The, 152, 177
"Ringo's Theme," 181
Robert Fraser Gallery, 232
"Robin Hood," 98
Robinson, Red, 138, 179, 246
"rock and dole," 28
Rock and Roll Revival, 286
"Rock Island Line," 7
Rock of Gibraltar, 278
Rohne, Dorothy "Dot," 45
"Roll over Beethoven," 117
Rolling Stones, The, 107, 116, 122,
    123, 126–28, 157, 167, 170, 171,
    177, 181, 252
Ronettes, The, 145
Rory Storm and the Hurricanes, 29,
    37, 101, 102
Rossington, Norman, 170
Rowe, Dick, 88, 89, **90,** 108, **122,**
    169
Rowe, Tommy, 152
Rowlands, John, 178
Royal Academy of Dramatic Arts
    (RADA), 76
Royal Albert Hall, 120, 122
Royal College, 232
Royal Command Variety
    Performance (Nov/63), 129
Rubber Soul, 199–205, 206, 246, 247
*Running, Jumping and Standing Still
    Film, The*, 162
Rustics, The, 89
Rydell, Bobby, 138

Saint Joan, 26
Savile Row, 269, 277, 278

Scaffold, The, 38

Scala Theatre, 166

"Scrambled Eggs," 192

Screaming Lord Sutch, 123

Scott, Ken, 267

Searchers, The, 53

Searle, Robert, 195

Second Brandenburg Concerto, 234, 252

Sellers, Peter, 165

Sentimental Journey, 306

Sgt. Pepper's Lonely Hearts Club Band (album), 149, 206, 213, 233, 236–48, 268, 287, 288, 291, 292, 294, 309, 314

"Sgt. Pepper's Lonely Hearts Club Band," 237

Shadows, The, 42, 119, 314

Shankar, Ravi, 230, 231, 318

Shannon, Del, 120

"She Came in Through the Bathroom Window," 291

"She Loves You," 117, 125, 126, 131, 132, 134, 138, 141, 145, 149, 246

"She's Leaving Home," 246, 247

Shea Stadium, 197, 198, 223, 224, 226, 314

Shenson, Walter, 161, 163, 165, **195**

Sheridan, Tony, 40, 44, 50, 67, 68, **69, 71,** 75

Shindig, 177

Shirelles, The, 198

Shotton, Pete, 8, 9, 11, **13**

"Shout," 138

Shout!, 255

Silver Beatles, 29, 31, 36

Sinatra, Frank, 317

Skiffle, 7–9

Smith, Judy Lockhart, 95

Smith, Mike, 87, 89

Smith, Mimi, 3, 4–6, **7**

Smith, Norman, 96, 98, 105, 106, 118, 119, 139, 189, 194, 200, 201, 208

Smothers, Tommy, 284

Snow White, 262

Snow, Hank, 15

Snowden, Lord, 129

"Some Other Guy," 88

"Something," 265, 288

"Something/Come Together," 293

"Something in the Way She Moves," 288

Spaniard in the Works, A (Lennon), 194

Spanish Fire Dance, The, 31

Spector, Phil, 145, 307

Spector, Ronnie, 145

Spencer Davis Group, 257

Spielberg, Steven, 282

Spinetti, Victor, 160, 165, 166, 187, 258, 277, 316

Star-Club, 91–93, 95

Starr, Ringo

    interviews, **101, 107, 174–76, 183, 187, 229**

    joins Beatles, 99

    marriage to Maureen Cox, 183

Steele, Tommy, 137

Stewart, Les, 21

Stigwood, Robert, 254

Stockhausen, Karlheinz, 209

Stokowski, Leopold, 211

Storm, Rory, 62, 77

"Strawberry Fields Forever," 232–36, 247, 309

Styner, Alan, 61

Sullivan, Ed, 128, 138, **140, 151,** 159, 197, 276

Summer in New York City, 308
"Sun King," 291
Sun Record, 179
Sunday Times, 255
Sutcliffe, Millie, 24, 27, 29, 59, 60, 70, 92
Sutcliffe, Stuart, 23–31, 35, 47, 48, 52, 59–61, 69, 70, 73, 91, 92
Swan Records, 90, 130, 134, 135
"Sweet Georgia Brown," 71

"Taste of Honey, A," 118
Taylor, Alistair, 75, 83, 84, 85, 89, 98, 254, 273, 274, 275, 277, 281, 286, 309
Taylor, Derek, 86, 124, 128, 168, 178, 191, 274, 275, 277, 281, 316
Taylor, Iain, 12, 258
Taylor, James, 247, 288
"Teddy Bear's Picnic, The," 5
Thank Your Lucky Stars, 114
"That Happy Feeling," 70
"That'll Be the Day," 5
Thomas, Chris, 264, 267
"Those Were the Days," 260
"Three Cool Cats," 21
Tibetan Book of the Dead, The, 209
"Ticket to Ride," 190
Tin Pan Alley, 98, 193
"Tomorrow Never Knows," 209, 210, 213, 232, 266
"Too Much About Sorrows," 15
Top 40, 246
Top Ten Club, 49, 50, 53, 66, 68, 77, 92
Top Vocal Group of the Year Award, 126
touring, end of, 228
Townshend, Ken, 106
Troy, Doris, 282

Trudeau, Pierre Elliot, 300
Turner, Billy, 11
TV Cartoons, 262
"Twenty Flight Rock," 14, 40
Twickenham Film Studios, 269
Twist and Shout, 121, 122
"Twist and Shout," 90, 116, 119, 129, 138

UNICEF, 300
United Artists, 161, 162, 196
Upstairs, Downstairs, 234

Valentine, Dicky, 130
Valentino, Rudolph, 129
Variety Club, 126
Vartan, Sylvie, 161
Vaughan, Ivan "Ivy," 11–13, 14
Vee Jay Records, 90, 130, 134, 135
Vee, Bobby, 138
Vera, Diana, 168
"Verrueckt Beatles, The," 41
Victor Spinetti Fan Club, 187
Vincent, Gene, 14, 29
Vinton, Bobby, 138
Volmer, Jurgen, 45, 67
Voorman, Klaus, 45, 47, 66, 67, 95, 212, 243, 286, 312

Waller, Gordon, 160
War Game, The, 299
Warwick Hotel, 198
Washington Coliseum, 152
Watkin, David, 196
Watkins, Peter, 299
"We Can Work It Out/Day Tripper," 205
West, Mae, 244
Whalley, Nigel, 11
"When I'm 64," 232

"When the Saints Go Marching In,"
12, 16
"While My Guitar Gently Weeps," 264
Whitaker, Bob, 205
White, Alan, 286
White Album, 260–68, 288, 291
White, Andy, 106, 108
White, Paul, 136, 141, 147, 283
Whitfield, David, 130
"Whole Lot of Shakin' Going On," 62
Williams, Alan, 28, 29, 30, **35,** 37,
38, **42,** 52, **53,** 85, **311**
Williams, Hank, 15
Wilson, Brian, 241
Wings over America, 312
WINS, 146
"With a Little Help from My
Friends," 247
With the Beatles, 119, 129

"Within You, Without You," 239
Wolfe, Tom, 149
"Wonderland by Night," 68, 70
Woodbine, Lord, 30, 35, **38**
Woodstock Festival, 301, 304
Wooler, Beryl, 100
Wooler, Bob, 53, 59, 63, **72,** 73, 74,
77, 81, 84, 100, **126**
"World Without Love, A," 160
Wyman, Bill, 122, 171

Ye Cracke, 24
Yellow Submarine (film), 261, 262
"Yellow Submarine," 208, 210, 219
"Yesterday," 192, 193, 210
Yesterday and Today, 205, 206
"You Can't Do That," 175
"You Never Give Me Your Money,"
291